How I Grew

Books by Mary McCarthy

How I Grew

Mary McCarthy

HARCOURT BRACE JOVANOVICH, PUBLISHERS
SAN DIEGO NEW YORK LONDON

Thanks are due to the following people for help in obtaining pictures: Lisa Browar, Curator of Rare Books and Manuscripts at Vassar College, Carol Gelderman, Molly Johnsrud, Professor Léo Laporte, Frani Muser, and Marilyn Tuohy of the Annie Wright School. The pictures in the Vassar section are used through the courtesy of the Vassar College Library.
Thanks also to: The Reverend Edward O. Miller, Barbara Dole Lawrence (that memory-book!), Patricia Fowler, Carol Brightman, and Eve Stwertka.

––––––––

Chapters 2 and 4, in somewhat different form, appeared earlier in The New Yorker; other parts, in Vanity Fair and the Paris Review.

Library of Congress Cataloging-in-Publication Data
McCarthy, Mary, 1912–
How I grew.
1. McCarthy, Mary, 1912–   —Biography—Youth.
2. Novelists, American—20th century—Biography.   I. Title
PS3525.A1435Z468   1987   818'.5209 [B]   86-29480
ISBN 0-15-142193-5

Designed by Francesca M. Smith
Printed in the United States of America
First edition
B C D E

*To my grandfather, Harold Preston; my teachers,
Helen Sandison and Anna Kitchel; my brother,
Kevin McCarthy; my son, Reuel Wilson;
and my husband, James West. With thanks.*

How I Grew

1

I was born as a mind during 1925, my bodily birth having taken place in 1912. Throughout the thirteen years in between, obviously, I must have had thoughts and mental impressions, perhaps even some sort of specifically cerebral life that I no longer remember. Almost from the beginning, I had been aware of myself as "bright." And from a very early time reasoning was natural to me, as it is to a great many children, doubtless to animals as well. What is Pavlov's conditioned reflex but an inference drawn by a dog? The activities of incessant induction and deduction are characteristically childlike ("Why don't we say 'Deliver us to evil,'" I am supposed to have asked, "the way Mama does in Frederick and Nelson's when she tells them to deliver it to Mrs. McCarthy?") and slack off rather than intensify as we grow older. My "cute" question, quoted by my mother in a letter to her mother-in-law (apparently the last she wrote), may have been prompted by our evening prayers: did we already say the "Our Father" and the "Hail Mary" besides "Now I lay me"? At six, I was too young to have had a rosary.

Someone, of course, was "hearing" our prayers; my father, probably, for I speak of "Mama" in the third person. It is Daddy I must be questioning; Gertrude, our nurse, was too ignorant. And now, writing it down more than sixty-five years later, all of a sudden I doubt the innocence of that question. There was premeditation behind it, surely; play-acting. I knew perfectly well that children could not pray to be delivered to evil and was only being clever—my vice already—supplying my parents with "Mary's funny sayings" to meet a sensed demand.

It is possible (to be fair) that the question "Why don't we . . . ?" had honestly occurred to me in Frederick's listening to Mama order and being surprised to have "deliver," an old bedtime acquaintance, pop up in the middle of a department store. Or, conversely, as we intoned the Lord's Prayer, my mind may have raced back to Mama at Frederick's. Which had priority, which bulked larger in my teeming experience, which name had I heard more often, God's or Frederick and Nelson's? But if, in one way or another, the question had honestly occurred to me, the answer could not have been slow to follow, without recourse to a grown-up. No, that inquiry was *saved up* for an audience, *rehearsed*. For my father's ear, I was not so much reasoning as artfully mimicking the reasoning process of a child. In any case, as far as I know, this is the last of my cute sayings on record. After the flu, there was no one there to record them any more. Nobody was writing to her mother-in-law of the words and deeds of the four of us. With the abrupt disappearance of the demand, the supply no doubt dried up. Soon our evening prayers—we knelt in a row now, wearing scratchy pajamas with feet in them—underwent expansion. To "God bless Mama and Daddy" something new was added: "Eternal rest grant unto them, o Lord, and let the perpetual light shine upon them. . . ."

From an early time, too, I had been a great reader. My father had taught me, on his lap, before I started school— *A Child's Garden of Verses* and his favorite, Eugene Field, the newspaperman poet. But in the new life instituted for us after our parents' death almost no books were permitted— to save electricity, or because books could give us "ideas" that would make us too big for our boots. A few volumes had come with us, I think, from Seattle to Minneapolis; those would have been *Black Beauty*, the "autobiography" of a horse, by Anna Sewell, *Hans Brinker or The Silver Skates*, *Heidi*, and Dante and *Don Quixote* illustrated by Doré, but these two were for looking at the pictures on the living-room floor while a grown-up watched, not for reading. Someone, not our parents, was responsible for *Fabiola, the Church of the Catacombs*, by Cardinal Wiseman, and I remember a little storybook, which soon disappeared, about some Belgian children on a tow-path along a canal escaping from Germans—was it taken away out of deference to the feelings of our great-aunt's husband, the horrible Uncle Myers, who was of German "extraction"? At any rate these are all the books I recall from the Minneapolis household, not counting Uncle Myers' own copy of *Uncle Remus*, Peter Rabbit (outgrown), and a set of the Campfire Girls (borrowed).

Yet the aunts must have had a *Lives of the Saints*, full of graphic accounts of every manner of martyrdom, and where did I come upon a dark-greenish volume called *The Nuremberg Stove*, about a porcelain stove and illustrated with German-looking woodcuts? And another story with a lot about P. P. Rubens and a "Descent from the Cross" in Antwerp Cathedral? Not in school, certainly; the parochial school did not give us books, only readers that had stories in them. I can still almost see the fifth- or sixth-grade reader that had Ruskin's "The King of the Yellow River," with pages repeating themselves and the end missing—a fairly common binder's error, but for a child afflicted with book hunger, it was a deprivation of fiendish cruelty, worse than the arithmetic manual that had the wrong answers in the back. Those school readers also gave you "tastes" of famous novels, very tantalizing, too, like the chapter about Maggie and Tom Tulliver from the start of *The Mill on the Floss*, which kept me in suspense for more than twenty years, Becky and Amelia Sedley leaving Miss Pinkerton's, a sample of *Jane Eyre*.

Oh! Among the books at home I was nearly forgetting *The Water-Babies*, by Charles Kingsley (illustrated, with a gilt-and-green cover), which must have come from my father's library—I can feel a consistent manly taste, like an *ex libris*, marking little Tom, the sooty chimney-sweep who runs away from his cruel master and falls into a river, Don Quixote and his nag, Dante and Virgil, and Wynken, Blynken, and Nod, who "sailed off in a wooden shoe" one night, "Sailed on a river of crystal light,/ Into a sea of dew." (*Black Beauty*, on the other hand, which was a bit on the goody side, had surely been our mother's.)

When he died, my father (another Tantalus effect) had been reading me a long fairy tale that we never finished. It was about seven brothers who were changed into ravens and their little sister, left behind when they flew away, who was given the task of knitting seven little shirts if she wanted them to change back into human shape again. At the place we stopped reading, she had failed to finish one little sleeve. I would have given my immortal soul to know what happened then, but in all the books of fairy tales that have come my way since, I have not been able to find that story—only its first and second cousins, like "The Seven Ravens" and "The Six Swans." And what became of the book itself, big with a wine-colored cover? Was it left behind on the train to Minneapolis when we all got sick with the flu? Or did our keepers promptly put it away as unsuitable, like my little gold beauty-pins? In Minneapolis we were not allowed fairy stories any more interesting than "The Three Bears."

But stop! That cannot be true. Certainly I read "The Little Match Girl" and "The Snow Queen," with the little robber girl I loved so and the piece of ice in little Kay's eye that even then I understood to be a symbol, in other words over my head. There was a good deal of that in Hans Andersen—the feeling of morals lurking like fish eyes peering out from between stones in the depths of clear water. Except in "The Snow Queen," where the furs and the sleigh and the reindeer and Gerda and the robber girl made up for everything, I disliked those lurking morals; I hated "The Little Match Girl." And I was not fond of "The Ugly Duckling" either; I sensed a pious cheat there—not all children who were "different" grew up into swans. Was that why I was allowed to have Andersen, like a refined sort of punishment, in my room? And they let me have another book, printed in big type on thick deckle-edged paper and possibly not by Andersen, that contained a frightening tale about a figure named Ole Luk Oie who threw sand in people's eyes just as they were going to sleep. Not the same as the sandman; more of a bogey. Burying my head under the covers, for nights running I used to scare myself in my pillow-less (better for the posture) bed with this runic fiction, repeating the words "Ole Luk Oie" like a horrible spell. And in the morning, sure enough, my finger found grainy particles stuck to my eyelashes showing that he had been there. But maybe, if you knew Danish, the story was more boring than spooky, and the dread sand in the eyes was just a symbol of something in society.

Almost no books, but how then, while still in Minneapolis, did I learn about Loki and Balder the Beautiful and Frey and his golden sister Freya, goddess of love and beauty? That was not the kind of thing the Sisters of St. Joseph taught, and there were no comic books then to retell myths in strip language with balloons coming out of the mouths of helmeted gods and heroes—just the funny papers, which showed funny people like Olive Oyl and Miss Emmy Schmaltz. Probably the answer lies in *The Book of Knowledge*, a junior encyclopedia that someone finally gave us—proof that prayers were answered—and that our guardians for some reason let us keep and even use. They must have thought that it was a collection of known facts and figures and therefore no more harmful than the diagrams it carried of chemical retorts and the Bunsen burner. But to me, in that household, that red-bound set was like a whole barrel of bootleg liquor, cut but still the real stuff. Of course there were facts in it (there had to be), but you could ignore those; the main point was that it told you the plots of the world's famous books from the *Iliad* through *The Count of Monte Cristo*. If the Trojan Horse and the Cyclops were there (and Roland and Oliver), they would have had to have Thor and his iron gloves, blind Hoder and his arrow—at least the "basics."

Yet the suggestion leaves me unsatisfied. It does not account for the *intimacy* I formed with those scenes and figures of Norse mythology: how Thor lost his hammer, Odin's raven, the bad dreams of Balder, Sif's hair—you would think that I had had an entire "Edda for Children" hidden in the swing in our backyard.

Nor can I altogether account for the hold this material, however acquired, had on my imagination, for my so much preferring those gods and goddesses to the "sunny" Greek ones. Perhaps I liked the strong light-and-dark contrasts of the Northern tales. I was a firm believer in absolutes: the lack of shadings, of any in-between, made Asgard a more natural residence than Mount Olympus for my mythic propensity, just as clear, concise Latin was always more natural to me than Greek with all its "small, untranslatable words" (as Mrs. Ryberg at Vassar called them).

But there was more to it than that. For a juvenile half enamored of the dark principle, fond of frightening herself and her brothers with the stories she made up (or just a decided brunette with pale skin that she tried to see as "olive"), there was a disappointing lack of evil in Greek mythology. Obviously they did not tell children about the banquet of Thyestes, and all we knew of Jason was the *Argo*

6

and the Golden Fleece, yet the crimes and horrors that were kept from us "till we were old enough" (like the watches my brothers received from our Seattle grandfather) were the work of mortals and titans, not Olympians. Even in his worst moments, no Greek god could approach the twisted cunning of a Loki. I hated his very name, and yet in a way he "made" the story of the Aesir for me.

In fact, the notion of a thoroughly evil creature sharing in the godhead was thoroughly un-Greek, and I suspect that it did not sit well with me either at the age of nine or ten despite the spell of intrigue and danger he cast on those tales. I could not quite fathom why Loki should go virtually unpunished even for the awful act of plotting the slaying of Balder; did it have something to do with his mixed ancestry, half-god and half-giant? You would think the *least* he deserved was permanent expulsion from Asgard, and yet he crept back, assuming new forms. The weakness of the Aesir (even Thor) in dealing with him was mystifying; they seemed to treat him and his relatives as fixtures of the establishment—his deathly daughter Hel ruled over the nether world. Being already a "confirmed" Catholic, I associated gods with goodness and could not take a standpoint that identified them simply with power—as sheer power of evil, Loki merited worship certainly. If I was unable to see that, it was doubtless because my model for badness was Satan. Proud Lucifer (Loki was a real cringer and fawner) was cast out of heaven once and for all, and such power as he retained, below, among men, was helpless before the saving action of God's grace.

Yet now that I consider it, I can see that the appeal of Freya, Balder, Loki, and Company was, precisely, to my Catholic nature. The Prince of Darkness, despite his large handicap, *was* a power for us, a kind of god even if we avoided the Manichean heresy of picturing him as dividing the world in equal shares with God the Father. The only surprise is that the Norse cosmogony should have felt so congenial to me given the prejudice against real Norse-

7

men—the "Scandihoovians" of Minnesota—that Irish Catholics learned at their mother's knee. Evidently I made no
connection between the great battle of Ragnarok that was
to end the world and the local Olsens and Hansens. In the
same way, my grandmother, old Lizzie McCarthy, who was
"not over-fond" of Jews, never appeared to notice that Jesus was one, at least on His mother's side.

The sense of being at home among the Aesir, "speaking
their language," was all the more natural to a Catholic child
in that the Northern myths (though I did not guess it then)
show clear traces of Christian impaste overlaying very
primitive material. Balder, in particular, their pure-as-snow
sun god, is a lot closer to Jesus on Mount Tabor than to
Phoebus Apollo in his sky-chariot. The gods and Nature
weep tears for him, treacherously slain by an arrow of mis-
tletoe, as he descends like Christ crucified to the lower world,
but there is a promise of a Second Coming, when all will
live in harmony.

So it "fits," I suppose, that when I left the house in Minneapolis and, before very long, the faith, the gods of Asgard lost their hold on me. I have scarcely thought of them
since. Looking them up now, to reaffirm my memory, I am
amazed to learn that Balder has a wife (Nanna); I had imagined him as a bachelor like Our Lord or Sir Percival. Otherwise that Northern pantheon has remained surprisingly
fresh in my mind, as though deep-frozen in a snow-slide,
untouched by any process of wear or tear. I do not think
they figure in my writings even metaphorically, unlike King
Arthur and his knights, who turn up in the story of Peter
Levi (*Birds of America*). My passion for them was a crush,
which I got over so completely that the cure has left me
with a perfect immunity to Wagner. Though *The Ring* has
been "in" twice during my life, I have never had any interest in it.

But I am digressing in the middle of a digression, piling
Ossa on Pelion, we Latinists would say. I was talking about

books or, rather, about the scarcity of them that I had to endure between my seventh and my twelfth year. Yet losing the thread (or seeming to) has given me time to wonder about the truth of what I was saying. On reflection I see that I have been exaggerating. I cannot have waited more than a decade to read "Thumbelina" and "Puss in Boots," or "Snow White" or "Rapunzel" or "Rumpelstiltskin." If they were already old friends when I read them aloud to Reuel, it means that in Minneapolis we must have had the usual Grimm and Perrault fairy tales and that secretly or openly I read them.

Aladdin and his lamp, too—I have a distinct memory of a genie, somewhat pear-shaped, emerging from a cloud of smoke—Ali Baba, and Sinbad the Sailor, in one of whose adventures I first learned of the roc and pictured to myself fearfully its huge white fabulous eggs. Then there are books I feel I have read that I cannot remember in the Minneapolis house or "place" in the years just following: *Tanglewood Tales* and a *Pilgrim's Progress* illustrated with dark, Doré-like lithographs. But a Catholic home would not have had Bunyan; still less would the Sisters of St. Joseph have given it to us in school—almost better Foxe's *Book of Martyrs*. And yet I feel sure that I was a child—not a girl—when I saw the words "Apollyon" and "Slough of Despond" and essayed to pronounce them to myself. The volume with its gloomy illustrations "belongs" in the Minneapolis framework, more specifically in the glass-fronted bookcase in the parlor, and I can only suppose that, like the Dante and *Don Quixote*, it had belonged to our father, more catholic in his tastes than the rest of his family, and that our guardians were too ignorant to confiscate it.

It was not till I left Minneapolis, I think, that a book disappointed me. I could not finish Washington Irving's *The Alhambra*. That was in the convent, in Seattle. I doubt that such a thing could have happened in the Minneapolis time, for then I could read just about anything—I had an iron stomach for printed matter, like a goat's. To this day, I have a good digestion in this respect, which I must owe, like my generally good digestion and appetite, to the Blaisdell Avenue regime. The ability to read almost anything was the corollary, obviously, of deprivation, for, exaggerate or not, it is still true that we had very few books.

It is true, too, that at that time children by and large had a far greater power of absorption of the printed word than children do today, and there also scarcity was a factor— children's books were a comparative rarity, so that children "made do" with books written for adults. The change came between my generation and the next: a book like *The Water-Babies*, which I "ate up" as a child, no doubt like my father before me, was utterly resistant to being gulped down or even tasted by my son. And he rebelled against Cooper's *The Prairie*, even though it was being read aloud to him—a kind of spoon-feeding. You could blame that on the Hardy Boys, were it not for Henty and H. Rider Haggard, whom he read straight through and begged for more of.

On the whole, children's taste in books seems to change more slowly than adults'. *Heidi* and *Robin Hood* are still classics, and I have read the Howard Pyle King Arthur books not only to Reuel but to my husband's children, more than fifteen years his junior. But other old books have become inaccessible to young readers, as though placed out of their reach by the modern child's shrunken vocabulary. Stylistic mannerisms are another barrier. They can cause books to date alarmingly, like affected fashions in dress, and this applies equally to old and young. We cannot return to the favorites of our youth. It is as much as I can do to read Meredith now, though I devoured him as a girl, to the point where until recently I supposed that my sentences must sound like him. But when a couple of summers ago I reread *Richard Feverel*, I could not see the shadow of a resemblance; the problem was to get through it at all.

Charles Kingsley, a "muscular Christian," was a contemporary of Meredith's. There is an old copy of *The Water-Babies* (first published in 1863, four years after *Richard Feverel*) in the room where I am writing, inscribed "Harry from Uncle Louis, Christmas 1904." The two names are in my family, "Harry" on both sides of it, but the book is no relation; it came with the house in Maine when we bought it. Nevertheless the bookshelves that face me as I write are confronting me, eerily, with the classics of my childhood: *The Water-Babies*, Andrew Lang's edition of *The Arabian Nights* (same illustrations), *Black Beauty*, *Heidi*, *Rebecca of Sunnybrook Farm*, even Manly's *English Poetry*, where I found "Sister Helen" a few years later on a Tacoma boarding-school shelf. It is as if these ghostly volumes that had formed my persona had been haunting the house on the Maine seacoast that my husband was to buy in 1967.

But to return to the point at hand: *The Water-Babies*, which was written as a children's story on a theme of child labor, is extremely arch and fanciful, as much so as anything Meredith ever penned. On opening it yesterday, I felt sympathy with the reluctant Reuel of forty years ago; the only plain sentence in the whole narrative is the first one: "Once upon a time there was a little chimney-sweep and his name was Tom." In the same way a new look at the first chapter of *Vanity Fair*, borrowed from the Bangor Public Library, makes me wonder how this could have figured in the sixth-grade reader of St. Stephen's parochial school. Even if ruthlessly cut and preceded by a vocabulary, the need of which is emphasized by the markings in red ink of a previous borrower underlining the difficult words: "equipage," "bandy," "Semiramis," "incident to," "orthography," "sensibility." . . .

Well! Necessity is the mother of invention: the shortage of books in the Minneapolis house was compensated for by other kinds of reading-matter. We had the funny papers every afternoon and a whole section of them in color on Sunday. There was also the Sunday magazine section, which we were allowed to look at (I can't guess why), spread out on the den rug after church. I remember best the high-society scandals, constituent elements (come to think of it) of Henry James's "international theme"—Anna Gould, Count Boni de Castellane, the much-married Peggy Hopkins Joyce, the Marquise de la Falaise de la Coudray—King Tut, the Kohinoor diamond, the curse of the Carnarvons, and some medical curiosities. Then there were religious periodicals: Grandma McCarthy's blue-and-white *Ave Maria*, which I read in her upstairs sunroom, and old Aunt Mary's more low-brow *Extension*, sepia-toned, which I would "borrow" and keep hidden under my mattress; both of these carried short stories. In *Our Sunday Visitor*, sold after church every Sunday, you could read about the scary burning of crosses by the Ku Klux Klan on Catholic lawns, and there was a gripping Question-and-Answer column that advised you, if you were a doctor, which to save, the mother or the child, in a perilous childbirth—readers seemed to write in the same questions week after week, maybe in the hope of getting a different answer. In church after Sunday Mass there were also free distributions of tracts on foreign missions—that was probably where I learned of Father Damien and the lepers on Molokai—Catholics had a great appetite for reading about gruesome diseases, especially those involving the rotting or falling off of parts of the body. But in general the various tracts, flyers, illustrated brochures on missionary work extended our horizons almost like *The National Geographic* of Protestant homes.

That was all there was to the "media" then; the very word was unknown. There was no equivalent of *The Reader's Digest*; rotogravure sections of the Sunday papers were yet to come; radio was in the crystal-set stage—in our house Uncle Myers' envied toy. We were allowed to watch him listen with the earphones on his head. There was a unique occasion, however, when we were brought to my grandmother's house to listen to a radio "event" on a big set for which you did not need earphones; that was the Dempsey-Firpo fight (September 14, 1923). Unfortunately the knock-out took place early in the second round, almost before the fight had started, and there was nothing to do but tag home to bed, sadly (at least in my case) because Luis Angel Firpo had lost.

My passion for the Bull of the Pampas was a great laugh to the family. They did not understand that I had fallen in love with his name. Names were often the reason for my preferences—what else did I have to go by? And they are not such bad indicators: a man does not choose his name, but he can change it—witness Voltaire and Muhammad Ali. That a little girl should have a passionate crush on a prize fighter may seem odd, but here again the economics of scarcity were at work. It would have been more normal to be "crazy about" a star of the silver screen, but I had never seen one, unless maybe an episode of Pearl White in the days of Mama and Daddy. During the five years in Minneapolis, the only full-length movie I saw was *The Seal of the Confessional*, shown in the church basement. It was about a handsome priest who heard a murderer's confession and so had to keep silent, rather tiresomely, while an innocent man was going to the chair, but there was an exciting sub-plot about an atheist who was struck down by lightning when he defied God to demonstrate His existence. On Saturday mornings our neighborhood movie house let children in free to see the trailer for the coming Western, but those "tastes," while whetting the appetite, were of course not a substitute for the real William S. Hart. By the time I left Minneapolis and could go to the movies, the great days of silent film had passed.

Stage stars we never laid eyes on, nor vaudevillians. The only music we got to hear was a few records, e.g., "Over There," "Listen to the Mocking-bird," occasional band concerts in parks, the church organ, and military brasses in parades; our grandmother's "music room" contained a player piano, with rolls you inserted, but we were forbidden to work it. We knew John McCormack and Harry Lauder from their photos, Caruso, probably, too, and our great-aunts cherished a faded tintype of a figure called Chauncey Olcott, who, Webster's tells me, was "Chancellor John Olcott, 1860–1932, American actor and tenor," surely of Irish descent. In my grandmother's "music room," I eyed a big photograph of Mme. Schumann-Heink and was shocked by the monstrous bellows of her bosom.

No public figures entered our ken, except for Marshal Foch,

whom we saw in person—a trim little white-haired figure—
being welcomed by the city in front of the Art Institute,
across from Fairoaks Park. During the Harding-Cox campaign (1920), I pedaled our little wooden wagon up and down
our driveway shouting "Hurrah for Cox!" but the only basis
for my support was that he was a Democrat and I thought
my father had been one. I was impressed by President
Harding's death because Seattle had a part in it. Returning
from Alaska, he fell sick (surely from the seafood?) in Seattle and died in San Francisco. It was exciting to see our
birthplace "make" the headlines. From the McCarthy aunts,
uncles, and cousins we had already heard more than once
about the IWW mayor, Ole Hansen, Seattle had elected. The
initials, they said, stood for "I Won't Work," but I was less
interested by that than by his horrible first name, which I
probably identified with Ole Luk Oie, the bogey in the storybook. My happy memories of boulevards and grassy terraces and continual picnics in the backyard got muddied by
the McCarthy family's Republican politics and dislike of their
in-laws till I came to think of Seattle as a disreputable place
that had a dangerous district called Coon Hollow (I remembered that from my father) and an "I Won't Work" Ole for
a mayor.

Needless to say, on the visual side we were kept well
below the poverty line, just as in politics, reading, enter-
tainment. The house they had put us in was ugly, with an
ugly yard and a few ugly bushes like Bridal Wreath. For a
while we were allowed to use a stereopticon, with views of
the pyramids, and in my room there was a "Baby Stuart"
in a blue-and-white boy's dress. In a group of schoolchil-
dren, we could sometimes go to the museum, where, running away from home, I once hid behind the cast of the
Laocoon. But our clothes, faded, continually pieced, let out,
and let down, the repellent food we ate, my worn, dull
black, second-hand rosary were cruelly punishing to a sense
of beauty. Yet in this sphere our guardians were less effec-
tual. They could keep books out of our hands, limit the rep-

ertory of the phonograph, restrict our intercourse with the neighbors' children by penning us within a wire-net fence, but they could not stop us from using our eyes. The passionate pleasure I got from soap bubbles, rainbows—anything iridescent, including smears of oil on street puddles—from the funny "faces" of pansies, spurs of nasturtiums (which also concealed a nectar), freckles of foxglove, from holy pictures, spider webs, motes of dust riding on a sun ray, "Jack Frost flowers," dew, the white vestments at Easter, Easter lilies around the altar, all that joy was beyond our guardians' power of prevention. No more could they put a halt to it than they could keep us, fenced in our yard, from reading the sky-writing that spelled out "Lucky Strike" on the summer sky while we watched the words form.

Nature finds substitutes in the cultural realm, and how can I regret *Orphans in the Storm*, *Little Lord Fauntleroy*, Buster Keaton, early Harold Lloyd, the Little Pepper books, the "Patty" books, Jeritza, Mary Garden, when I had Balder and Freya, Thor and Sif, *The Book of Knowledge*, snowflakes, prismatic refractions, the seeds I planted one year on Good Friday that turned into frilly sweet peas?

The wryness I feel on looking back at Uncle Myers and the Sheridan sisters, on that jaundice-colored house with its attendant Golden Glow, Bridal Wreath, and gross rhubarb plant in the backyard, is almost wholly material. I don't mind about the cultural sustenance that was withheld from us— rather, the contrary. They seem to have hit on a formula for child-rearing that virtually forced us to use our imaginations. What I mind is the horrible food we were made to eat, the carrots I dumped out the window, the gristle and fat, the chicken necks I sucked to draw out the little white cord, the prunes, farina, and Wheatena. Here there was no compensation, no sensibilizing of the palate to shadings of taste; the envy with which we watched Uncle Myers put bananas on his corn flakes led only to my devouring thirteen in one fevered session in my grandmother's pantry in

Seattle—a *sickening* experience and my last encounter with the fruit.

The beatings with hairbrush and razor-strop I can still resent, but abstractly, as injustice. My body does not remember them as it remembers the carrots and parsnips, still refusing more than sixty-five years later the sweetish taste of the first unless camouflaged with mint, butter, caramelized sugar, and so on, and refusing the second absolutely. As to compensation for the physical abuse I received (and I count being made to stay outdoors in the snow for two hours at a stretch in sub-zero temperatures going down to twenty), I am not sure whether Nature has seen to that or not. Certainly those people, at least in this world, never had to pay for their crimes. Yet I do not think that I have tried to avenge myself on them in what I have written—they were dead long before I could use a typewriter. As far as I can tell, I do not *feel* vindictive toward them, have not for years, maybe not since I was seated on a train for Seattle with my other grandfather; my escape was my revenge. And if I triumph over them now, still again, recalling details of their regimen, it is because the tale of it makes me smile. Perhaps that is Nature's repair-work: over the years I have found a means—laughter—of turning pain into pleasure. Uncle Myers and Aunt Margaret, my grandmother, too, in her own style, amuse me by their capacity for being awful. It is a sort of talent, really, that people do not have nowadays or not in the same way. And, to the extent that my memory has been able to do justice to that talent in them, they have been immortalized, which is to say that Uncle Myers and his pedometer have been condemned to eternal derision.

Not his razor-strop, mind you. That is not funny. Yet if he had only that to speak for him, I do not think he would "live" as a character. The pedometer humanizes, which is the first step toward immortality. Nevertheless there are moralists who think I ought not to laugh or get an audience to laugh with me during a public reading at the figure of Uncle Myers, my old persecutor. What they overlook is the fact that as the injured party I have earned the right to laugh. My laughter is a victory over circumstances, and insofar as it betokens a disinterested enjoyment I imagine it to be a kind of pardon. I had the choice of forgiving those incredible relatives of mine or pitying myself on their account. Laughter is the great antidote for self-pity, maybe a specific for the malady. Yet probably it does tend to dry one's feelings out a little, as if by exposing them to a vigorous wind. So that something must be subtracted from the compensation I seem to have received for injuries sustained. There is no dampness in my emotions, and some moisture, I think, is needed to produce the deeper, the tragic, notes.

What I have been saying may suggest that already in Minneapolis my intelligence was at work organizing those painful experiences so as to get the upper hand of them. But that is not so. Far from jesting to myself bitterly on the theme of our deprivation, I literally did not think about it. In our parents' lifetime, as the reader has seen, I reasoned, with childish logic, trying to put together pieces of the puzzle children live in. Now that had stopped. I made no effort to subject the thing that was happening to us to any process of understanding. Perhaps I was too stunned to use my intelligence outside of school. The fact that what was happening was incredible, not to be believed in as real by children who had been loved and spoiled by their parents, may explain the absence of thought.

In another sense, thought—at least on this subject—was superfluous. The explanation was always simple—no mystery. If I was beaten with a razor-strop for having won a prize in a city-wide essay contest, I had no need to ask myself why. I was told why; it was to keep me from getting stuck up—logical, given our position. And it was easy to find the cause of *that*; it was simply that our parents had died. They were in the cemetery, bedded side by side; we had been shown. And God was not going to send us any new parents. Nor would we want to be taken by the Protestants, out in Seattle, in comparison to whom Myers and Margaret were the lesser evil, and we should be thanking our stars for that.

If you started to question any of it, you bumped up against God's will, which was higher than thought—as every child knew. The alternative to thought was prayer. Since it would go against God's will to ask for Mama and Daddy to come back from heaven, I suppose I prayed, in my novenas, on my rosary beads, for our grandmother McCarthy to take us (or, better still, just me) to live with her. My exploits of running away may have been aimed at that, too, though the conscious intention was to escape punishment by hiding, in the confessional box, behind the Laocoon. But on the whole it was wiser to pray for intentions that God would fully approve of, such as getting our parish priest to give in to my pleas for confirmation though I was still below the age.

The arbitrariness of punishments was another deterrent to thought. No pattern could be discerned, and it was not worthwhile to make the effort to see one. Of course there were other things to think about, had I been inclined. For example, the German helmet and unexploded shells that our handsome uncle Louis had brought back to his parents as souvenirs of the Great War might have led me to wonder about the place of wars in God's scheme. Children do make such general reflections. Reuel, aged seven (have I written this?), announced to me one evening that he had decided that slavery was "a good idea, but quite mean," and, again, one summer, a few years later, he wrote me from Cape Cod: "Dwight is trying to give up progressiveness, but I think it's too late." No such thoughtful reflections (which are different from the logical reasoning common in children) were ever framed by my own young mind. Perhaps Reuel's reflectiveness only showed that he was spending his impressionable years in not just one but two intellectual households. Certainly he was much occupied with distinctions, as when he observed after his first term in boarding-school: "You're an intellectual, but my father's a literary man."

In my case, dreams substituted for thought. The bits and pieces of history and legend I was picking up were fuel for my dreams, going up like bonfires, rather than building blocks for a picture of the world. I dreamed of becoming a Carmelite nun, like the great St. Teresa, who was half my name-saint; it was the reputed harshness of the discipline that appealed to me. For me, excess was attractive almost per se: not to be a mere nun, but to be a *cloistered*, silent, non-teaching nun, in rope sandals, with a rope around the waist, continually fasting, and praying two hours a day in her cell. At the same time, not fully satisfied by this effaced, selfless, brown-clad vision, I pictured myself as an abbess. Under my able administration were devoutly girded nuns singing the offices and at my right hand a chaplain, like Teresa's St. John of the Cross.

This dream conflicted with another. I was to marry the Pretender to the throne of France, and, fighting side by side with him, commanding my own troops, I would win back his throne for him, place the crown on his head, and become queen myself. "Queen Marie Thérèse"—my name would be the same as Louis XIV's Spanish consort's. To choose between these high destinies was hard. But at length I saw a way to reconcile them. First I would marry the Pretender and win back his throne for him; having done that and become queen, I would abdicate and retire to a convent, where I would be elected abbess. But I could no longer be a Carmelite; none of the strict orders accepted women who had been married.

There was another problem connected with my ambition. Should I marry the Duke de Guise, the actual Pretender, or his son, the Count de Paris, who was nearer my age? The Duke de Guise seemed the better bet; though old, he had the acknowledged kingly title, while the Count de Paris was a bird in the bush. Moreover, my source (the Sunday magazine section) did not show any pictures of the Count, so that I had no idea what he looked like. Whereas you could see plenty of photos of the Duke, gray-haired but erect in his bearing, thin-waisted and extremely tall. Or am I fusing newspaper likenesses of the modern Pretender with the old Duc de Guise, head of the anti-Protestant League, a giant seven feet tall, who was felled at Blois by order of Henri III, measuring his full length (I read somewhere) at the foot of the king's bed? Such leakage or "running" as of non-fast colors is a common occurrence in the memory.

There are also unaccountable holes. What made me choose "Clementina" for a confirmation name when my wish was finally granted ("Perseverance wins the crown," said old Father Gaughan)? It must have been for St. Clement, an early pope, though I am unaware of having had any special devotion to him. In fact, I remember nothing of any Clement, only the funny fact of becoming Mary Therese Clementina McCarthy. What I do remember from that time is an ardent devotion to St. Agnes, symbol of purity, with her white woolly lamb. It was *her* name I wanted to take at confirmation, and how and why I was re-routed to St. Clement I cannot imagine. My only clue comes from San Clemente, on the Aventine, the church of the Irish Dominicans. Did a young priest on Bishop O'Dea's staff, preparing me for the sacrament, infect me with a bug he had picked up from those Irishmen during a year in Rome? In any case, the author of the "Epistle of Clement" (ca. A.D. 96), designed to heal a rift in the church of Corinth, seems a peculiar choice.

Otherwise my mental life consisted of dreaming, greedily reading whatever I could, telling stories to myself and my brothers. In school I wrote poems and was a champion speller, my nearest rival being a pale blond Polish-American boy named John Klosick, who sat in front of me and whom I loved for his delicacy of frame and feature. My only stage appearance was as "Iris" in a playlet about the flowers. I had wanted to be "Rose," the heroine, but with my glasses and nervous mannerisms probably I was not pretty enough for the leading part. No doubt I consoled myself with the reminder that irises were the fleur-de-luce, the royal flower of France; in my crepe-paper costume of purple petals and a crown I could therefore feel quite important in flower-land. For the Greeks, as I could have gleaned from *The Book of Knowledge*, I was the personification of the rainbow and the messenger of the gods—nobody had told me that I was also the sister of the Harpies. When the day of the performance came, I was reconciled to my part and prepared to shine. Aunt Mary had taken great pains over my costume, more elaborate than the others, the tiers of scalloped petals fitting my form like a real dress. Yet my first full-scale public humiliation was in store.

When the curtains parted, we were revealed drawn up in rows simulating a flower garden. As a tall, nodding bloom, my place was at the end of the front row, stage left. During rehearsals I had learned the parts of the other flowers as well as my own. It was the same mistake—excessiveness—I had made with my first writing exercise as a first-grader in the convent by dotting my "e"s for good measure as well as my "i"s, so that instead of starring (as I had expected) I was placed at the bottom of the class. Now I let my lips move along with the voices of "Rose," "Violet," and "Daisy" as they stepped forward one by one and recited their lines. I am not sure whether this accompaniment was audible or just visible to the parents and relations out front. And I cannot decide whether I was aware, myself, that my lips were moving like a prompter throughout the playlet, whether in fact I intended to be noticed ("Look at Iris! She knows the whole play") or whether I was oblivious, absorbed in the performance—the first theatre, I realize, that I had ever seen. I am inclined to think it was the second because of the slap in the face my pride received when my aunt Margaret came up to me furiously at the end of the play. I don't recall the words she used to bring me to my senses, only the derision in her voice—typically Irish, by the way. It's possible that she mimicked the movement of my young lips with her old ones. I suppose she felt humiliated before all those parents, and some priests, too, probably. Or she angrily considered the work Aunt Mary had put into my costume only to have me put the family to shame. At the time, though, it did not occur to me to imagine her feelings. In my fury, instead, I dared to strike at her (that must have been the time) with a Catholic periodical she was carrying, folded, under her arm and that, sobbing, I wrested from her. The sequel I don't know. I remember only the awful impiety of hitting out at her on the street and my wild heavy breathing. Afterwards did we walk home together, heading for Uncle Myers' razor-strop, my petals burning me like the shirt of Nessus?

It was not the last time that my lips moved visibly during a school performance accompanying (even improving on) the other actors as they pronounced their lines. But when it happened again it was in Seattle, at the Sacred Heart, and the correction was administered kindly, softened with praise for my execution of my own assigned part. For a long time, even before I had renounced my Carmelite vocation, nothing could deter me from my wish to be an actress. My writing, though I was held to be good at it, interested me less. I now suspect that my stage ambitions were merely the vehicle for a hope to be acclaimed for my beauty; that must be a large incentive for both sexes to choose careers in the theatre. With my glasses and straight hair I was far from beautiful, but I was not resigned to that. I would study myself in the mirror, frizz my hair with leather curlers, make earrings out of wire and colored beads of glass, and decide, tossing my dark head, that I had a gypsy allure. As my looks finally improved once I had got rid of the glasses (and some braces they had fastened on my upper teeth), I invented other personae (one modeled on the Madonna), giving fuel to my dreams of the stage. It was not till my junior year in college that I began to guess the truth: that I would never be an actress.

It came home to me in the Vassar Outdoor Theatre. We were doing a dramatization of Chaucer's *The Knight's Tale*, put into modern English; I had been cast in the part of Arcite, the second male lead. In the last act, having just been killed by a fire-breathing dragon (a stage effect contributed by the Chemistry Department), I was lying stage center, spotlit, on the grass when I heard a great laugh from the audience—forgetting that I was supposed to be dead, I had pulled down the short tunic of my orange oilcloth costume, as though it were a skirt. And now I perceive that it was all of a piece, consistent, that stage behavior of mine: onstage, unless I was actually speaking my assigned lines (i.e., "acting"), I forgot that an audience could see me. Actors do not do that.

Earlier in that chastening performance—with my husband-to-be, a real actor, watching critically from a front row—titters should have warned me that a cardboard tower, my prison, was noticeably shaking as I quaked with stage fright; to lean against it for support had been a mistake. In school and college, I was given leading parts (usually male) by teachers and student directors because I wanted them so badly and because by that time I had the necessary looks and voice to pass for an actor, not just the ability to learn lines. But I had no more vocation for it than I had to be a Carmelite nun or queen of France. The fact that I was so rarely given the *female* lead (in *The Knight's Tale* I had longed to be the Fair Emily, a votive of Diana, with whom both the young knights are in love) ought to have tipped me off sooner. My stage appearances, testifying to my need for applause, belonged to my dream life; they had little to do with the life of my mind.

When I was rescued by my Protestant grandfather from the evil spell of the house on Blaisdell Avenue, one of the immediate effects was the opening up of libraries to me. His own, in the first place, in the tall Seattle house looking out over Lake Washington where I was now taken to live. Then there was the library of Forest Ridge Convent, where he was sending me as a five-day boarder (so that I would not lose my religion) and where I had spent a few weeks as a day pupil when Mama was still alive.

My grandfather Preston's library was strong on sets. The oak shelves, going all the way to the ceiling, held the complete works of Dickens, Frank Stockton, Tolstoy, Sienkiewicz, Bulwer-Lytton, Dumas, and the complete Elsie Dinsmore books, which had belonged to my mother when she was a little girl. The convent had all of Fenimore Cooper, some Washington Irving, and Stoddard's *Lectures*, with illustrations. During the sewing hour a nun read *Emma* to us, Booth Tarkington's *The Gentleman from Indiana*, and *A Tale of Two Cities*. I am not sure where I found Longfellow's *Tales of a Wayside Inn*, containing as one chapter "The Saga of King Olaf"; I had hated "Hiawatha," all too reminiscent of the civics of Minnehaha Park and Minnehaha Falls, but I loved those tales, and they are the main reason I know something of European history—Normans, popes, and German emperors. It was a shock, then, to discover rather recently that "Robert of Sicily, brother of Pope Urbane and Valmond, Emperor of Allemaine," who learned the lesson of humility one Easter Sunday in Palermo, was not an historical figure; all my life, from the age of twelve on, I had been taking him for a minor Angevin.

Despite the efforts of the Forest Ridge librarian to "direct" my reading (e.g., Stoddard's *Lectures*), I was gobbling books in both libraries, in the same spirit as had led me to eat those thirteen bananas one right after the other in Grandma Preston's pantry, with the result that I could never eat a banana again. It was not like that, luckily, with reading, though, now that books were multiplying before me like the loaves and fishes of the miracle, I did become somewhat more picky.

With Dumas I had a special problem because of my religion. There was a set in the Preston library, a dozen or so purplish volumes, and I could not keep my eyes off them, though I knew that the only Dumas not on the Index was

The Count of Monte Cristo, which I had already read. The craving was worst for *The Queen's Necklace*, because it was about Marie Antoinette's diamonds and the Cardinal de Rohan. Will power, however, enabled me to resist. But when I lost my faith, toward the end of my second year in the convent, there should have been no further hindrance. The pleasure path lay open. And yet by some quirk familiar to me in later life, now that Dumas had become accessible, I lost the desire for him. So far as I can remember, I never got around to reading *The Queen's Necklace* or, if I did, I never finished it. That applies to *The Three Musketeers*, too. To the best of my knowledge, the only book of Dumas I have read all the way through is, precisely, *The Count of Monte Cristo*—God is not mocked, I guess.

I missed out on Scott's novels (though he was not on the Index), just as I had on Dumas. I came to him too late, when my first hunger for fiction was sated. Something like that happened with the Little Colonel books and quite a number of older girls' classics. Basing my judgment on *A Girl of the Limberlost* by Gene Stratton Porter, I may have decided that they were too young for me. The exception was the enchanting *Rebecca of Sunnybrook Farm*, a favorite with George Orwell, too, which I read several times, having "fallen" for her handsome father, Lorenzo de' Medici Randall. I think I had read *Little Women* already in Minneapolis and now I read *Jo's Boys* and liked it even better, just as I liked *Through the Looking-Glass* better than *Alice in Wonderland*. My tastes were perverse.

I preferred boys' books to girls' books. Like Reuel in the next generation, I loved Henty's *Along the Irrawaddy*, and I made my grandfather subscribe for me (in his name) to *The American Boy*. Yet the only Kipling I read was *The Light that Failed* and "Wee Willie Winkie" (both school), and *Kim* when I was an adult. *The Jungle Book* and *Just So Stories* I missed, because they failed to come my way when I was "right" for them, i.e., in Minneapolis. I was a case of uneven development, like Lenin's description of the leaps and bounds in the progress of backward countries—or I was rising on one side, like a half-baked biscuit—and thanks to that had few terms of reference in common with the schoolmates I was meeting. Unlike them, at the age of eleven, I had never seen a movie (not counting *The Seal of the Confessional*); the children's books I *had* read dated back to my parents' childhoods; I was unaware of the *St. Nicholas* magazine and, when I finally heard of it, supposed it had something to do with the St. Nicholas Day School for girls in Seattle, where the Protestant upper crust went. I arrived among my Sacred Heart contemporaries like a dropped stitch in time and in some ways I never caught up—I was twice married and driving a car before I could ride a bicycle.

In Seattle my tastes in reading all at once became curiously adult. On weekends I now read trash for adults instead of trash for children: *True Story*, *True Confessions*, movie magazines. The effect of this low-grade reading-matter was to make me sometimes impatient with "slow" traditional books. That was probably why *Ivanhoe* bored me so when we "had" it my first year in high school, while "The Lady of the Lake," which could be declaimed, was as exciting as a play, especially the great unmasking: "These are Clan Alpine's warriors true./ And, stranger, *I* am Roderick Dhu"— a fierce character whom, naturally, I thrilled to far more than to the tame heroes. In fact, my mental life toward the end of my time at Forest Ridge was at a dead low. The loss of my faith had produced no countervailing benefit. Having started, almost by accident, to doubt the reality of God, I lost interest in the subject when I discovered to my surprise that there was no real proof that He existed. Religion left me, to return, if at all, in later years as an amused interest in theology. And I had no other object of thought. Sex remained a closed book despite *True Story* and *True Confessions*, from which I merely concluded that one must be careful not to sleep with a man (not even drop off for a minute) or a baby would begin growing inside one. My interest in my own body centered on my breasts, which I kept a close watch on, hoping they would grow; there were ads in those magazines that recommended creams and massage, and I was tempted to send in for free samples, just as I was tempted by advertisements for a puzzling thing called a truss, which to my ears had a salacious sound—I cannot remember whether a free trial was offered. What I lacked, above all, in this whole field was reliable information.

My ignorance, not so very remarkable in a bright girl (in my experience, sexual wisdom seldom keeps pace with the "higher" kind), points to what was a crucial problem for my development, the real obstacle to the birth of a mind in my teeming brain—the fact that I had no friends. It ought to have alarmed my grandparents if they were watching (which apparently they were not) that I had no one of my own age to talk to, no one to confide in, no one I dared ask, for example, what a truss was. I could not trust my uncle Frank's wife, named Isabel, active in the younger married set, not to make fun of my strangeness—a thing about myself that I sensed without being able to see. I did not take to my new classmates—a "Pat," an "Eileen," a "Joan," with red hair, freckles, and dandruff on the uniform. Mothers of these and others (I think of a stick named Jane Miller with glasses and a stiff brother, Vincent) invited the class for tables of lotto followed by ice cream and cake on a Saturday, but I was always glad to go home when my grandmother came to pick me up in her electric. None of those girls was ever invited to our house, and at the time that did not strike me as peculiar since nobody but a relative had been allowed to put foot in the house in Minneapolis. When at last a popular girl from the class ahead was demoted to be my deskmate (a punishment for talking in study hall) and responded kindly to my overtures, it was partly from pity, I now see, and a willingness to be entertained. We did not share thoughts. Yet friendship, I believe, is essential to intellectuals. It is probably the growth hormone the mind requires as it begins its activity of producing and exchanging ideas. You can date the evolving life of a mind, like the age

27

of a tree, by the rings of friendship formed by the expanding central trunk. In the course of my history, not love or marriage so much as friendship has promoted growth.

When, at my own urging, then, in the year 1925, I entered a public high school in what is now the black district of Seattle, it was not as though I were leaving a circle of friends behind to embark on the unknown. Certain Sacred heart presences—Marie-Louise L'Abbé, Julia Dodge, Janet Preston, Marjorie MacPhail, the Von Phuls, the Lyonses, the Danz girls, little Abbie Stuart Baillargeon, Eugenia McClellan, Susie Lowenstein—are stored in my memory like fall leaves pressed in a school book, but though I cannot forget their names, faces, figures, the awareness was not mutual. I had arrived among them a stranger from Minneapolis and to those I most worshipped I remained that. At Garfield, again, I knew nobody; I had no former classmates from a city grade school to serve as a launching pad. The convent I had left behind was utterly remote from this new milieu—no connection, another planet—and when, in the second term, the exquisite Julia Dodge appeared among us, as a transfer from Forest Ridge, it was like the transmigration of a soul from a distant heavenly body. Nobody among my new acquaintances could believe that I knew her, and she showed no recognition of me.

I did not last long at public high school; my grandparents, wisely, withdrew me at the end of the first year when, crazed by liberty, I almost ceased to study. Since the loss of my faith was proving to be permanent, more than an adolescent's caprice, we decided that I should go to a Protestant boarding-school, where there would be little stress on religion. The choice lay between St. Margaret's School, in Victoria, B.C., the Anna Head School, in Berkeley, California (where Helen Wills had gone), and the Annie Wright Seminary, in nearby Tacoma. Needless to say, I longed to go to Anna Head, which in fact was a good school, and my grandparents leaned toward Annie Wright, where they could come to see me in the car on occasional Sundays, bringing

28

fruit and cookies and a flowering plant for my room. The principal, a Miss Preston, established a good rapport with my grandfather, and thus my fate was decided.

In other words, accident—the coincidence of a surname and the driving time from Seattle—determined my entire future. Had I got my wish and gone to Anna Head, I would have become Californian and I would not like myself now. I prefer being a Puget Sound type that had gone east to college, as could happen, though rarely, to Seattle girls; from Anna Head, I would probably have continued on to Stanford, or even Berkeley, and become a sorority girl, a Gamma Phi, maybe, like my mother at the University of Washington. As to what I might have turned into had St. Margaret's in Victoria been elected, I cannot even guess.

On the choice of one's secondary school, one's course in life seems to be plotted, and often there is no consciousness of a choice being made, no visible bifurcation of the ways: from grade school one continues to the neighborhood high school (as my parents did) or one goes to the boarding-school where "everyone" in the family has gone. Here the part played by chance seems all but unnoticeable, and the future appears to flow inevitably from the past. With relatively rootless people, often transplanted, like myself, destiny's decisions, on the contrary, may appear highly capricious. I think of Reuel studying school catalogues and voting for Andover—a preference I could not account for until in a corner of a photograph in the Andover catalogue I noticed a Ping-Pong table. In a similar vein Edmund Wilson overruled Milton Academy (girls, proximity to Boston, a good curriculum) for the self-evident reason that T. S. Eliot had been a Milton boy. In fact Reuel was sent to Brooks, in *North Andover*—a decision that had something to do with the size of the headmaster's dog.

But my own fates may have pronounced while I was still in public high school, months before Annie Wright was even thought of or a single name-tape sewed on my underclothes. It may have happened on the day I got my first

29

library card from the Seattle Public Library—an important, even self-important, day for me, although I cannot call it the happiest of my life, as Napoleon is supposed to have said of the day of his First Communion. Nevertheless I remember the feeling of power conferred on me by the small, ruled piece of cardboard still empty except for my name typed at the top and my signature below. I was in the main downtown branch (not far from the YWCA, where I used to swim all by myself on winter Saturdays in the pool), and the fiction shelves frightened me with a bewilderment of choice—a sensation bordering on panic that one can get nowadays in a too well furnished supermarket. The power of choice I held affected me as an urgency, forcing me to take out a book before I was fully prepared, hurrying me to make up my mind as though behind me there were a crowd of other borrowers. Summoning resolution, I picked a book from the shelves and advanced to the counter. It was *The Nigger of the Narcissus*. The librarian looked at me; I looked back at her. She took my card and tucked another one, stamped, in a flap at the back of the volume. I had the impression that she might say something, but she let me walk away. In my mind was only the vaguest notion of who Joseph Conrad was or had been.

2

It was in public high school that I became conscious for
the first time of a type of person that we would now call
an intellectual. In those days the word for such people col-
lectively was "intelligentsia," borrowed from the Russian
and scarcely used any more, as though the Bolshevik Revolution, in eliminating the social grouping, had consigned
the term to "the ashcan of history"—a favorite receptacle.
"Intelligentsia" had included bohemians—artists and musicians, people like Pasternak's parents—as well as *narodniki*,
nihilists, teachers, doctors, sometimes combining several of
these vocations in one person as in Turgenev's Bazarov. It
was the enlightened class in society. The characters typically found in Chekhov—army officers, country doctors, small
landowners fond of musing on large ideas, students—all

belong to the intelligentsia, whatever their occupation or lack of it. They are an epiphenomenon of increased education, hence choiceless in a sense and rather sad; the intellectual, on the other hand, is self-chosen, even when produced in quantity. The term took hold in the thirties, encouraged by Marxism and the depression. In Garfield High School, on the edge of the Madrona district in Seattle, probably neither term was familiar in the year 1925, but the thing existed and was recognized.

Like most big-city high schools, ours had a star system, expressive of the fact that we were a juvenile mass society. The biggest and most powerful—galaxies distant from a speck of a freshman like me—were the football stars (Larry Judson); then came the track stars (the fleet Bill Albin); then the basketball aces (for some reason less glamorous, although a cheering section of us, wearing beanies and waving pennants, accompanied them to whatever high-school gym they played in, all the way to Ballard, even, or West Seattle). Besides the athletes there were the thespians (Larry Judson, again, in a brown business suit, and black-haired Kathleen Hoyt, who had an "English" voice, very affected, wore a cloak, and was coached by her mother) and the literary "lights" who edited the school paper (the famed Mary Brinker, who married Mr. Post, the English teacher, and thus became Mary Brinker Post, and tiny Estare Crane of the single black side spit curl, who married the wit Mark Sullivan, but of him more anon).

Garfield had no academic stars, awing the rest of us with their straight A's. I don't think grades played any part in the politics of the school, which may be why I let mine sink to D-minus even in French and English, my best subjects. My grandparents thought it was because my head had been turned by boys, after two years of deprivation with the Ladies of the Sacred Heart; no doubt they were partly right, since when an end was decreed to Garfield and I was sent the next fall to the Episcopal boarding-school for girls in Tacoma, my marks at once shot up.

But boys and their effect are not what I want to talk about here (I was not allowed to "step out" with them anyway); rather, I want to trace the onset of intellectual interests in me that I can place during that year. At first this was merely curiosity, awakened by the discovery of what appeared to be a new species of being. We had not had any intellectuals in the convent, unless I count the Mistress of Studies. There had been none in my family (although my father with his invalidism and irregular law practice might have qualified for the old intelligentsia), and I would not find any at Annie Wright Seminary. This does not mean that brains and scholastic achievement were undervalued in those schools; almost the contrary. In the convent medals for excellence in our subjects were awarded every month like the wide blue, green, and pink moire ribbons some of us got to wear over our left shoulder and across the chest for good conduct, and books were distributed at the end of term as prizes for scholarship. I don't recall prizes at Annie Wright, but we had a number of coveted academic privileges and honors, the crowning one being to be chosen valedictorian at Commencement, which was almost as good as having been May Queen.

The quality of the teaching at both Forest Ridge and Annie Wright was greatly superior to what was offered at Garfield (this cannot have been a matter of better pay, since the nuns received only a cell and unenviable board), and the high quality of the instruction was sensed by the pupils, even the dull ones, as a special kind of electricity given off by certain teachers. There was nothing of the sort at Garfield; maybe some of the teachers were feared; most of them, I felt, were despised. But at the convent, as at Annie Wright, a few (Madame Bartlett, Miss Dorothy Atkinson, Miss Hayward) were the objects, almost, of a cult. There was much vying to be noticed by them, sit by them at table, have them (at the Seminary) as chaperons for shopping trips and playgoing, and these were not the most indulgent or youngest and prettiest teachers but the most stiff, sallow, severe. To the more formidable Madames in the convent (Mère Bartlett, in particular, with her shadow of a moustache) legends of prowess clung—how they had been educated at the Sorbonne, how they had read all the forbidden classics on the Index under a special dispensation from the archbishop—and around the more austere women in the Seminary, e.g., Mrs. Hiatt, the widow of a cleric, who wore a gold watch and chain, we wove fables of loss of fortune that had lowered them to the sad point of teaching us.

Of course, the closed, single-sex atmosphere of boarding-school encouraged such an attitude in the girls: at the Sacred Heart the piano lesson, chaperoned by an old lay nun dozing in a chair, was our unique encounter with a man outside the confessional; at Annie Wright the only males we saw during the week were Mr. Bell, the chaplain, who sometimes "took" the morning service, the janitor, an incomprehensible old Lancashireman, the gardener, an incomprehensible old Yorkshireman, and Major Mathews, the riding-master (married). Having no better food for our hungry imaginations, naturally we romanticized our teachers' mental acquirements and surely graded some of them higher than they deserved. Even so, the comparatively low esteem in which the teachers at Garfield were held seems rather remarkable. It must have been related to the lack of attention given to high marks, though which was cause and which effect is not clear.

The "exception" teacher at Garfield, I gather, had been the above-mentioned Mr. Post. He was already in the past tense when I entered, having left (to become a writer?) a summer or so before, but he was still spoken of with reverence by boys and girls who had not had the luck to "have" him in class. What he had taught in the way of English I never found out, but I think he owed his unusual status not so much to his classroom performance as to having been adviser to the newspaper and the yearbook—media-functions that connected him with the reigning star system of the school. I picture him as a sort of coach to Garfield "teams" of budding journalists, which had moved on to the U, across the canal; some, like Mark Sullivan, were already "making their letter" on campus by editing the college newspaper, yearbook, humorous magazine. Certainly Mr. Post had the kind of popularity enjoyed by a football coach, and, just as a Husky quarterback trained on Seattle playfields could aspire to be named All-American and enter the Hall of Fame, so a member of one of Mr. Post's "winning" high-school teams could hope to have a story accepted by *College Humor* while still an undergraduate and eventually make it to the Seattle *P.-I.* or Colonel Blethen's *Times* (our afternoon paper, the *Star*, was lacking in prestige) or even go east and become a columnist like Hearst's O. O. McIntire or the real Mark Sullivan, a then-famous pundit.

Today journalists are not considered intellectuals. But in 1925, in the West, high-school and college newspapers seemed secure stepping-stones to literary and intellectual fame. There was no such thing as "creative writing" then; there were no "Writers' Workshops," no "writers in residence." Rather, the cub reporter was the man of destiny in our still half-pioneering Far Western cities, just as in the small towns of the prairie the newspaper editor was the town philosopher. Jack London, Frank Norris, Dreiser, Mencken, Ben Hecht, Burton Rascoe had blazed the trail to the city room or afield to the foreign correspondent's tent— in Seattle we did not know yet of "Bunny" Wilson and Hemingway, who had been making their start in the same way. Such figures as Mencken and Dreiser, rather than V. L. Parrington (*Main Currents in American Thought*), actually teaching in the English Department of the University, were the intellectual giants, resembling Rodin's "Thinker," that our locals sought to emulate. Giants and titans, like Dreiser titles or Gutzon Borglum likenesses hammered into a mountain face, peopled the cultural scenery, above all west of the Mississippi. The sheer size of the country gave the effort to write a narrative an epic thrust, and the notion of genius, hard for Americans to relinquish, was still very much alive in the pages of our school yearbook. The genius (I now slowly perceive), like the intellectual, is a product of mass culture.

I have only to summon up in memory the hushed study halls of Forest Ridge and Annie Wright, with the *surveillante* or teacher-on-duty raised above us at her desk on the dais, I have only to see morning chapel, with the girls in dark-blue serge uniforms and black net veils, like widows, intoning "*Oui, je le crois*," or else in Episcopalian middy blouses and bare-headed tuning up on "Sun of my soul, Thou Saviour dear, It is not night if Thou be near," to admit that an intellectual cannot be the product of an elite education. Rough plebeian democracy is the breeding-ground of the class of intellectuals, springing up like the dragon's teeth to fight and kill each other down to the last five men before they can found the City.

Yes. I think of evening chapel at the Seminary: the day girls are gone; the organ plays; the boarding department stands up in its poorly fitting colored-silk dinner uniforms to sing the dirge for the day ("Now the day is o-over, Night is dra-awing ni-igh," my favorite), whereupon our principal, Miss Preston, dark-eyed, in a polka-dot dress, kneels down on her stout knees at her prayer-desk and clears her wattled throat to begin the Collect for Aid against Perils, "Lighten our darkness, we beseech Thee, o Lord," in her deep New England voice. Stubby Miss Preston is a Smith woman; *her* favorite hymn is Number 117 (Bunyan's "He who would valiant be"); she cries easily, like her billowy blue-eyed counterpart, Madame McQueenie, the acting Reverend Mother of Forest Ridge; they are both fond of taking repentant girls onto their slippery laps—Miss Preston's, usually silken in the evening, being worse. Now our voices follow hers in the General Confession: "We have left undone those things which we ought to have done. And we have done those things which we ought not to have done. And there is no health in us"—how true! Chapel and study hall, Church of Rome and P. E. merge. I listen to the scratch of pens, the bell of the *surveillante*, the soughing of the organ, the creaking of pew benches, and I could weep for it all, for the waste of it.

Those hard-working women, our teachers, not always brilliant themselves, gave a sound education, tried to inculcate good morals and a respect for excellence, and accomplished hardly more than a finishing-school. What they taught (like the art of making buttonholes we had to master in sewing class in the convent) was never used afterwards. Or only by that tiny percentage that was going to teach school itself or find some other employment for Boyle's Law and the subjunctive after French verbs of saying, thinking, and the like, when uncertainty is conveyed. Annie Wright prepared you for college, that was the idea, but you did not need any special preparation to go to the University of Washington, and in my year—1929—only two of us went on to an institution that required College Boards. The Ladies of the Sacred Heart made no pretense of college preparation; they had a so-called College Department, consisting of two years, for the tall, blue-ribboned older girls like the Lyons sisters, and that was it. What both schools imparted to their graduates was something like old-fashioned "accomplishments," but these were mostly out-of-date (those buttonholes!) or bizarrely irrelevant to the future lying ahead. Was Latin prosody a grace that would sit prettily on a girl who was going to marry a lumber executive? And the *pas de chat* and correct ballet positions we were taught at the convent, the schottische and polka we got at the Seminary, how were we going to use them? In the years of the tango and the Charleston, we were learning clog-dancing.

In a sense, I suppose, I was the chief beneficiary of Forest Ridge and Annie Wright in that I was able to find a use for what we learned. I don't mean that *Sans Famille* and "Belling the Cat" served to get me into Vassar, though, multiplied, evidently they helped. I mean that I was peculiarly fitted to "get the good out of" the convent and the Seminary, not because I was more gifted or cleverer than my

37

classmates but because, thanks to Garfield's plebeian incentives, I was an intellectual by the time I reached Annie Wright. And no one else was.

I will explain. A superior education, such as, on the whole, we got in those private schools, can only be used by those it was not intended for. By the fluke of having gone—for a single year—to a big-city high school, I happened to be one of them. The point of a private school in the U.S.A. is to represent in its curriculum the purest conspicuous waste. Unlike the English public schools, our private schools do not aim to prepare a ruling class to govern—the exception used to be Groton. Our usual private schools are not vocational schools even in that remote sense. If there is anything "exclusive" (aside from the cost) in the whole system of private education, it is the *exemption* of a class of students from evident vocational goals. Some at Annie Wright strove harder for grades than others, but this seemed to be a matter of temperament, rather than need. There were no grinds (that I remember) among us. As with high jump and shot-put, the act of surpassing rivals in doing a sight translation was performed for its own sake or for purposes of showing off. I am not saying that there were no professions besides teaching for which Latin could not some day be useful. There was medicine, for instance. In our class at Annie Wright, besides a future French-teacher, we had a future doctor. Yet if those two girls—and I—profited from the curriculum, it was through the fact of being—or becoming—anomalies.

Just to make it clear: I am in favor of the teaching of Latin and Greek, plus one modern language, on the secondary-school level or even earlier. It is probably the best way of teaching history—Western history, evidently, to which as a nation we can claim an inheritance. But I believe that this has no meaning, even as a utopian dream, unless the entire nation's children are given the "basics" of a culture we all share, as Jews and unbelievers, like it or not, once shared the culture of Christendom. When the classics are offered as ornaments or status symbols for the few, they become otiose, and this had happened at some point during the Coolidge era: the public high school of a New England mill town, say Fall River, Massachusetts, on the retirement of its old-maid classics teacher, ceased offering Latin and even Greek to the progeny of mill workers and thus obliged the owners, who wanted "advantages" for their children, to send them "away" to school. (This was a sign, evidently, of an impoverishment of our culture as a whole. It is the same with food: in countries with a superior cuisine—France, Italy, China—allowing for regional variations based on climate, everybody eats the same diet, though the rich have more of it and more often; in nations famous for bad cooking—England, the U.S.—rich and poor have utterly different food cultures.)

For Latin to be rescued from oblivion (to which even the Church has relegated it), there would have to be general agreement on its absolute value and desirability—not just some faint persuasion of its utility, such as the argument now put forward that it can help teach ghetto children English, however true that contention may be. The average intellectual today has no Latin; indeed, he may have no language other than English. Though the class of intellectuals can trace its ancestry to the clerks and pedants of the medieval and Renaissance "schools," learning is no longer an earmark—it is optional, and the lack of it avoids confusion with the horde of academics. Here is a better criterion: an intellectual, as opposed to a dutiful classroom performer but like the "upstart clerks" of Elizabethan times, is always self-made. Finally: it is a mistake to think that an intellectual is required to be intelligent; there are occasions when the terms seem to be almost antonyms.

But to return to Garfield. Instead of study hall, there was an auditorium in which school assemblies were held, though not every morning, and sometimes the school band played. Since you were expected to study at home, you did not have your own desk here in which you kept your books and equipment. We each had a locker for that purpose, and we hung our coats, scarves, and so on, in an adjacent hall lined with hooks. I cannot remember what provision there was for overshoes and rubbers; it hardly ever snowed in Seattle, but it rained a lot.

Nor can I remember where and how we ate. I think some brought school lunches, to be supplemented with milk from the school cafeteria, and some brought money and bought food there, and a few bought more glamorous and unwholesome food in nearby eating-places catering to the fast crowd. Certainly we did not go home for lunch. And what strikes me now, looking back at that big high school, is a sense of being adrift, having no settled place in it.

It was mainly not having a desk, I imagine. In the grade-school "room" and the study halls of boarding academies, the pupil's desk holds the tools of his trade ("Student")— pen nibs, blotters, ruler, compass, books, pencils, erasers, plus the usual contraband—and bolts him firmly into the system. For all eternity I am the eighth-grader who sits next to one of the Berens twins, pretty, dark Louise, and behind "Phil" Chatham (whose father's name, spelled "Ralph," is pronounced "Rafe"), on the dictionary side of the room, four rows from the front, where the Mistress of Studies is on watch. In chapel, it was height that determined your place: big girls in the back pews, little girls in front. The effect to be made, entering two abreast in procession, was the main concern of our supervisors. Since growing girls grow at different rates, continual readjustment was required. This was particularly true at the Seminary, where our principal had processions on the brain. On a great occasion like Founder's Day, prepared for by many a rehearsal, suddenly at the last minute a teacher with a measuring stick would pass along the double line of girls and move some of us ahead or back; then another teacher would move us again.

At table, evidently, we had our established places. A

Seminary "table" consisted of ten or twelve girls moving every second week to sit with a different teacher till the "top" table headed by the vice-principal, Miss Justine Browne, was reached, after which new tables were formed. By what sort of shuffle those combinations were made up, nobody knew. Why the "two Gins"—Virginia Barnett and Virginia Kellogg—were sometimes put at the same table, although roommates, while I repeatedly drew one of my *bêtes noires*—a pale, spectacled, black-haired, sneering underclassman by the name of Catherine MacPherson—was beyond understanding. In general, if there was a principle to be discerned, it was the negative one of keeping friends apart, to insure that Miss Preston's golden rule of "M.C.G." ("Make Conversation General") would be maintained. In the Forest Ridge refectory, conversation was limited by having to be in French, by retreats (when the only utterance permitted was "Passe le sel"), by Lent and Advent, and by sudden arbitrary silences imposed by the *surveillante*'s clapper. There, too, our place at table was not chosen but assigned. It was all decided for us and sealed by our napkin ring marking the spot like the name-tapes sewn to our clothing. Similarly, with our library book, the precise hour of our weekly bath (which we took under a canvas shift so as not to have to see our bodies), we occupied the station to which God or some Madame in her infinite wisdom had seen fit to call us. Garfield, by contrast, was a churning millrace of apparent free will.

Here the classrooms were long, and we sat in rows, rather than around an oak table, seminar-style, as we had at the convent. In those long classrooms, the teacher, up front by the blackboard, seemed a great way off, and it was possible not to be called on if you made yourself small. I was quite often unprepared. In freshman English, we had the Old Testament and *Ivanhoe*—both boring. Instead of the English history and French history, with kings and favorites, that I had learned by heart in the convent, Garfield started us with World History, which did not have any interesting people in it—nobody like Warwick, the King-Maker, Jack Cade and Perkin Warbeck, or Ganelon, the traitor. The result is that I can still name you the rulers of England and quite a few of their prime ministers, down to whiskered Lord Palmerston; the Capets and Valois did not stick with me so well. At the Sacred Heart, in eighth-grade French, I had been memorizing Victor Hugo (*"Cette étoile de flamme,/ Cet astre du jour,/ Cette fleur de l'âme,/ S'appelle l'amour"*); Garfield's Intermediate French was all exercises and grammar.

At home, having finished *Rienzi, the Last of the Tribunes* and "The Outcasts of Poker Flat," I felt I had outgrown my grandfather's library. *Pickwick Papers*, one of his great favorites, had put me off Dickens for years to come. I had loved *A Tale of Two Cities*, when it was read aloud to us during sewing class in the convent by a tiny, Irish-accented Madame, and some of *Oliver Twist*, but I could not abide "Boz" and refused to open anything with a name like *Martin Chuzzlewit*. In my school crowd, insofar as I had one, nobody read; our entire mental apparatus was bent on grading boys and girls in terms of appearance, dress, antecedents, though the last category was not too important unless it conferred mystery. Our curiosity, such as it was, centered on a white-faced fat boy who had entered with us and was said to be a "morphodite."

Except for the few boys who played musical instruments, it was unusual for Garfield's students to have "interests." There was a girl who painted—a dainty blonde named Ebba Rapp who wore uneven hemlines and a jabot—and I went to her house for her to do my portrait, a pastel head-and-shoulders that my grandmother kept for a long time. But I don't remember ever entering our Seattle art museum; nor did I go to a concert till much later, when they had "Symphonies under the Stars" at the stadium in the University, with Michel Piastro conducting. Yet Seattle was an artistic town. It had a Ladies' Musical Club, run by my great-aunt Rosie, who had gone to Vancouver once with Chaliapin, the Cornish school of drama and art, which also offered eurythmics, a stock company, and (soon, if not already) a repertory theatre run by Mr. and Mrs. Burton James. But none of this seems to have "related" to the adolescent population, which entertained itself by eating sodas and sundaes, swimming and diving in the various lakes, playing popular records, and going with dates to the movies—something my grandparents would not let me do.

I could go to the movies with *them*, sitting in loge seats—a torment; I did not wish to look "different"—to the Saturday matinee of the stock company with my grandmother and one of her sisters, go shopping with her in her electric, take a family ride in the Chrysler around Lake Washington after Sunday lunch, pick out "Marcheta" to myself on the piano, persuade my married uncle's friends to hear me recite "Lord Ullin's Daughter," play practical jokes on the telephone ("Have you got Prince Albert in a can? Well, let him out"), and once or twice a year go to a tea-dance at the DeMolay Temple (Masonic) in ribbed silk stockings with a coerced partner who, like me, had never learned to dance. I could send in coupons from the cheap magazines I read for samples of nail polish, freckle cream, bust-developer, put Cutex nail polish on my mouth in the guise of lipstick when I thought my grandmother was downtown, make messes in the kitchen trying over-ambitious candies like marshmallows—a sticky, gelatinous mixture hopefully (note correct use of word) cut in cubes and rolled in floury sugar. I had dropped piano lessons on leaving the convent; the only sport I knew how to do was swimming (breast stroke, side stroke, overarm side stroke; no crawl); I was unaware of masturbation—except maybe for boys? In short, I had no real occupation, and my sole real interest—the stage—required an audience.

At Garfield I tried out faithfully for skits and playlets that were done outside class hours under the coaching of a teacher. This was independent of the regular school play (*Dulcy*, that year, by George S. Kaufman and Marc Connelly, starring a "Dumb Dora"); it was more like what is

43

now called a workshop, held in a disused classroom in the school basement without lights, scenery, or costumes, and with only a faithful few signing up for it regularly. I hardly know how to tell this, but one afternoon, in a sketch we were doing—for practice, with only the teacher watching— I was cast as Larry Judson's wife. Yes, the captain of our football team. He was a senior with dark-reddish curly brown hair, reddish-brown eyes, and well-cut manly features, possibly a dimple in the sturdy chin. If I remember right, he played end, my favorite position. What possessed the teacher to cast me, a freshman and only thirteen, opposite Garfield's idol, with whom I was secretly in love? And that was not all. In the playlet *he had to put his arm around me* and hold me to his chest, though the "heart" he pressed me to was a little too high for my head to rest against without stretching—I had not yet got my full growth.

That this should have been happening to me was so like a dream that today I ask myself whether it was *not* a dream. Odd that a football star would want to be an actor. And yet there was Paul Robeson, who had been All-American at Rutgers and then played on Broadway (1923) in *The Emperor Jones*. In any case, after that, Larry Judson smiled at me whenever he met me in the mid-morning tidal flow around the bulletin boards in the main hall—a faint, full-lipped smile that told me, I guessed, that he remembered. And once, it seems to me, as I was skirting the school playfield, a ball thrown or kicked by him hit me in the midriff, making me feel like St. Francis receiving the stigmata. But this memory is very fuzzy. I am not sure whether it was a football or a baseball or even a tennis ball and maybe I have imagined the whole thing. When I was sent off to the Seminary, I lost sight of him. I only know that he did not become an actor, did not play football for the U, perhaps did not *go* to the U. I wonder whether anyone still alive, besides me, remembers him treading the boards at Garfield and could tell me what became of him.

But I truly did play his wife; all at once I am completely

sure of this, for I have recalled an odd detail. That dark-brown suit, almost chocolate-colored, a real man's suit, smelled when he "clasped me to his heart." It was not an armpit reek of stale sweat announcing that the suit needed a trip to the cleaner's; it was more of a closet smell, as though the suit had been hanging quite a while in an airless space. And it was somehow a *mature* smell, reminding me now of the collective B.O. of my grandmother's clothes when I got a whiff of them all together in her closet. It belongs to the aging process; I have noticed it on my own clothes in these last years when they have spent a winter in an unopened closet without benefit of mothballs. Maybe it has something to do with the oily or tallowy secretions of the sebaceous glands. Could my "husband" have been wearing a middle-aged man's suit? That might have been passed on to him from an uncle who had died? I try to recall whether it was two-piece or three-piece. Did I encounter any vest-buttons in our hug? I am not sure. All I can bring back is a sense of the color and heaviness of the cloth, which "put age on" him, giving him a sedate, settled look.

Now something else comes back to me that I had entirely forgotten. *Larry Judson was Jewish.* I do not know how or when I learned it, certainly quite a bit after we played husband and wife. I think a Jewish friend told me, as if it were a thing I should have known already. To me, though, it was a stunning surprise. "Larry *Judson*?" I was shocked. I was a quarter Jewish myself and I had already had a Jewish love-object—my second cousin, Burton Gottstein, in his sophomore year at the University, velvet-eyed and lustrous as a black pearl. At the Sacred Heart I had decided that the degree of consanguinity (we were actually first cousins once removed) could not prevent our marrying in the Church if he would consent to take instruction. Now I had left the Church, so Larry's Jewishness should not have bothered me on that score: no need to be married by a priest. Anyway marriage was no longer in my mind—a sign surely that I was maturing. Just worshipping him from not too far off

45

was enough. Why, then, was I so taken aback? It was a sort of disillusionment, like learning the real names of one's favorite movie stars—I could have slain the relative who brought me the tidings that Ricardo Cortez was plain Jake Krantz. On the screen he would never be the same for me. In Larry's case, though, I was able to accept the undeception. The suit and the mature smell, I guess, had prepared me for swallowing a dose of reality. In my soul, without knowing it, I was getting ready to be sorry for the boy-man.

At that point I had not given much thought to Jews or what it meant to be one. There were several kinds evidently (corresponding, I now see, to the degree of assimilation): the kind represented by my grandmother and her sisters; another represented by their brother, Uncle Elkan Morgenstern, and his huge-breasted little wife, Aunt Hennie (in that family girls were fat and boys went through some rite at the age of confirmation called the bar mitzvah with presents and a party afterwards, where you got sweetbreads and mushrooms in patty shells, cheese puffs, and Crab Louie); and still a stranger kind, in funny clothes, whom I used to look at from the Madrona streetcar, which went by their houses—the poor Orthodox Jews from the Pale.

In the Pale, which Larry's parents probably came from, little boys wore long dark trousers and resembled little men. Philip Rahv used to tell me, years later, of how he had felt marked as an immigrant in a Providence, Rhode Island, grade school by the Old Country long trousers his mother dressed him in. And I remember how Philip used to call my five-year-old Reuel "little man." In 1925–26, in Seattle, I could have known nothing about the Pale and its customs. Yet on the broad porches of those multi-family dwellings—wooden tenements—that I stared at from the streetcar, I had seen quite young bearded men wearing shiny black hats and thick dark suits and old bearded men in black skullcaps and their undershirts and, no doubt, pale boys, too, looking old and solemn for their size. And nearer home, our next-door neighbors, Mr. and Mrs. Gerber, afflicted with heavy accents, had two long-nosed sons, Len and Sid, who dressed "old" and kept apart from the neighborhood. Unlike my young uncle Harold and his friends, they were destined for "business," I heard, as though it were a vocation, like the priesthood. Larry's brown suit may have spoken to me in a foreign language that I was nonetheless vaguely able to decipher of a fate in store for its wearer—a doom of premature manhood already thickening his jowls. That was the price he would have to pay for his parents' being poor Jews—a price Burt Gottstein, who belonged to "their" best fraternity and would soon join a smart brokerage house, would know nothing about.

I am guessing, of course. All I am certain of is that Larry, our school star, disappeared from my ken as though swallowed up. Maybe his parents moved. My memory of him stops with the suit, the hug, the piteous little "racial" realization framing the whole like a black mourning border. And I remember nothing further of those after-school dramatics. Maybe I ceased to sign up for them because the teacher failed to give me another leading part. Or spring came, and I got interested in the track team, following them to meets in the afternoons, which might have made a "conflict" with the acting workshop: I traded Larry Judson for Bill Albin.

(A few paragraphs back, I was wondering whether anyone could tell me what became of Larry Judson. Since I wrote—and published—those words, two people have told me, one of them being Larry Judson himself. He remembers treading the boards and thinks the teacher was named Miss Aiken— Yes! But his letters, two by now and both very nice, say he is only partly Jewish, a quarter, like me. And for fifty-two years he has been married to a Miss Birdie O'Rourke. The man's suit is explained by facts he relates: he was older than the rest of us, working his way through high school as a salesman for *Pictorial Review*, the way others worked their way through college.

But there is another stage episode of my Garfield year, which I do not know where to situate. Perhaps quite early, before Larry and the skit. The problem is that the person it happened to, the heroine of the occasion, has become unrecognizable to me, so that I cannot account for her feelings and behavior. That is not true of the convent: in my slightly spotty blue serge uniform, unrelieved by any good-conduct ribbon, I am my familiar self, younger. But in trying to describe what I can remember of the Garfield time, I have been noticing a contradiction. From the record I know that I was wild about public high, to the point of losing my head and having to be removed by my grandparents. But what I put down does not sound that way; it sounds scornful. Evidently the self that felt the attraction of Garfield's mob scene has been sloughed like a snake's skin. Or brutally killed, leaving me, the person I am now, as the sole survivor. "I know not the man," St. Peter said, denying Jesus, and I can say, with greater truthfulness, of that thirteen-year-old pennant-waver, "I don't know that child." In what I am about to relate the disassociation is almost complete, resulting in big patches of amnesia. I do not even know what I looked like or what I wore that year—no photographs have survived from the period.

Once upon a time, then, I appeared on the stage at Garfield before a good-sized audience and scored a real success. It was an event, I think, for freshmen, designed to bring out the talents of the entering class—something like "amateur night" in the movie theatres and vaudeville houses of those days, when volunteers mounted the stage to do solo acts and were judged by the amount of applause they received. If I reconstruct it right, you could sing or yodel or tap-dance or play an instrument such as the banjo or you could recite, but it had to be something light—nothing on the order of "Lord Ullin's Daughter." I had chosen a comic monologue by the Canadian humorist Stephen Leacock: "I had a little dog and her name was Alice." It was meant to be delivered in a doleful deadpan voice that would make the recitation all the more hilarious. Well, I brought the house down—a slightly untoward surprise (even though I had aspired to it), as I had always thought of my muse as tragic. They clapped and cheered and possibly stamped; if there was a prize, I won it. Then why does a clear recollection of that red-letter day, as if too painful, refuse to reach consciousness?

I can see several answers. First, they were laughing *at* me, rather than *with* me, or, as we used to say in boarding-school, I was being funny-peculiar, not funny-haha. Perhaps so: the recitation may have succeeded in a partly unintended way, causing an *excess* of applause. Second, plagiarism. Could I have pretended to have written that skit myself? And then did some teacher confront me with my theft? Possibly. There was a precedent in my history: back in grade school, I had stolen copiously from *Our Sunday Visitor* for my prize-winning essay on the Irish in American history. Still, that was different: *then* I did not know it was wrong; *now* the uneasiness surrounding the blank in my memory may suggest guilty feelings. Yet a temptation to steal somebody else's words was not my thing; perhaps I was too conceited for it. *So*, third, my claque.

Probably the real answer lies there. But to explain I shall have to go back and account for the improbable fact of my having a claque. It was the crowd from Mercer Island, halfway across Lake Washington, whom I had come to know slightly the previous summer through staying with the Berens twins from Forest Ridge. Today Mercer Island is reached by a bridge and is much like any other outlying section of the city. But in those days you took a ferry to get there; it was rural, and behind its farmland and dark spruce trees rose Seattle's claim to fame in our geography books—snow-capped Mount Rainier. Looking across from my grandmother's tall house on moonlit nights, I saw the moon make a silver path across the black lake water that corresponded with the daytime route of the ferryboat. The band of rooters occupying the first rows of our Garfield auditorium on the day of "Alice" came whooping to school on the ferry every morning and went home by the same means every night—

the tooting ride back and forth seemed to have welded them into a vociferous unit like the anvil chorus. I shut my eyes and try to see that cheering-section individually, but they have stuck together in a lump, like candy in a coat-pocket, like their fatal watchword—"Let's stick together, kids." In the blur I can pick out only one face, that of Josephine Hoey (pronounced "hooey"), their leader: glasses, pale eyes, pale lashes, skin the color of junket, fish mouth. When she laughs, she chortles; her fattish shoulders shake.

Yes, this was the reception committee that had welcomed me to Garfield, where I had thought I would know nobody. From the first day they had "taken me under their wing," showing their pride in the act of adoption by trumpeting my convent nickname (the mysterious initials C.Y.E., which they mistook for "Si," as in "Silas") whenever they caught sight of me: "There's Si McCarthy!" "Hey, Si! Hey, there, Si!" In the summer, they must have heard the twins greeting me at the ferry, and of course it was the Berens twins, known to most of Mercer Island at least by sight, who were responsible for the bit of red carpet put under my feet at Garfield.

At Forest Ridge, the two girls were boarders, a class ahead of me, but in the summer they lived on the island with their widowed mother, a realtor who wore a beret at a sporty angle on her prematurely white hair, smoked cigarettes in a holder, and painted big circles of crimson rouge on her cheeks. That summer they had had me over two or three times to spend the night with them in their bungalow; they were sorry for me, I guess, because I could not win the popularity I coveted (the twins were *very* popular) or, lacking one parent themselves, they could imagine how it felt to lack two. (In fact, it was not clear whether Mr. Berens had died or whether he had deserted Mrs. Berens; he was never alluded to in my presence, and his relict had all the earmarks of what was then called a grass widow.) I loved staying with the two of them—lively Louise and studious Harriet—going to bed in the starlight on their screened sleeping porch, and I loved the island, which was woodsy and informal even for the West. I was impressed by the knowledge that Mrs. Berens "worked," unlike other convent mothers, and wore big pearl earrings even around the house. The twins helped with the cleaning and washing up, and I envied them; in my grandmother's house, I was not trusted to do anything of importance. On Saturday nights there was dancing—or was it a movie?—in a barn down the road, and Mrs. Berens let us go, not even bothering to look in herself as a chaperon.

It must have been on one of those Saturdays that, thanks to the twins, I met my first "man." His name was Armour Spaulding (which said tennis to me); he was twenty-one and smoked a pipe. One night, in his white oxfords, with the pipe glowing, he walked me home along a path through the woods, under a moon, no doubt, with the dark lake water lapping the shore. Possibly Mrs. Berens had deputized him to escort me home; he may have taken me for older than I was. Anyway he sounded quite interested by my flow of conversation and courteously drew me out when I hesitated. For about a year I lived on the memory of it, as if on stored-up energy, though I never saw him again and all I retain of him is the name, the pipe, the shoes, a close-cropped, somewhat bullet-shaped head, perhaps a white shirt and dark-blue blazer. He must have cast a spell of glamour over the whole of Mercer Island, in reality not very classy, he and the popular, kind-hearted twins and their trouper of a mother.

At Garfield the contingent that welcomed me and seemed proud to count me among them probably knew Armour Spaulding, but I never asked. Instead, I lingered around a sporting-goods store that carried Spalding rackets, as though the surname would make him materialize like a genie reporting for duty at the rubbing of a lamp. Meanwhile I acquiesced gratefully in the sponsorship of the Mercer Island entity without being especially drawn to any of its members. But before long I became aware that I had let them take me over too quickly. Those friendly millstones were pulling me down to their level. And that dawning suspicion, I now conjecture, was what has made me efface the success of Alice and her dog from my memory: I was ashamed of it then and there, stricken *in medias res*. As I stood on the stage receiving plaudits, I must have wished to drop through a trap door, like the one in the Metropolitan Theatre that, according to Aunt Rosie, was utilized by Harry Houdini for his famous disappearing act. But no such luck. I was left with a hatred of Stephen Leacock, of the loyal chortlers and stampers, and of the side of myself that wanted their mindless applause. But I have no recollection of my emotions. If some psychoanalyst is moved to tell me "You felt imperiled by success," I do not deny it: I *was* imperiled by success and at the age of thirteen apparently had the sense to know it.

Having lowered myself to the limit of degradation (thank God no member of my family was there), then mercifully dropped into an oubliette, in mind, if not in body, I began to "space" my meetings with the Mercer Island crowd. They must have considered me, rightly, an ingrate. The Berens twins, too, faded from my life. Several years later, home from college for the summer, I saw Louise again; she, the pretty and vivacious one, had become an elevator-starter at Frederick's. And didn't my grandmother tell me that Mrs. Berens was in jail for embezzlement? My present self is shocked that I did not try to "do" something for Louise, my old desk mate. Today I would, but perhaps that only shows that today I am more of a hypocrite.

Yet there is a little more, I suspect, to the "Alice" episode. At that very time, as I now reckon it, I had probably made my first intellectual friend, if "intellectual" is the right word for "Ted" (really Ethel) Rosenberg, whose organ of reflection was perhaps less fully developed than her bump of sensibility. She had a broad, coppery, high-cheekboned face, like an Indian's, short, black, curly hair, like a boy's, a thin, flat-chested figure; she wore brogues and soft loose vests of deerskin. Her green prominent eyes, flecked with brown, had a riveting gaze and widened shyly with excitement, and her voice, always husky, got softly breathless when she spoke of her culture heroes and heroines, some of whom were dead and some of whom were right there in our school.

She came of a family of intellectuals, very close-knit and loving, who did not seem to have any other relatives. There was a sister, Matilda, called Till, who worked in a doctor's office, a tall, gaunt, rabbinical-looking older brother, Dan, who was a graduate student in the Speech Department at the University and talked in a slow, careful voice, and a little brother, Jess, who, at least in my memory, played the violin. The father was a tailor; the mother kept the house, read, baked, and benevolently listened—she was active in Aunt Rosie's Temple De Hirsch (Reformed). I had never met a family like this before; the nearest I had come was Aunt Rosie, who played solitaire all night in a downstairs bedroom lined with signed photographs of opera stars and pianists, and her husband, Uncle Mose, who subscribed to the *New York Times*.

I am not sure how I got to know Ted, who was at least a class ahead of me. It was a question, I think, of *my* becoming aware of *her* becoming aware of me. This could have happened in the cafeteria, in the hall in front of the bulletin boards, or even on a chilly bench at the side of the sports field during football practice, for Ted's hero worship fully embraced athletes. The intellectuals at Garfield were equipped with radar for finding each other, though they themselves, the diviners, would have been barely noticeable to eyes less skilled than their own. Among the incoming freshmen, somehow, Ted had picked me out as someone worth knowing, like a connoisseur looking over a Whitman's Sampler and sensing which one would have a liqueur cherry underneath the chocolate coating. Some feature of me had caught her attention—something about my appearance, something she had heard about me, something she had heard me say. However our acquaintance started, my first clear memory of Ted is connected with a book.

In those days modern literature (like "creative writing") was not taught in school *or* in college. You read it, relying on tips from friends. As with Prohibition liquor, you had to know somebody to get hold of the good stuff. Professional librarians were no help. The circulating library at Frederick's had recommended *The Peasants* by some Pole who had won the Nobel Prize to my grandmother, who had been reading it for months, scarcely making any progress. I had heard of a sensational novel about flappers—*Flaming Youth*—and of *Three Weeks*, by Elinor Glyn, but the existence of modern literature, apart from such titles, was a secret "they" had succeeded in keeping from me till I met Ted. And when she introduced me to *Green Mansions*, by W. H. Hudson, after school in the deserted locker room, it was on a note of confidentiality. The Modern Library imprint awed me, as though it were a sort of guarantee or the password of some exclusive set. I did not notice that the book had first been published in 1904.

Thus at a time when I was close to failing most of my subjects, my real education was getting under way. If this overlapped with "Alice," no wonder I felt mortified. Ted could have been in the audience, and what would she have thought? Being far more a loving soul than a critical spirit, she might have tried to see the best in Stephen Leacock. The critical spirit was me. Borrowing her eyes, I would have looked on myself far more harshly than it was in her nature to do.

In the friendship that began, she was the guide, scout, pathfinder; I was the follower. Yet my character was more decisive and sharper than hers. Once I was initiated into this new, arcane region, I promptly judged. The one-way traffic in limp leather volumes that moved from her locker to my school-bag did not always go smoothly. I did not like all her treasures. And, though I usually tried to hide it so as not to disappoint her, I think she generally knew when I felt let down.

It started, in fact, with *Green Mansions*, with that girl, Rima, who was meant to be the spirit of the South American rain forest and flitted about, naked, among the trees. Somehow I had been led to expect, possibly by the glow of Ted's countenance, that some torrid scenes were coming—Rima was not naked for nothing. But in reality, alas, she was; she violated that literary principle—wasn't it Chekhov's?—that a loaded gun hanging on the wall in the first act must go off in the last. Yet Ted, I perceived, did not mind Rima's being a disembodied spirit; she liked her better that way. That was one of the pitfalls of modern literature, I soon learned; it did not always live up to its promises. I had been let down already by Conrad's *The Nigger of the Narcissus*, when I took it out of the public library the year before, thinking that the dirty word "nigger" in the title was going to couple perversely with the white narcissus bloom, but then "Narcissus" turned out to be the name of a boat. *Marius the Epicurean* was another misleading title, a real cockteaser (or *allumeuse*, if you prefer) for the expectant young reader.

To be truthful, what I was hoping for from books described as modern or daring (and from classical sculpture) was to see the fig-leaf stripped off sex. Someone had finally told me the rudiments of the act, but I did not feel wholly convinced that *that* was what men and women did. There was the usual difficulty in picturing respectable people, i.e., my grandparents, doing it, and in fact something in the sexual conjunction does arouse a natural skepticism, whoever the parties involved: "For Love has pitched his mansion/ In the place of excrement." But unless someone has experienced sex or a close approach to it, stories and poems do not tell much about it; if one has, they may act erotically as reminders. In my case, what might have been helpful were scientific manuals (unavailable), but even with scientific manuals (remember *Ideal Marriage*?), some prior knowledge or practice is generally required for full enlightenment. It is something like the Uncertainty Principle: if you are distant enough from the experience to need instruction, you are too remote to be benefited. Possibly blue movies shown in the classroom by a teacher with a pointer are what is really wanted. Or is the famous "need to know" of children just another *ignis fatuus*?

At any rate I felt the need, and Ted apparently did not. At the same time, I could tell that for her there was a strange vibration in *Green Mansions*, something thrilling and esoteric, that remained hidden from me. Now I know its name: literary art. We called it beauty then, and for a long time I had trouble perceiving it without being nudged, at least when it was of human manufacture; I could recognize it in sunsets, dew, wild flowers, fireflies, snowflakes, and the like. The excitement that literary art could produce in someone like Ted confused me, therefore, leading me to look for a set of thrills and revelations that literature does not give.

My own preferred authors that year were Adela Rogers St. Johns and Thyra Samter Winslow (both *Saturday Evening Post*, if I remember right), and the English Berta Ruck, an Enid Blyton of her time, who wrote about the Land Girls of World War I. But I did not try to proselytize, except now and then my grandmother. Ted, meanwhile, was eagerly sharing her heap of treasures with me: Pater, of course, Oscar Wilde, Whitman's *Leaves of Grass, The Crock of Gold*. When she gave me one of her Paters (it may well have been the deadly *Marius*), she wisely sugared the pill with the whispered tale that Pater had done his utmost to save Oscar Wilde from ruin by pleading with him not to publish *The Picture of Dorian Gray*. "It will bring us all down," he cried, weeping, having taken the train from Oxford to London to stop him, but the reckless Oscar persisted. I do not know where Ted got this literary anecdote or whether she invented it. I have never seen it in any book. Indeed, I have never seen it stated that Pater was a homosexual.

The romance of this story, for Ted, lay in the suggestion of a liaison between the two men; that is obvious to me now. Later, I gather, she became an overt lesbian, moving to California and changing her name from Ethel-Ted to Teya, though I have learned to my surprise that, some time before that, she was married briefly to a tennis star called Billy Newkirk. But at Garfield in her crushes—all purely mental, I assume—she did not distinguish between the sexes, any more than between football and track; she distributed her love equally between Larry Judson and Bill Albin. I thought of her then as a sort of deep-voiced boy; somewhere in my mind or in a lost album is a picture of her playing baseball, with springy legs spread apart and a catcher's mitt. More girlish, though, was her perpetual weaving of romances, as though to cover the nudity of everybody's life. She spun her webs around Kathleen Hoyt and her tartan cloak, around Estare Crane and her spit curl; it must have been she who told me Larry Judson was Jewish. She was sweet on my grandmother, whose tragic story she seemed to know, just as she knew about my parents, and I could never tell whether it was as a beautiful woman that Augusta Morgenstern interested her, or as a Jewess, or as the wife of Harold Preston, for she was sweet on him, too, and so was Till. My grandmother, in turn, liked them both and put down her book to chat with them, which was rare with her when I led a friend into the living-room, with its shirred pongee shades and fancy grass wallpaper.

Our friendship that first year was almost entirely bookish, on a separate plane from the other friendships I was beginning to make: with a pug-nosed Virginia who lived in Denny Blaine; with Mary McQueen Street and her sister, Francesca, who lived on 35th Avenue but really came from the South; with Ethel Scott and Mildred Dixon, who already dated and lived in a run-down section of mainly two-family houses and grassless front yards. . . . I ask myself whether it was because Ted was Jewish that I did not try to mix her with the others, but actually none of my new friends mixed; I went to each of their houses separately in the afternoon— my grandmother's strange inhospitality made it too hard to ask them home in the evenings. Besides, the bookishness into which Ted with her shining eyes had initiated me was a bond between us that kept us apart at times even from her sister.

I wish I could chart her enthusiasms, as a service to intellectual history. Beyond those I have already mentioned, I remember Aubrey Beardsley, Lord Dunsany, possibly Vachel Lindsay, because he came from Spokane. Among the influences reaching me through her, it is not always easy to distinguish the aesthetic movement from celebrations of "queer" sex. But I gather it was not always easy for the evangelists of both or either in their day. *Their day*: the peculiar thing about the modern authors Ted reveled in was that they were nearly all antiques. This was probably more of a commentary on Seattle than on Ted. Our city, despite its artistic reputation (or perhaps because of it), was remote from the vanguard; its most advanced circles might have still been reading *The Yellow Book*.

Aestheticism, unfortunately, was the key. Clearly there was not much roughage to stimulate the brain in those on the whole limp leather volumes that were coming my way. Anatole France, eventually ("The Procurator of Judaea," *Thaïs, The Red Lily*), but no Shaw or Wells. I ask myself how it happened that Ted never discovered Joyce. But wait! Now that I think of it, I can recall *Pomes Penyeach*: "Rain on Rahoon falls softly, softly falling,/ Where my dark lover lies./ Sad is his voice that calls me, sadly calling,/ At grey moonrise." Surely that is an *ex libris* of Ted's, marked by her inspiration (including my belief that Rahoon—actually the Galway cemetery—was in the South Seas, a confusion maybe with Rangoon, the capital of Burma). Still, I have no memory from this period of *A Portrait of the Artist* (not yet a Modern Library title?), which would have given us more to chew on.

I try to bring back a typical evening at 712 35th Avenue during the spring term at Garfield; the year is now 1926. My grandfather's chair is vacant; he has put down *The Life and Letters of Walter Hines Page* and gone to his club for a rubber or two of bridge. In *her* chair my grandmother, who by now has probably finished *The Peasants* by that Pole, is reading another long dull book, this time by a Dutchman called Couperus, who did *not* win the Nobel Prize. I am lying on a sofa with a mystery story, *Cleek of Scotland Yard*, or a new Berta Ruck, *Leaves of Grass* having fallen from my hand. My young uncle Harold, a sophomore at the U, is in his quarters off the landing with his cronies. The telephone does not ring, which is just as well, since if it should be a boy for me, I shall have to refuse any date he proposes and get him off the line as fast as I can without his guessing that I am only thirteen years old and for that stupid reason prohibited even from flirting with him on the telephone. All at once there is a thundering on the stairs; my uncle and his friends are going out.

They have names for each other like Goose and Flamingo; a fat one, Don Dickinson, older brother of Kenny Dickinson, is called the Toad, and they call me the Niece. Our big gaunt maid Lavinia is Leviathan. Two of the troupe are still seniors at Garfield—John Lewis and Paul Janson—and of course they know my age and condition of servitude. My uncle comes into the room and kisses my grandmother's cheek; " 'Night, Niece," he adds, waving. It is too early, still, for me to go to bed, and I have nothing left to read but the paper and *Leaves of Grass*.

Rescue, however, is in sight, though I do not yet realize it. Among Harold's cronies is one who does not call me the Niece as regularly as the others, who sometimes stops to talk to me in the downstairs back hall, who went to Garfield and had Mr. Post, knew Mary Brinker, and far in the future will marry Estare (Esther?) Crane of the single black spit curl and work for the Seattle *Times* before dying young. That is the Mark Sullivan whom I mentioned earlier. Some time soon (if he has not already started), he will undertake on his own hook to correct my reading. The first thing will be to try to cure me of Adela Rogers St. Johns.

Mark was a tall, somewhat knobby boy with a red face (hence Flamingo, I suppose), a blinking, flannelly Irish type very different from the male McCarthys with their green eyes and thick dark lashes. His teeth were poor, and I did not think he brushed them enough, which was true of a number of Harold's friends. He wore slightly ragged sweaters, usually red, and his socks hung down. He was the son of a Seattle policeman and had a sister named Marcile. Every summer my grandfather took him with us to Lake Crescent in the Olympic Mountains. He and Harold shared a double cottage, and I shared one with my grandfather that had two rooms with separate entrances—my grandmother stayed home in Seattle, not liking the mountains and being afraid of the water because of some experience with a rowboat when she was young. She had box lunches packed for us to take on the ferry to Port Townsend, whence we rode on the train to Port Angeles and then a rattly bus past dark-green Lake Sutherland to Singer's Tavern on beautiful Lake Crescent, "a jewel in the heart of the Olympics," as the publicity leaflet said. My grandmother was happy shopping at Frederick's every day; my grandfather was happy playing poker and bridge at Singer's with his contemporaries, Judge and Mrs. Alfred Battle, Mr. Edgar Battle, Mr. and Mrs. Boole, Colonel Blethen of the *Times*, and every morning leading a party of walkers up to the Marymere Falls. He approved of the food in the hotel dining-room; one night, after dinner, he sent a dollar bill to the chef "with my compliments."

Mark and Harold, the Flamingo and the Goose, would never dance in the evenings to the two-piece band of young-lady musicians on the hotel porch, but they played golf and tennis a lot and at least once a summer took me along, to climb the peak called Storm King, though never the redoubtable Sugar Loaf, across the lake. Once Mark, all by himself, and without any trail, explored the hidden waterfalls that rose above Marymere like a secret winding staircase with green overgrown landings cut into the mountain side. I believed—and it may have been true—that he was the first person ever to have followed them to the top. At my pleading, he promised to take me with him the next time he undertook it, but probably my grandfather told him no, too dangerous for a little girl, and I remained unfulfilled—to this day I am a romantic of waterfalls. He and Harold did not go in swimming, I think—maybe because of the icy lake water—but my grandfather always made one of them accompany me in a rowboat when I took one of my "championship" swims to Rosemary Point, the next resort, and perhaps Mark, out of his good nature, occasionally watched the after-breakfast diving exhibition I put on at the hotel pier.

At Singer's he and Harold were mainly spectators of the human comedy, which included a lounge lizard from the East, me pumping the player piano, my grandfather's watchfulness over my virtue, the framed poems and mottoes on the walls of the big card room ("Down to Gehenna, or up to the Throne,/ He travels the fastest who travels alone"), the golf on the five-hole course.

Mark, who was a humorist, wanted to be a reporter or feature-story writer—at the U he was on the daily paper and magazine—and premonitions of the blue pencil led him to take up an ironical attitude to red-faced Colonel ("General," by preference) Blethen, which pleased me, since I did not like the Blethen boys, Bobbie and Billy, and it did not wholly displease my grandfather, who considered the newspaper-owner a "martinet."

The authors Mark admired ought to have been a counterweight to Ted's "pashes": Mencken, above all; Nathan; Dreiser; Ben Hecht; Carl Van Vechten; Ernest Boyd. I can fancy an invisible struggle of the two opposed forces for possession of my mind, except that I do not think Mark saw enough of me during his visits to Harold to be aware of Ted's influence. Nor (the same as with Ted) was I always responsive to his urging: Jim Tully, the hobo poet, was as lost on me as Marius the Epicurean. And, again, there was my expectation of sex: Mark's favorite book, which he left for me one night on the back-hall table, was *Mademoiselle de*

Maupin, in English, by Théophile Gautier; the heroine dressed in men's clothing, and the book was reputed to be "hot," but if there was anything erotic there, I was utterly unable to find it. It was another disappointment, like *Green Mansions,* that I kept to myself. Other recommendations of Mark's misfired. I preferred *Tom Sawyer* to *Huckleberry Finn*—an error; it should have been the opposite. I was too young for Dreiser's *The Genius,* a well-thumbed volume which was left for me on the hall table, too; *Moby-Dick,* likewise, was way over my head—that I had seen the movie, *The Sea Beast,* with John Barrymore, was more a hindrance than a help. Nevertheless Mark was having his effect. I was soon reading *The American Mercury* and had induced my grandmother to subscribe to *Vanity Fair,* a Condé Nast publication that I could look at the day of its arrival in the sewing-room, along with her *Vogue.* And he had made me seriously wonder about Berta Ruck.

Even before summer, I must have already suspected that I would not be returning to Garfield. I do not remember whether, finally, that was cause for grief or not. Maybe I was glad, on the whole, to be removed from the excitement of boys, since it would be two more years before I would be allowed to go out with one of them—my grandmother had statutory ages for everything, sixteen for boys, fourteen for real, non-ribbed silk stockings, fifteen perhaps for lipstick (Tangee). The E, the D, and the several D-minuses that came my way at the end of the grading period were fresh arguments for a change of scene. Meanwhile, in the last days of the term, while my grandfather from his office was writing in for boarding-school catalogues, I found that I had made my mark at Garfield High, albeit ambiguously. Despite Ted's briefings, our school intellectuals had been known to me only by sight. *But they knew me.* When the yearbook, edited by *them,* came out in due course, that became clear. There I was, almost the only freshman so singled out, on a page of that year's memorable personalities with an appropriate sport, hobby, or pastime listed opposite each. I never sought to learn who or what had "elected" me to that company—a hidden enemy or just some senior having fun on the basis of information supplied by one of my associates. I could choose to think that it was teasing or I could choose to think that it was meant to hurt, but this was how, toward the bottom of the page, I appeared: "Si McCarthy. Tiddledy-winks."

3

In my first year at Annie Wright Seminary, I lost my virginity. I am not sure whether this was an "educational experience" or not. The act did not lead to anything and was not repeated for two years. But at least it dampened my curiosity about sex and so left my mind free to think about other things. Since in that way it was formative, I had better tell about it.

It took place in a Marmon roadster, in the front seat—roadsters had no back seats, though there was often a rumble, outside, in the rear, where the trunk is now. That day the car was parked off a lonely Seattle boulevard; it was a dark winter afternoon, probably during Thanksgiving vacation, since I was home from school. In my memory it feels like a Saturday. "His" name was Forrest Crosby; he was a

Phi Delt, I understood, and twenty-three years old, a year or so out of the University and working for his family's business—the Crosby Lines, which went back and forth across Puget Sound to points like Everett and Bremerton. He was medium short, sophisticated, with bright blue eyes and crisp close-cut ash-blond curly hair, smart gray flannels, navy-blue jacket, and a pipe. He had a friend, Windy Kaufman, who was half-Jewish and rode a motorcycle.

He believed I was seventeen, or, rather, that was what I had told him. Afterwards I had reason to think that while I was adding three years to my age he was subtracting three from his. So in reality he was an old man of twenty-six. Probably we were both scared by what we were doing, he for prudential reasons and I because of my ignorance, which I could not own up to while pretending to be older. My main aim in life, outside of school (where I could not hide the truth), was to pass for at least sixteen.

We had met at Lake Crescent that summer. I was staying, the same as every year, in a hotel cottage with my grandfather, who approved of the American-plan food, the great Douglas firs, the dappled morning walk up to misty Marymere Falls, the bridge games and poker and the five holes of golf. I hated golf (one of the joys of growing up was that I would not have to play it any more), but I could swim and dive in my new "Tomboy" bathing suit (maroon-red turtleneck with a long buttoned vest that tended to rise over your head when you dove and little separate pants underneath) and know that I was watched from pier and porch by admiring older people awed by my long immersions in the icy water. I could teach myself to row. I could switchback (adding a new word to my vocabulary) up old bald-pated Storm King with my uncle Harold and his friend Mark, eat a box lunch at the summit and run all the way down. The changeless idyl began with a ferry ride to Port Townsend; then there was the train ride to Port Angeles and the opening in our compartment of an unvarying shoe box of exquisitely packed thin chicken-liver sandwiches and deviled eggs, then the jitney ride through the mountains to our destination, which really was crescent-shaped and a bright celestial blue.

In this paradise, there were no boys for me, though—only the horrible Blethens and an ass named Warren Boole who was going to Lawrenceville and had a nose with nostrils like a bellows. I could vamp him, I found, in my new green tiered dress—made for me by my grandmother's dressmaker, Mrs. Farrell—and some perfume and earrings, but it was not worth it, too disillusioning to see him "turn on" like a wind-up toy while his indulgent parents watched. Then, with the summer almost over, *he* came to Singer's Tavern in the Marmon, I don't know why, possibly just as a predator, looking around. He found only me, to judge by the result.

I would have expected him to be interested in "Missy" Lewis, a tall fair beautiful girl with braids around her head who went to the Anna Head School in California and was eighteen years old. But maybe Missy was too well protected by her married brother Richard and his stout, dark, golf-playing wife or by her own straight-browed look of virtuous reserve or simply by the fact that she stayed home in their group of cottages after supper. Anyway he danced with me the first night on the hotel porch, to the two-piece female band, and the next morning he took me rowing on the lake, down toward the steep bulk of green Sugar Loaf Mountain, till my grandfather, straining his eyesight on the pier, angrily waved me back to the hotel landing. By lunch-time the gray car and its driver were gone (was he sizing up Rosemary Point, down the lake, supposed to be less exclusive?), but that night he danced with me again, holding his cheek closer to mine and softly singing into my ear a song that was new that summer: "Sweet Child."

"Sweet child,/ You're drivin' me wild./ That's puttin' it mild./ Sweet child, I'm wild about you." He made it "our" song, private, extremely suggestive, and I was dizzied by the thought that a liability, my age, was turning into an asset through the pulsing of his voice softly beating into my ear. Meanwhile in the big main lounge my grandfather at the poker table with Judge Alfred Battle, Mrs. Battle, Mr. Edgar Battle, Colonel Blethen, Mr. and Mrs. A. J. Singer noticed nothing wrong—he would not have been aware of the words of a popular song. Through the glass doors, if he looked, there was only ballroom dancing to be seen. To me, though, the tune "called" like the pounding of a tom-tom deep in the jungle. It needed only a bar or two hummed in his baritone to have me throbbing with excitement the next day as he walked me along a path through the woods. We were following Marymere Stream to where it emptied into the lake at a little sandy beach, which for some reason was seldom visited—the walk from Marymere Falls turned off toward the hotel a little farther up. Now I ask myself whether "Forrie" Crosby had been at Singer's before or did he find this secluded spot, protected from the wind and from prying eyes, by a natural talent, like a dowser's?

We were alone in that small sunny cove at the edge of a cool woods of maidenhair ferns and virgin spruce. His arm was around my waist; he was turning me toward him. Then, before we could kiss—he had full, rather flat, sensual lips, shirred like tight-pulled material—my grandfather came thundering down the path. He had an air of being in the nick of time and perhaps he was—compare Don Giovanni and Zerlina's fearful shriek. I was ordered back to my room in our cottage, and my grandfather, I gather, then "told the man off." I could have wept when I heard that he had "given the fellow a first-class scare"; in his high-laced shoes (or was he wearing golf knickers and the appropriate footwear?) that pillar of the bar association would have carried quite a lot of conviction.

Probably I did weep; his persistent chaperonage seemed expressly directed at robbing me of any chance in life. Though kindly and well disposed most of the time (Lewis Stone was his favorite movie-actor), he was a tinder-box when anything off-color was mooted; when I teased him one morning for helping Miss Thompson, the pretty brown-eyed violin of our duo, down from a teetery log bridge into his outstretched arms, he went red in the face and shouted. Nor was this the first time he had thundered onto the scene when I was alone with a man by the lake shore. The previous time had been with that gigolo Mr. Jones from New York, who had asked me to take his picture with a fish he had caught, and afterwards Mark Sullivan and my uncle Harold had delighted in doing imitations of the imagined scene: Mr. Jones holding the salmon-trout in one hand and my thirteen-year-old form in the other; Mr. Jones dropping the salmon and fleeing into the woods as the Honorable Harold Preston, breathing heavily and adjusting his spectacles, rounded the corner.

Still, there was a difference. I had been angry with my grandfather over the Mr. Jones episode because his absurd suspicions made himself and me ridiculous. The whole hotel was laughing. Now it was my grandfather's *interference* that made me resentful. His suspicions, possibly over-alert, were not absurd. They were well grounded in Forrie Crosby's age as compared with mine—"sweet child." I am not sure, though, whether I sensed that then, whether, amid my wails of protest, I knew in my soul what the seductive fellow was "up to." But I know it now. It seems to me also that Mark and Harold did not find this episode quite so risible as the other.

Like my grandfather, like any of the hotel guests, they were able to see that the interest of a twenty-three-year-old (or twenty-six-year-old) ordinary sensual man in a fourteen-year-old girl must have some ulterior purpose. In the earlier case, it was possible that poor Mr. Jones (suspected of being a mulatto because of his yellowish eye-whites) had really wanted to have his picture taken. But it was hard to find an innocent explanation to cover the present case. And if one could have been found, I would not have wanted to hear it. Anything that *sought an explanation* for his interest in me was too wounding to my self-love to be borne. To have people wonder about that interest, searching for clues, told me the one thing that I was closing my ears to: quite simply, that I was a juvenile. If he had taken Missy Lewis rowing on the lake, no one would have thought anything of it; her brother, *in loco parentis*, would not have been on the pier frantically waving them back.

I myself, I guess, felt no need of a theory to account for the observable data. He had fallen in love with me, I must have told myself. It happened constantly in books and films: two people danced together and immediately were "smitten"—Dan Cupid's arrows. I was a little young, but people often told me that I seemed older than my age, because of all the books I read. Just as one example, *he* thought I was seventeen. . . . It was typical of my grandfather's outlook to treat me purely in terms of my years. And of my sex. Although surprisingly broad-minded in some ways—about leaving me free to choose my own religion and not trying to censor my reading matter—he had the hidebound idea that socially girls needed more control than boys. He did not stop to consider my feelings: I had not been out of sight of the hotel more than ten minutes when he came rushing out after us. And now his old man's vanity was satisfied to have driven my swain away. That afternoon, the Marmon was gone, before we could even say good-bye. But in September I would be going to Annie Wright—I had made sure on our walk that he knew. He would write to me, he had promised, holding me close. When a man declared he would write to you, that was a real sign.

Did I really believe all this? Did I dream of being "pinned" by his fraternity pin? Or did I suspect that at the first opportunity he was going to be my seducer? I had got plenty of warnings, certainly, from the *True Story* and *True Confessions* I read. Or (most likely) did I simply stop thinking and let myself be carried ahead like Maggie Tulliver on the flooding river in *The Mill on the Floss*? The fact is, I have hardly any recollection of what went through my mind between the time he left Lake Crescent and that wintry afternoon in the car with the celluloid side-curtains buttoned or snapped down. At Singer's I know that I took walks—sentimental pilgrimages—in the late afternoon to our little lonely cove, once with Mrs. Judge Battle (Madge), my favorite grown woman, in a natural-silk loose-fitting suit and wide Panama hat—strangely, I was happy, with the tall, beautiful woman in the golden light. And I can hear myself pumping out "Sweet Child" on the player piano over and over till someone complained.

In Seattle, he telephoned soon after we got back, but my grandmother, when she heard me talking to him, called out to me to hang up. Grandpa must have told her something. "Just tell him you can't see him." I hung up promptly, surprising her. I hadn't been eager to talk to him while she listened. What I really feared, however, was that he would find out, thanks to her interruptions, that I was not allowed to get telephone calls from men or boys. But then at the Seminary letters from him started coming, and I answered: "*La sfortunata rispose.*" Each girl had a list of ten approved correspondents handed in by her family, but that applied only to the letters we wrote; the authorities never bothered with any incoming mail but packages (those containing food had to be shared), and you could always give your outgoing letters to a day girl to mail or drop them into a box yourself during a school walk.

Well, it was not a flood of mail that poured in from him— a single sheet every week or so covered on two sides with round broadly spaced writing. My own letters must have been much fuller. Not only fuller but also passionate. Alas, I no longer have the packet of letters from him tied up in string that was stored in a trunk of papers in a warehouse at the time of one of my divorces and never reclaimed because I did not have the money to pay the bill. Yet it hardly matters: his letters were unrevealing, no doubt deliberately so.

He almost always ended with *"Hasta la vista"*—probably he had taken an elementary course in Spanish—which to me was the most heartfelt moment in his correspondence; I was under the spell of songs like "Marcheta" and "Valencia," of shawls and castanets, and supposed *hasta* meant "haste." It was a blow to learn from our school Spanish teacher that the phrase was a standard formula like *Au revoir* and *Auf Wiedersehen*. His letters showed a fondness, too, for such phrases as "Young feller, me lad"), addressed to himself ("Forrie, young feller, me lad"), which he used in conversation as well. The effect on me of this variant of "old man" (as I take it to be) was of a natty worldliness. He signed himself "Forrest," with a flourish, occasionally "Forrie" in smaller writing—proof, I feared, that he wrote to some other girl or girls more familiar with him than I was and did not always keep us straight. He put no return address on his envelopes and instructed me to write care of the Phi Delt house, not at home or at work. His home, I learned—from him or the telephone directory—was Federal Avenue (Capitol Hill), still a good neighborhood then. Years later, I saw the house, square, fairly well proportioned and without architectural interest.

I did not judge his letters, even if I could not help noting some mistakes in spelling, all the while I was covering the heavy white paper with kisses of joy. I was in love with him, whatever that meant. I did not let myself judge his letters and yet I knew them by heart and was extracting every drop of meaning contained in them, both what I wanted to hear and what I was afraid to. If I had been able to submit specimens to a love laboratory for tests of sincerity, I could guess what the pronouncement would have been. In other words, despite my young years, I knew too well the man who was writing to me, knew him better every week. I did not like his handwriting, so round and sloping, or the way he made his "r"s; without being a graphologist, I sensed a character deficiency in it. And I shrank almost bodily from eye contact with *"Hasta la vista,"* once I had been told what it was. None of this, however, could restrain me from hoping that my instinct—or my intelligence?—was wrong. The best means of ignoring the shortcomings of those letters, which I nonetheless *hung* on as liaison with a future, was to keep reliving Lake Crescent—the past. I was able to summon up the eyes, the voice in my ear, the full, flat, sensual lips, a wristwatch, gray flannel and navy-blue worsted. His physical being and accessories (including the Marmon) had style—they matched each other and the whole entity named Forrest Crosby—and style, a quality strangely lacking in his correspondence, was for me the same as allure or even S.A., as we called it then. I was a sucker for style. The total absence of that quality from the letters I was getting may well have been the result of excessive precaution—they might have told more of their author if I had not been virtual jail bait.

In my room, after evening study hall, I wrote to him and mooned over his image. Annie Wright had assigned me as a roommate the unpopular one of our two Jewish girls, but we had asked to be separated after the first weeks. This left me free to think of him and only him; what should have been fresh impressions—different girls, teachers, food, rules, new surroundings, a new (to me) religion—barely reached me. And for the first and last time in my life I did not talk about the man I was wildly in love with. It was scarcely a matter of choice: I had nobody to confide in. I could tell my love only to him. I had no friends yet; that would come next term when I got to know girls from the class ahead. For the moment there were only my classmates, hopelessly juvenile—their only interest was basketball.

Nonetheless, as often happens with lonely young creatures, I found companionship. In poetry. Indeed, I wonder whether poetry would have any readers besides poets if love combined with loneliness did not perform the introductions on the brink of adult life. By luck, on the study-hall shelves, I came upon Manly's *English Poetry, 1170–1892*—the volume I spoke of a while ago as turning up here in Maine and where then, in my hour of need, I encountered the Cavalier Poets. "Go and catch a falling star," "Why so pale and wan, fond lover?"—I had the conviction that Suckling, Donne (whom I took for a Cavalier), Carew, and the others were writing directly to me and about me. In Manly, later in study hall, I would find "Sister Helen" and Thomas Lovell Beddoes, and Thomas Hood, but the insouciant Cavaliers were tied to Forrest Crosby.

The girls could not get telephone calls (calls from our families went through Miss Preston, our principal), so it must have been in one of those letters that he told me when and where to meet him. Thanksgiving would have been our first chance. At the time, the Seattle girls at the Seminary traveled by boat, a two- or three-hour trip, with a chaperon, although I once took the "interurban"—a cross between a streetcar and a train that was a little less slow—and by my senior year the new Seattle-Tacoma highway had changed all that, making weekends, even Sundays, in the bigger town possible. But in my sophomore year it was different. I remember the quantities of baggage we took with us and the effect of seeing the seniors in peppy furs like caracul and pony, topped by little hats—they were dressed to kill for the "big" football game at the University stadium and the house parties that went along with it. At home, we must have had the usual Thanksgiving bird, carved by my grandfather and preceded by Olympia oyster cocktail. Then, with palpitating heart, and pale as death, doubtless, I met Forrest Crosby, on the next afternoon. But no. I think there were two meetings, two days running: for *it* to have happened the first time, without some preliminary, would have been going too fast.

But *how* did we meet, since he could not come to my house to get me? At my age, a hotel lobby was too exposed. No, it was on a downtown street corner, after three, when the light was beginning to fade. If I was seen, I could be downtown shopping or going with a girl to a movie. It seems to me that it was on Union or University Street, not far from the Public Library, that I waited, but only for a few minutes; he was almost on time.

After that, there was nothing to do but ride around or park. He could not take me tea-dancing at the Olympic Hotel; he could not take me to the movies; he could not take me for a sundae or a toasted-cheese sandwich at one of the usual meeting-places in the University district. If it was on Saturday, he could not take me to the football game—the last of the season. In November, he could not take me swimming or rowing. Roadhouses, where we might have danced, were hardly ever open in the afternoon. The necessity of not being seen and reported to my grandmother meant that none of the ordinary ways of passing the time were open to us, which was bound to leave us in the end with no recourse but sex.

Hence I might say that what happened was my grandparents' own fault; *they* had forced me into clandestinity. If I had been free to meet him innocently, I would not have met him guiltily. This was true up to a point and in a general way. The tight rein they tried to keep on me while my contemporaries were allowed to run loose was a mistake and kept me from having any easy or natural relation with boys; I never even learned to dance with one of them properly. Moreover, the prohibitions I labored under led me into all kinds of deceptions. I lied to my grandparents about where I had been, with whom, how long, and so on. I lied to my partner in deception, in this case Forrest Crosby, because I was sure he would despise me if I avowed my inexperience, and I lied to other girls to keep them from knowing of my trammels, in short from discovering all of the above. This lying became a necessity, imposed by my grandparents in the first instance, but then the habit was formed, as the wish to appear other than I was permitted to be dominated every social relation except those with my teachers.

Yet, true as all that may be, the other truth is that my grandparents' prohibitions were far from being the cause of what happened to me on the passenger seat of that Marmon. Had they let Forrest Crosby come to the house, he would have seduced me with greater ease, probably on their own living-room sofa after they had retired.

Hold on! All the time I have been writing this, a memory has been coming back to haunt me: *he did come to my house.* In the summer-time, after Lake Crescent, and for some reason—perhaps sheer surprise at the daring of it—my grandmother let me receive him. On the living-room sofa, after she had gone up to bed. And he did start to seduce me right then and there, with the lights on. He was on top of me when something happened. Someone interrupted us. Perhaps it was my grandfather, returning from his club, who surprised us and told Forrest to get out of the house. Or Harold came in, and Forrest hastily left of his own accord. Anyway, we were on the sofa (the only time I ever was, with a man), and he fled, and after that he wrote to me at Annie Wright. I did not see him again till that wintry day, probably in Thanksgiving vacation.

On that first afternoon (I think) we drove around, we talked, we parked and kissed each other and maybe went a little bit further—I am not sure. I was wildly excited but not sexually excited. At the time, though, I was unaware of there being a difference between mental arousal and specific arousal of the genital organs. This led to many misunderstandings. In my observation, girls tend to mature as sexual performers considerably after puberty, contrary to common belief, and this is confusing for young men and for the girls themselves, especially when mental development, with its own excitement, has far outdistanced the other. I do not know the explanation but am sometimes tempted to agree with the theory that the orgasm in human females is learned from the male.

In any case, the excitement, almost ecstasy, I felt in that first embrace is hard to remember back to, since sex, by now familiar, gets in the way. Surely that bliss had more to do with love, with the tremulous persuasion that his kisses and caresses and murmured words were proofs of an eagerness for me that could only mean love on his side, than with anything like estrus. Possibly, from the signs, he himself felt that I still needed a bit more preparation, since after a while, if I recall right, he started the motor and drove me to a corner near home.

If I recall right, it was at that same corner (Union and 34th) that he picked me up the next time. And this time, the Saturday, I was more nervous. It was not that I was greatly afraid of being seen—I could lie. No, I think that I knew now what we were going to do. And I did not want to. Having finally realized what was in the cards, had been in the cards since Lake Crescent, I was scared silly. Maybe he then explained to me in so many words what we were going to do, which should have been a good move in principle; it would have made me more scared temporarily, when I saw the inexorability of what was coming, but it would also give me time to get used to the idea while he drove rapidly along the boulevards, looking for a lonely place to pull off the road. When he found one that satisfied him, he stopped the car and looked steadily at me with a faint amused smile. I must have appeared piteously tense.

As if resigned, he drew me to him, settling my head on his shoulder, and started asking me about Annie Wright and the different girls there. Like Scheherazade, I was only too pleased to talk. I must have told him about the Quevli sisters, day girls who seemed to be the prize cultivars of the school, or my desk-mate in study hall, Ellin Watts from Portland. . . . Then something prompted me to mention a small jazzy senior who wore bobbly earrings, a lot of lipstick, and a "fun" fur coat and had a peculiar name—De Vere Utter. "Lady Clara Vere de Vere", some sarcastic teacher had said. He nodded. "Windy fucked Vere Utter," he observed. The casual way he dropped that, as a datum of passing interest, froze me in his "easy" embrace. What could I answer? I was horror-struck.

Unless he was one of those men who like to talk dirty to anybody they are about to sleep with, he was exerting himself, probably, in the cheeriest way he knew, to diminish my fears of what, buttoned in his fly, lay in store for me: if a popular Annie Wright senior had done it with his friend Windy, no need for me to feel strange. He could not imagine, I suppose, that this was the first time I had heard that word, though I must have seen it scrawled on Minneapolis fences on the way to the parochial school. Of course I knew what it meant: to fuck was to do *it* straight, with no love, the way men did with prostitutes. And he was preparing to fuck me. The message had come through clear and strong.

I did not turn a hair, so far as he could see. But I felt as if I had died. I thought dimly of Vere Utter and how she would take it if she guessed that Windy had "told." I was distantly sorry for her, seeing her screwed-up little monkey face and short buck teeth with a smear of lipstick on them and the dance step she tapped out on the forward deck of the ferryboat—poor Vere. I don't seem to have felt the same pity, in anticipation, for myself, that is, to have foreseen what Forrest would be telling Windy about me. Perhaps I was still trying to think that with me it would be different: what he was starting to do as he unbuttoned himself and pulled aside my step-ins would not be that f- - -ing.

In fact, he became very educational, encouraging me to sit up and examine his stiffened organ, which to me looked quite repellent, all flushed and purplish. But in the light of the dashboard, I could not see very well, fortunately. He must have thought it would be interesting for me to look at an adult penis—my first, as by now he must have realized. Then, as I waited, he fished in an inside breast-pocket and took out what I knew to be a "safety." Still in an instructive mood, even with his erect member (probably he would have made a good parent), he found time to explain to me what it was—the best kind, a Merry Widow—before he bent down and fitted it onto himself, making me watch.

Of the actual penetration, I remember nothing; it was as if I had been given chloroform. How long it lasted, whether or not we were kissing—everything but the bare fact is gone.

It must have hurt, but I have no memory of that or of any other sensations, perhaps a slight sense of being stuffed. Yes, there is also a faint recollection of his instructing me to move, keep step as in dancing, but I am not sure of that. What I *am* sure of is a single dreadful, dazed moment having to do with the condom. No, Reader, it did not break.

The act is over; he has slid under the steering-wheel and is standing by his side of the car and holding up a transparent little pouch resembling isinglass that has whitish greenish gray stuff in the bottom. I recognize it as "jism." Outside it is almost dark, but he is holding the little sack up to a light source—a streetlight, the Marmon's parking lights, a lit match?—to be sure I can see it well and realize what is inside—the sperm he has ejaculated into it, so as not to ejaculate it in me. I am glad of that, of course, but the main impression is the same as with the swollen penis; the jism is horribly ugly to me, like snot or catarrh, and I have to look away.

Soon he drove me back to what was turning into "our" corner—34th and Union, at the end of the Madrona car line, near what I think was the Piggly Wiggly store. I got out of the car and quickly walked the four and a half blocks home, past Mary McQueen Street's house and the little new Catholic church with the modern stations of the cross. Nobody saw him with me, and there were no telltale traces on my step-ins for the maid to find when she washed—if the hymen was punctured, it did not bleed, then or ever. I have no memory of what story I told at home to account for my afternoon, nor of what I thought and felt that evening. Since it was Saturday, did I go with my grandparents after dinner to the current attraction at the Coliseum or the Blue Mouse— Seattle's quality movie-houses? I wonder what was playing that Thanksgiving week in the year 1926.

The next day there would have been the inevitable Sunday lunch with my married uncle, Frank, and his wife, Isabel, my uncle Harold, who had to have a special first course because he did not eat tomatoes, and maybe Aunt Alice Carr or Aunt Eva Aronson (both in fact great-aunts). We would have started with a thick slice of tomato on a bed of crabmeat and alligator pear topped by riced egg yolks and cut-up whites mimosa style and Russian or Thousand Island dressing, the whole surrounded with a chiffonade of lettuce, and we would have finished with ice-cream (possibly peppermint at that season, made with candy canes) cranked that morning on the kitchen porch by the old gardener-driver and left to ripen under burlap; in between would have been a main course of—very likely—fried chicken, and at the high point of the meal my grandfather would have said "Allee samee Victor Hugo," referring to a restaurant in Los Angeles. On this Sunday I would have been spared the after-lunch ride around Lake Washington, for I would have been driven to the dock in good season (a favorite expression with my grandfather) to catch the ferryboat back to the Seminary.

I wish I knew what was going through my head during that meal. Was I accidentally remembering parts of the day before ("WINDY FUCKED VERE UTTER") and trying to push the recollection away? Or was I feeling superior to my tablemates because I knew something they would never guess? Since yesterday afternoon I was no longer a virgin—how horrified Aunt Alice Carr with her spindly legs and old-maidish ways would be, how her frizzy head would tremble on the weak stem of her neck! For an insight into my state of mind I try thinking now of Emma Bovary at table with Charles after one of her trysts. It is not hard to guess what *she* felt. Boredom, obviously, excruciating boredom. And a Seattle Sunday at 712 35th Avenue could have given cards and spades to Yonville L'Abbaye. It was not that my grandfather, taken by himself, was uninteresting to talk to— that applied to my grandmother, too—the tedium was in their life. So, given the fact that I was old for my years and had read *Mademoiselle de Maupin*, if not yet *Madame Bovary*, I may conclude that my supreme emotion that Sunday in the bosom of my family was something between exasperated boredom and haughty disdain.

In any event I would not see them all for several weeks, not until Christmas vacation. And now comes another hiatus in my memory. Of the time in school between Thanksgiving and Christmas I remember only insignificant details having nothing to do with him, such as reading *The Merchant of Venice* after lights out in my closet by means of a bridge lamp laid on its side and shaded by a bath towel, such as Sir Roger de Coverley and isoceles triangles and Vachel Lindsay's two nieces whose parents were missionaries in China. On a more personal plane, I remember singing a new (to me) Christmas hymn, "A Virgin Unspotted," as we marched in procession into chapel, and the strange emotion that came over me as I caroled the words out, my heart singing for joy in Mary Virgin, though Mary I was and virgin I was not. In the Episcopal hymns and liturgy, I was experiencing what psychiatrists call "ideas of reference." With the Advent hymns now posted in chapel I recognized my Jewish relations and raised my voice for their safety: "Rejoice, rejoice! Em-ma-a-anuel will ransom captive I-i-israel." Without ever recovering a trace of the faith I had lost in the convent, I was falling in love with the Episcopal church. I did not believe in God's existence but, more and more, as Christmas approached, I liked the idea of Him, and chapel, morning and evening, became my favorite part of the day.

Meanwhile I must have been in correspondence with Forrest, whom I still could not call "Forrie." I feel sure that we were writing to each other because how else did we arrange to meet on that same corner on an afternoon of Christmas vacation? But here comes a peculiar, almost unnerving, thing: not only do I not now remember how we made the date, but until a few days ago I had forgotten that we ever had one. In my memory the image of him standing by the car and holding up that transparent sack of rubber or fishskin was the finale—CURTAIN. If you had asked me, I would have said that I did not see him again till many years later, when I was grown up.

Well, that is true, but not the way I have been remembering it. The truth is that somehow or other we did make an arrangement to meet. I was on the corner, waiting, and he never came. I do not know how long I waited. I went into a drugstore and pretended to look at magazines; I went into a grocery store—the Piggly Wiggly—and looked at the fruit. I walked up and down the sidewalk. I counted the Madrona streetcars. I dared not linger more than an hour lest people become curious. 34th and Union was not far from where Mark Sullivan lived. I promised myself that if the Marmon had not appeared when three streetcars had reached the end of the line I would give up. I tried counting up to a thousand. I decided that he must have come while my back was turned, in the drugstore, so it could be my own fault. Finally, stopping every few steps to look over my shoulder, I walked slowly to the next corner, took a last look behind me, and then went rapidly home. In my memory this day, too, as it comes back to me, feels like a Saturday, and I have the feeling that I posted myself on the same spot the next day, in case there had been a mistake. But the next day I did not wait so long.

Why didn't I telephone him? At fourteen and a half, I did not have the courage; actually, I am not sure I would today. He had told me not even to *write* to him at home. If I had tried to reach him at the Phi Delt house, I would have got some pledge—besides, they were on Christmas vacation. There was nothing to do but wait till I got back to school. Then if he did not write me, I would write him. If today there is something "philosophical" in my attitude to grief or disappointment, it may have been born then.

I think he wrote me when I was back at Annie Wright, but I may have sent him a cry of wild reproach to which his letter was an answer. In any case, it was short, the shortest he had yet penned, and offered no real excuse. He was sorry but he had been "held up"; for the rest, it was one of those letters of commonplaces of the "Hope you are fine and painting the school red" type. Something like that. And no "*Hasta la vista.*" But the awful thing was that *it was not signed.* Not even a pusillanimous "F," which he had put on his last letter, I now seem to recall. Just a wavy line after the last sentence.

The letter cut off all hope. It told me, among other unbearable things, that my grandfather's judgment had been right. The letter was like a signed, or, rather, unsigned, confession. And I was too young to be able to pardon him, which might have sweetened the bitter dose for me. Children do not pardon. Far from forgiving, I could not even understand. I knew that men tired of girls who gave themselves too easily, but so suddenly, so soon? Had I failed, in the car, to move the way you were supposed to? And, having failed on my first trial, would I ever get a chance to do better?

"Hell hath no fury like a woman scorned" I read with interest in some book I had spirited into study hall. But the saying did not seem to be apposite. I had no means of dealing with the pain I was feeling; nothing like it had ever happened to me. I was in torture, but there was no one I could tell, no bosom I could fling myself on. My grandmother was too old and unsympathetic, and anyway my lying ruled her out. I could not tell a teacher, least of all the severe Miss Dorothy Atkinson, the English teacher with puffs of ash-blond hair over her ears and glasses on a chain whom I admired. Tears did not help without a comforter; I would have preferred to howl, but you could not do that at the Seminary, even if you did not have a roommate the walls were too thin. I did not consider suicide; that came later, when I no longer had a reason for it.

My sole resort, as often happens, was him, the cause of the pain. I could write to him, and I did, a very long letter, which I spent hours revising and maybe polishing since it was the last, I guessed, that he would ever receive from me. The burden of it was that I hated and despised him: I was grateful to have seen him finally in his true colors so that I would never have to see him again. While loosing the vials of my wrath, I may have alluded to his faults of spelling—I hope so. I was desperately burning my bridges, so as to give myself no encouragement for expecting an answer.

In full awareness of the consequences, I folded the thick screed into a big envelope and addressed it to him. But before putting on the stamp I wrote "I love you" in the place the stamp would cover. Not altogether satisfied with that, I carefully turned it upside down, which in stamp language meant "Look underneath." Then I gave the letter to be mailed. In terms of gambling, it was a weakly hedged bet I was placing. The chances of a grown man's looking under a postage stamp were piteously small, even with the nudging of the wrong-way-up Lincoln or Washington. Boarding-school-girl code anyhow—how would he know it? The only way he could have discovered those three little words would have been if the stamp had fallen off the envelope. My message had the same fate as the note to the fairies I had put into a rose in Uncle John's garden in Duluth one summer evening.

My love slowly withdrew from him, like a puddle drying up. For months, maybe a year, I kept looking for the Marmon whenever I went downtown in Seattle, especially in the vicinity of Seneca and Spring Streets, where I felt his numen at the wheel of every automobile. Sometimes I would think I saw the car's hood, heavy-set on the high chassis, coming toward me, but when I looked more closely, the car, although gray and a roadster, would be a different make. There could not have been many Marmons in Seattle.

Were there many Forrest Crosbys? Luckily not, perhaps. Yet he was scarcely an original. He was banal, even in the hold he had on my awakening sensual imagination. It was not only the bright-blue eyes, the crisp hair, the pursed, amused mouth, but also, I think, the car, the pipe, whatever shoes and socks he wore. It was his accessories that seduced me, as in an advertisement, and they included his name, which, like so many names in Seattle (Armour Spaulding!), seemed pseudonymous, creations of a press agent.

As they said of such men a bit later, he was a wolf, but a wolf with consistency of style—apparently he did not find sheep's clothing becoming. What was unusual about him, probably, was the priority of style over substance, also the fact (which might seem to be contradictory) that he "wanted *only one thing*." Most men, in the end, want much more.

I suppose I am sketching the outlines of a Don Giovanni, one of the few I have known. That would explain what he "saw" in me. It was not my being pretty (I am not sure I was, and, till the senior yearbook, no photo exists to say yes or no) or "fresh." It made no difference whether I was intelligent or stupid, passionate or cold. In the "boundary situation" (Karl Jaspers) constituted by the chill seat of a roadster, those qualities buttered no parsnips. What he wanted from me was what Don Giovanni wanted from fat and thin, chambermaid and lady, old and young: *"il piacer di porla in lista"*—that was all there was to it. That his organ and sperm repelled me suggests that on my side the attraction did not go deep despite the superficial power it exerted. It was like a kind of hypnotism, which I believe does not go deep either. I obeyed his command to open my legs, having gone too far not to finish the task, but it was chiefly my muscles that submitted; my mind held itself apart, not finding him, to my surprise, very interesting. In the same way, a hypnotist can make you carry out any quantity of orders but he cannot make you do anything that goes against your nature. Just as nothing can force us to *like* a hated vegetable, so I could never respond in depth to the man made manifest in those colorless letters. *Hasta la vista.*

I have been able to verify this judgment, for I met him again ten years later, and at that time, within his limits, he "fell for" me, and I had, I suppose, a kind of revenge. It was through Windy Kaufman that we met again; Windy was still his friend and still drove a motorcycle. I forget how I came to know Windy, but he took me riding with him more than once on his motorcycle. My family was shocked, but I enjoyed it, and my grandmother knew his mother. Mindful of what had happened to Vere, I took care not to give him "ideas," as we used to say, though I dared not let myself hope that Forrie had failed to confide in him—whenever my name was mentioned, did Windy observe "Forrie fucked her"? I could not guess from his demeanor. Then one day when he telephoned ("It sounds like that Kaufman fellow"), he proposed spending the evening with some other people at the house of a friend of his.

That was Forrest, in his Federal Avenue house, sitting with a pipe at one end of a long leather couch—very little changed, less changed than I was myself. But he recognized me—perhaps Windy had prepared him—and seemed pleased; probably he had forgotten the circumstances that had terminated our connection. The next night he telephoned, and I took the call in my grandmother's bedroom. No longer needing to hide anything from her, I told her who it was. But she had no recollection of the name.

The ending is obvious. He wanted to take me out, and I refused. He called once or twice more, but it was always the same: I would not go out with him. He still had some sort of allure about him: there was a little of Humphrey Bogart (not yet a film actor) in his deep, dry voice. But I was not tempted. I did not want another seduction, this time on a hotel bed or on his parents' "davenport"—that would cost me the ground I had regained. But he pretended not to understand my refusals. "You go out with Windy," he argued. At the same time he seemed quite well aware of the cool tit-for-tat that was continuing by telephone, and in some way it amused him, as if he were outside it, like a Ping-Pong game he watched while applauding my sometimes deft returns. There were high spirits in those repeated Noes of mine. I was laughing at the whole position; it was gratifying to my pride to see his renewed desire for me as a species of regret. It was clear to me now that cowardice had been the villain that killed his appetite. And he, behind the plaintiveness, behind the coaxing and wheedling, was chuckling for some reason himself. My refusals told him, doubtless, that he was still and forever my seducer—to all eternity: if I went out with Windy (his Leporello), it was because the servant presented no danger.

He never married, and the next time I came back to Seattle, married myself for the second time and with a baby to show my grandmother, I heard he had died. It gave me a funny feeling to hear that: I was just twenty-seven, and the first man I had ever slept with was gone. I wondered whether I could have something like an Rh-positive factor that did not combine well with the males I associated with: Mark Sullivan was dead, my first husband was dead, as well as the young man I had left him for—John Porter; and now Forrest Crosby. Of the series I would miss him least (most of all I would miss my grandfather, who had died "in good season," a year and a half earlier, aged seventy-nine), but still his passing, putting an end to a rake's progress, would leave a little rip or tear in the fabric of my life not easily rewoven.

4

When I went that fall as a boarder to Annie Wright Seminary in Tacoma, my uncle's friend Mark had offered to write to me. His letters did not start arriving till after Christmas vacation but then they "saved my life." Could this homely red-faced boy—by now a junior at the University—have guessed the significance for my social standing at school of having a regular male correspondent even though I was only fourteen? My classmates were mostly a year older but still hopeless babies, not yet weaned from the food packages sent by their mothers, which, despite the rule about sharing, constituted for them the most interesting part of the mail. Poor Jean Eagleson and Barbara Dole, poor Frances Ankeny, Ruth Sutton, Clover Rath, Mary Ellen Warner—if any boy wrote to them, it was a brother.

The girls I admired and wanted to copy were juniors and seniors, some of whom had fiancés who wrote every day. To those girls, who were not all as unapproachable as I originally feared, it was irresistible to pretend that Mark was mine. His letters, running to several pages, tended to bear it out, and a bloodstone ring given me by my great-aunt Alice for Christmas made a "perfect" engagement ring. In case doubts were inspired by the flat stone in its filigree silver setting (to carry 100% conviction it should have been a solitaire diamond), I explained that Mark was poor and bent on being a great writer. He had chosen the blood-stone, I added, to match my green eyes.

The center of my life, though, during that second term in Annie Wright's new buildings, gabled, dormered, case-mented, and beginning to be creeper-covered, with a clois-ter to walk in on rainy days, which had a camellia tree blooming beside it, was not a man or a boy but Mary Ann Lamping, a senior. Every night after study hall I sat in her room till bedtime with the rest of her clientele, doing my best to amuse that fair-haired, dry-spoken engaged girl, who came from a "social" family in Seattle (her father's name was Roland), wore a black riding-habit with a stock and bowler hat, was not going to the U after graduation but heading instead for a big wedding with ushers, and already had a "settled" air about her that was part of her allure. An absence of drive was part of it, too: her clipped, dark-blond hair was untouched by marcel iron or water wave; she had indolent, slightly broad hips and elegant tapering legs, never crossed, never folded under her, never wound around a chair leg, but squarely held apart, giving her the lap of a young matron as she sat in her armchair idly buffing her nails. Unusually for a senior, she did not have a roommate; she had no "best friend" in her class and took no part in school activities—riding was not considered an "activity," not being a team sport or competitive, and cost extra.

In Lampie's ambience, a fiancé's lack of "family," his not having a car or belonging to a fraternity, ought to have been severe liabilities, yet these shortcomings in Mark, if she knew of them, seemed to leave her indifferent. I never had to admit to her that Mark's father was a policeman, since she never asked; the "engagement ring" elicited no sign of disapproval (never more, anyhow, in her case, than a mild wrinkling of the short, lightly freckled nose) or quiet comparison with her own sparkler, and, looking back, I cannot decide whether she was sweet-natured—rare in a social girl— or lazily permissive, disinclined to raise questions. Although she had to hear parts of Mark's letters whenever one came (they were over her head, I imagine), only once did she query me about him, and that was to wonder aloud where he took me dancing when I was home. The Butler Hotel, I answered, lying. A safe choice: though my uncle Harold went there (he liked the band), Lampie never would.

Mark's motive in writing me was surely kindness. He had a fiancée and didn't need another. But there must have been something in me that brought out the pedagogue in young men, and he was still taking an interest in what went into my mind. He may have feared that Annie Wright would be just a fancy finishing-school—the same fear that my real (or semi-real) fiancé voiced about Vassar three years later. Mark's letters (typed with two fingers, newspaperman style) were tutorials of a sort, recommending books, making cryptic jests, copying out lines of poetry, maxims of Schopenhauer, aphorisms. Like Don Marquis's archy, he never used the shift key or any mark of punctuation beyond a few dots.

> how odd
> of god
> to choose
> the jews

he wrote, quoting Hilaire Belloc, he said, and always signed himself "mark," typewritten like that. I cannot remember how he closed his letters; it was my first husband, not Mark, I think, who used to type "S.L.S.O.C.Y.K." at the end of his, meaning "So long, sweet one, consider yourself kissed." No, it couldn't have been Mark because the funny acronym (looking like a Polish surname) was in capitals and had periods. When Dwight Macdonald called his dissident magazine *politics* (and note the small "d" in what is more commonly written "MacDonald"), I at once thought of Mark. That was in the forties, but they were the same generation. For a young male of those days (cf. e.e. cummings, a forerunner, born 1894), such graphic devices, like armorial bearings, were a "statement," a machine-age manifesto. They took their cue from the typewriter, with its upper and lower cases indistinguishable on the keyboard, like Everyman at birth; the elimination of the shift key was a kind of capital punishment. Females were unaffected by this revolution. In handwriting, distinction was sought at our school in the cramped practice of backhand (which in fact did express quite well the personalities of those laboring to perfect it), or in florid capital letters (I practiced and practiced on my "M"s and "C"s), while in the other hemisphere the aristocratic Isak Dinesen, writing of her African farm on an old Corona, strewed capitals about with a munificent feudal hand: "the trunk of an Elephant," "the Native People."

An additional motive for Mark's writing me was no doubt the act of writing itself. Probably he sat down to the typewriter late at night after a party, the way someone else— my uncle Harold, for instance—might tickle the ivories on the piano. I was receptive, and he was literary—the editor of the college magazine. In his free time, he was writing squibs and short stories and sending them to *College Humor* and maybe the old *Life* and *Judge*. Among the modern books he was reading that year, I remember *Count Bruga* (1926), *The Mauve Decade* (1926), *Nigger Heaven* (1926), and perhaps Huneker's *Painted Veils* (1920). And it was during that year (1926–27), my first at the Seminary, that he got into trouble with the U for an issue of the magazine he had published and mainly written, the February number, evidently—the offending lead piece was called "Lincoln Apple Sauce."

He must have sent it to me at school; there was no other

way I could have got hold of it. It was a shellacking of Abraham Lincoln or, more precisely, of the Lincoln myth, as I now realize. But at the time I did not distinguish between the two, and in that I was no exception. In suspending Mark, the University (which had just fired its liberal president at the instance of the governor) was punishing him for blasphemy against the martyred President as much as for irreverence toward the Lincoln myth. Perhaps the two were all but inseparable, just as Christ cannot be pried loose from Christianity or Communism from Stalin despite many "highly motivated" attempts. Perhaps all efforts at repristination are doomed to failure because anti-historical, like over-cleaned frescoes, which always look so glaringly new, worse than fakes. In any case, "Lincoln Apple Sauce," which pleased me inordinately, very much grieved my grandfather, not only for Lincoln but for Mark. He felt Mark had done himself a lasting injury at the very start of a promising career. My grandfather, a lifelong Republican, was a democrat, one of the few I have known, but he must have thought that the upward-mobile son of a police officer had to watch his step on the swinging rope-ladder of success.

"Lincoln Apple Sauce" owed its inspiration to Mencken, obviously. It was a piece of debunking. But that was not why I liked it. My reason was simpler: I hated Lincoln. All through school, and in the convent, too, our teachers had the habit of confronting us with opposites and making us choose between them. Evidently it was a form of head-counting, but its purpose I cannot guess. A pet opposed pair was Washington and Lincoln (later on, in college, it would be monism and dualism or Voltaire and Rousseau), and at Garfield High the previous February they had made us fall into line on opposite sides of the gym and march to music to show our preference. Even in the convent, where you would expect Mount Vernon to outshine a log cabin and a powdered wig a scraggly set of chin whiskers, Washington's claque was always smaller, and that was enough, naturally, to keep me loyal to it.

Actually I did not care all that much for Washington. I

was bored by the cherry tree, by the "Father of His Country" label, by Martha Washington's neckwear, by his flat red Gilbert Stuart face. Among presidents my real liking was for Jefferson, with Martin Van Buren second, but in school they never gave you that choice. And if the alternative to Washington was Lincoln, I had no hesitation about where I stood. My sympathies were aristocratic, which was also to say with the few against the many. Yet my dislike of Lincoln did not mean that I was pro-slavery. I had mentally freed my slaves long ago, in the wake of John Randolph and John Calhoun. But I was passionate about states' rights, which made me support the South in the Civil War.

In any conflict I was almost automatically for the losing side; that was an appeal that George Washington lacked. I loved Bonnie Prince Charlie, Mark Antony, Vercingetorix, Beauregard, General Jeb Stuart, the absurd Charles the First, and despised any victory that was not won against fearful odds. One might think that John Wilkes Booth's bullet would have softened my heart to Honest Abe. But no. His myth was stronger than the bullet, and the myth was too uncouth, too plebeian, for me. It was not till I was much older, nearly thirty, that I developed a real sympathy for and interest in Lincoln. But it was his intellect and, above all, his melancholy that did it. Neither had a place, naturally, in the common Lincoln applesauce, which Mark was deriding.

It should be evident from his literary tastes that Mark did not share my aristocratic views, even though, like Mencken, he hated and scorned the "booboisie." Yet Mencken in later life became what is called a reactionary, and maybe that is how a true hater of the bourgeois (look at Flaubert) is pretty well bound to end. By what criteria, if not simple lack of money, can the antique *demos*—"the people"—be told apart from the mass of middle-class boobs? In a country like America, which has shed its proletariat, except for coal-miners and an under-class of permanent relief clients, no distinction is visible. In any case, Mark did not live long enough to sour into a reactionary. When he died (of TB, I think) during the war, he was arrested at a stage of pure misan-thropy—normal in a newspaperman.

At the University he was soon reinstated, and the only penalty I remember his suffering was the confiscation of that issue of the magazine. I continued to be proud of his te-merity, and for a while he kept on writing to me, probably till he finished the University and found a job on a paper. It seems to me that he did not come to Lake Crescent with us the next summer and that, shortly after, our correspon-dence ceased. Maybe he got married. But he had been there when I needed him, like a pair of water wings; his letters saw me through my sophomore year. After that, I was *somebody* in the school, even when under a cloud; the teach-ers had noted me.

My sophomore year marked, too, the first time I was turned loose in a library, like a colt in green pasture. There was no librarian to hover over me; I was usually alone in the tall, dark-paneled room lined with books, not just sets as in my grandfather's library at home but modern books. And there were periodicals laid out on two round tables under central lamps where you could sit and leaf through *L'Illustration*, *The Illustrated London News* and *Punch*, as well as (I think) *The Virginia Quarterly Review*, *The Yale Review*, *Scribner's*, *The Century*. It was like entering a house with a little table all set as in a fairy tale. I would climb up to ex-plore the shelves and bring down booty—all of Sinclair Lewis, for instance, to choose from, including one called *Free Air*, featuring a filling-station; Galsworthy, of course (*The Forsyte Saga* and a new one in a violet cover called *The White Mon-key*, about Fleur); Arnold Bennett (*Clayhanger*, *Hilda Less-ways*, *The Old Wives' Tale*) and Wells's *Ann Veronica*; a whole line of dark-green volumes (*Fortitude*, *The Green Mirror*, *The Dark Forest*, *The Duchess of Wrexe*) by an author, Hugh Wal-pole, whom no teacher admired as much as I did. In twen-tieth-century books the taste was mainly English. I remember May Sinclair but not Willa Cather or Ellen Glasgow and am unsure about Dreiser. . . . I can see a yellow volume,

though, with a colored sketch of a Friend on the linen cover—
Hugh Wynne, Quaker, by S. Weir Mitchell, America's first
psychiatrist.

But the great thing was to find the complete Tolstoy. I
raced straight through it, and the volume that really struck
me was not *War and Peace* or even *Anna Karenina* but *The
Death of Ivan Ilyich*. I think I had fallen in love with the title.
Of *War and Peace* I remember most my disappointment with
Natasha for marrying fat Pierre after Prince Andrei. The let-
down was familiar; it was what happened to the reader when
an author was a moralist and had to punish his heroine for
her own good. I knew the sensation from having heard *Emma*
read aloud in the convent—by the little whiskered Madame
who also read *A Tale of Two Cities* and *The Gentleman from
Indiana* while we learned to make buttonholes and sew a
French seam—well, you know how the story ends, with
"headstrong" (read "high-spirited") Emma forced to marry
Mr. Knightley. In *Anna Karenina*, I of course fell for Vronsky
and did not notice his bald spot, any more than I had the
sense to notice Prince Andrei's small white hands.

Did I know that Tolstoy was better than Hugh Walpole?
Unfortunately I am not really sure. What I do remember is
my immense surprise on learning that my grandmother had
read Tolstoy, indeed all the Russian classics, which she spoke
of, tartly but half-fondly, as "those old books." She and
Aunt Rosie had gone through them when they were young
and—wonderful to think of—when the books were still
young, too.

Poetry at the Seminary was kept in study hall, rather than
in the library. It was there that I discovered Swinburne and
"So we'll go no more a-roving" after the Cavalier Poets.
None of this can have furnished material for letters to Mark,
who was fonder of prose than of poetry and more partial to
Americans and to French than to the English. That year he
was talking of *Jarnegan*, the new book by the hobo named
Jim Tully, now forgotten—if you look "Tully" up in a current book of reference, you are told "See Cicero." In the

summer he brought me *The Hard-boiled Virgin*, by Frances Newman, a new writer thought by us in Seattle to be H. L. Mencken's mistress.

Mencken, in fact, was the taste-maker, not only for apprentice journalists like Mark but for various young provincials seeking a direction. I remember trying to read *Thus Spake Zarathustra*—a typically limp volume lent me by my Garfield friend Ethel ("Ted") Rosenberg, who normally would have been more likely to press *The Rubáiyát* on me or Rabindranath Tagore. Indeed, putting the donor together with the title, I supposed I was being initiated into some new branch of Oriental wisdom. I did not know that Nietzsche had been launched by Mencken more than twenty years before, and perhaps neither did Ted. Yet it was he who had made *Zarathustra* a must for young aesthetes like her, who considered themselves far beyond the reach of his influence. More consciously a Menckenite and somewhat older (though surely still in her twenties) was Miss Dorothy Atkinson, a Vassar graduate and *American Mercury* subscriber, who in sophomore English was giving us *As You Like It*, the de Coverley papers, *Silas Marner*, "L'Allegro" and "Il Penseroso," Macaulay's essay on Johnson, and Thomas Huxley's "On a Piece of Chalk."

Like that reading list (more or less standard in private schools at the sophomore level, though we did not suspect it), Miss Atkinson was exacting and in appearance severe. She wore her ash-blond soft hair in funny puffs or whirls over her ears and her folding eyeglasses on a long chain or ribbon, had pale, slate-blue eyes, thick milk-white skin, and a satiric way of talking. Though I had her only that one year at Annie Wright (her successor, very different, was her popping-eyed younger sister, Miss Marjorie Atkinson—*Macbeth*, Burke, "Lycidas," the *Essays of Elia*—whom I made cry one day), Miss Dorothy Atkinson must count as a major influence in my life since it was in order to be like her that I went to Vassar.

Her room at Annie Wright was across the corridor from

mine, and I used to bring her the stories I was beginning to write, one of which—"A Wife and Mother"—she advised me to send to H. L. Mencken. It was unlikely that he would take it, she explained, but he might return it with comments and possibly words of encouragement—he had an interest in new, young writers. She was wrong in my case; I never heard from him. But to be given that advice by her, the cool essence of bluestocking, was flattery enough; I was amazed.

The stories I wrote (in study hall, behind the screen of an open textbook) were gloomy satires on respectability and received ideas. Long ago, someone—myself, I suppose—saved them, and then they must have been sent on to me when my grandmother died and the Seattle house was sold. Anyway here they are. On ruled exercise-book paper, the kind we used for our themes, they confront me with a total absence of early talent. Miss Dorothy Atkinson must have been out of her mind. The heroine of "A Wife and Mother," unalluring to begin with, in a few pages reaches an acme of repulsiveness ("She is more than fleshy; she rolls in fat. Her English is poor; her whole person carelessly tended. She has plenty of flashy jewelry and wears it often"), along with a complacent, self-made, Republican husband ("Old honest Abe is his ideal"), who calls all foreigners Wops. "So they live on, contented, average American citizens. . . . The wife and mother of whom sentimental songs are written." Poor Mencken.

Another one tells of a prostitute named Gracia (the Wife and Mother was Daphne), whom we first meet as a department-store clerk selling cosmetics. She loses her job because, at twenty-seven, she is losing her looks ("she would soon join the ranks of the waddling, middle-aging women who insist on buying their clothes in the 'Misses' section"); next she is seduced by a coarse Jewish businessman "with great pouches under hard bright eyes"; when, after six months this Mose Nordstrom tires of her ("The brute!" "The cur! He couldn't have me again now if he wanted to. . . .

He was really awful fat and funny looking, anyhow"), Gracia, now a "middle-aged, fussy, dumpy woman," gets work as an usher in a cheap movie-house, where she meets solitary men and, unaware of what is happening, seeing each of her clients as a new Prince Charming, sinks into professional vice. The final sentence sums it up. "What did she amount to? What was she? Just another prostitute with ideals." The theme of both stories is self-deception, reality being represented by fat; both heroines have a grave figure problem; both "waddle."

Another, unfinished or only partly preserved, "The Story of a Suicide," seems to have started out as an essay—"Those People Called Suicides." Both story and essay begin with a quotation from the Gospels and proceed: "Life is a wild, bitter, brutal thing, a thing that sears, that kills. Life is the reason for death. Most people picture death as a grim, old specter, whose all-destroying hand reaches out and clutches us. But to many, death is a calm, white spirit with a soothing hand, and a tender eye, that takes us away from that horror, life, when we are able to bear it no longer. To some it comes voluntarily; they are usually the ones that it hurts. But to those who cry for it, beg for it, pray for it, it does not hearken, so they are driven to summon it against its will. These people men call suicides."

Beside this passage, a hand has written in the margin: "Very good, Mary—I like your theme but don't make it [illegible] inhuman—I hope, Mary dear, that this version of suicide isn't your own!" So I had turned the essay in as a class theme. More important, to my surprise, I notice that the "y" of the teacher's "Mary," just like mine even today, has a long sweeping flourish of a tail, and that the "i"'s are dotted with circles, just as mine were before Miss Kitchel in freshman English at Vassar discouraged the practice. Till this moment, I never knew where I had got those circles from: what Vassar gave, apparently, Vassar took away. As for the fear that I might be thinking of suicide, I can't decide whether Miss Atkinson (for of course it was she) was being whimsical with her gay little exclamation mark or whether she was worried. A little of both perhaps, which would be the Vassar way.

A fragment of still another story, "What Doth It Profit a Man," has to do with suicide, too. A young woman, Diana Stone, seemingly pregnant, waits in vain for her lover to return to her in the woods by a mountain lake, where she lives. "Ordinarily she would be described as a tall, slender, green-eyed black-haired creature with a glowing natural complexion. But tonight the sorrow, the regret, the pensiveness of her face, as she stood gazing at the beauties of the mountain lake, made her beauty a matter beyond any doubt." Her man, named Keith, had left her. "Oh, God, why should it be?" It was finished. "Perhaps he had never cared, never meant those fond caresses, those words, those looks! Perhaps she had been just one more girl to pet with. . . . Keith . . . the man of her dreams had gone . . . she was alone, alone to face the consequences." For they had done more than pet. They had sinned and sinned gravely against the great commandment. After he left her, he intended to write, to ask her to forgive and to marry him. "But the lure of his bachelor life was too strong and the letter remained unposted." Nevertheless "his thoughts and dreams were haunted by those gay, yet wistful eyes of Diana Stone. He should marry her, by all the rights on earth, he should. He hesitated, for his will was weak." Finally ("her time was near") she wrote to him. "One pleading childish letter ending with 'I tell you, no matter what happens I will love you forever and ever, Keith darling, from your waiting Di.'" But her letter, misaddressed, had been too long in reaching him. When he got it, he at once telephoned for a ticket on the next train. "For he loved her, really, you see." But by the time he reached the familiar house in the woods she had taken strychnine. That night, she died. And: "The man that left the house that evening had snow-white hair."

If Miss Atkinson saw "What Doth It Profit a Man" (which looks earlier to me than "The Story of a Suicide"—heroine

Ardena Passy), it can hardly have occurred to her that Di's misadventure was rather autobiographical. Yet the strange thing is that this tritest and trashiest of all my study-hall narratives is the only one to correspond with anything in my experience. Underneath the embroidery I recognize "Keith," a girl's green eyes, a mountain lake, a path through the woods, seduction and abandonment. Except that I was not pregnant and did not have a glowing natural complexion (my skin was rather pale) the account was not far from the truth, while in none of the other tales, despite what a reader might surmise, is there the slightest trace of direct experience: I myself had no figure problem and, unlike poor Daphne of "A Wife and Mother," no pimples. The sole reference to real life that I can find in these determined-to-be-lifelike fictions is the first name of Gracia's Jewish seducer: Mose. Uncle Mose was Aunt Rosie's husband. I cannot imagine what prompted me to give his first name (unless it was the only one I knew that sounded Jewish or, to be frank, Jewy) to a coarse little rotter; I *liked* Uncle Moses Gottstein.

This brings us up against the mysteries of creation, from which trash seems no more exempt than "serious" literature. Even with trash, sources, like Psyche's Cupid, hide themselves from the light of inquiry. But, apart from Uncle Mose, apart from the absence of waddlers from my personal history, another puzzle rises to meet me as I study those numbered pages of crumbling yellowed paper with torn holes running down one side. What made me write those things? If they had been autobiographical, like so many juvenilia, there would be no need to ask the question. Or if a teacher had set us to writing stories. But I was not responding to any visible pressure, from within or without.

If I could ignore a strange ferocity of treatment, I would say that the urge that seized me was purely literary, by which I mean an urge to write words on paper regardless of any connection with myself or the world immediately surrounding me. In "Suicides," for example, it is almost as if my motive had lain in the epigraph: "I am the Resurrection and the Life" (John xi: 25–26), which opens the Episcopal burial service. This was one of my favorite passages from the New Testament and doubly dear to me because Dickens had used it in *A Tale of Two Cities* as a lead-in for the dissipated Sydney Carton's valediction ("It is a far, far better thing that I do, than I have ever done; it is a far, far better rest that I go to, than I have ever known") as he steps up to replace his high-born rival, Charles Darnay, at the guillotine while the knitting women count. I think I may have written both essay and story simply to have a pretext for setting down in my own hand those tremendous words from the Gospel. If that is so, I sensed, in my fifteenth year, that I belonged to the order of scribes.

In fact (now it comes back to me), those very words of Holy Writ are bound up with my awakening to literature: in the convent, during sewing hour, the tiny black-eyed nun, Irish or French, is reading to us from Dickens in a deep voice with a strongly rolled "r" the indictment of the tribunal ("Charles Evrémonde, called Darnay") to be followed, next week, by the speech of the dissolute barrister ("'I am the Resurrection and the Life, saith the Lord'"), while, bent over my embroidery hoop, like Kant awakening from his dogmatic slumbers or the child Samuel hearing the Lord's call in the house of the high priest or Archimedes in the bathtub, I feel the short hair rising on my scalp. A voice has summoned me, from the lips of a small hoarse old Madame with gray hairs straggling out from under her pleated wimple. Come to think of it, those words recur, uncannily, as though completing the circle, in my last novel, *Cannibals and Missionaries*, and in *The Group*, though maybe the strangeness is not so strange if you know that in both cases the dearly loved John xi: 25–26 is cropping up at an Episcopal funeral.

It is true that I was fond of epigraphs, scriptural or not, that over a text I liked to set headings, like tomb inscriptions, which gave me great pleasure to copy out and had little to do with the story. Among these same Annie Wright relics, I find entire poems—Edna Millay, Margaret Widde-mer, unidentified others—written out as though for com-monplacing. Yet I cannot think that such an instinct for magical safekeeping, for the tracery of groups of words carefully indited in my ornate hand with those fish-eyed "i"s, was my whole motive in writing. I spoke just now of a "ferocity" of treatment. Or "vehemence," I could say. I cannot escape the impression that I wrote in anger. The aesthetic urge was secondary. I had "something to say." Those waddling Daphnes and Gracias had got under my skin.

But, as I say, I did not know any women like that. There were none in my family—both my grandmother and my mother, I was often told, had been in their time "the most beautiful woman in Seattle," and my other grandmother, while stout, was solid and bulldoggy—and I was in no dan-ger of becoming one myself. A school picture shows a thin, somewhat tense girl, a little taller than average, not too dif-ferent from "Diana Stone," allowing for some romantic footlighting. Those Gracias and Daphnes must have repre-sented, for some reason, the enemy. Clearly they embodied some thing or quality I hated with passion. That cannot have been fat or shortness of stature, however displeasing when combined, but moral traits—triteness and self-deception. In my study-hall compositions, they are allied, occurring to gether like elements in the periodic table. And in fact I be-lieve I was right to have noticed that: triteness, the resort to well-worn counters, is an evasive device that protects you from reality's rough edges, which may hurt if you bump into them. But is reality, or truth, always so uncomfortable? That is not my opinion now (truth produces elation, surely, because of its closeness to beauty), but I evidently thought so when I was fourteen, for what was I doing but rubbing my heroines' noses in it, furiously, as though to wake them up? E.g., You are a prostitute, fat stupid Gracia, admit it, don't pretend you do it because the fellows find you irre-sistibly attractive; you are the same as a streetwalker, no matter what, like the Pharisee, you tell yourself: "God, I thank thee, that I am not as other men are." That was what the anger, the ferocity, the vehemence were all about. They sound excessive because the provocation is not disclosed. What was biting me, after all? Even if I was surrounded, at school and at home, by triteness and hypocrisy (and adolescents do feel that), why take it out on a notion of the average housewife, the average prostitute—in other words on total strangers?

But wait! A thought has struck me. "Fat and shortness of stature"—who does that remind me of? Why, Aunt Hennie, of course, Uncle Elkan Morgenstern's wife, my grandmother's sister-in-law; it was a family we did not see as much as once a year. But though immense-breasted Aunt Hennie, no more than five feet high, could not be viewed as exactly a waddler, her daughter and granddaughters— my second cousins—had certainly inherited a tendency to put on weight. I could scarcely have been afraid of coming to resemble the Morgenstern cousins (the Preston body structure, plainly, did not come from that side); in fact, the way they looked, together and separately seemed very alien to me. Doubtless the feeling was mutual—by all indications, they were clannish, Temple-going Jews who, unlike Aunt Rosie, did not mix. Then was my ferocity, unknown to myself, directed at the "Jewish connection," at what my mother in a letter to her mother-in-law had called "the Hebrews"? (My father, for his part, referred to "another Yiddisher fellow" when writing to his brother, Uncle Lou.) I rethink "Mose Nordstrom." It is true that I liked Uncle Moses A. (for Abraham?) Gottstein, but it is also true that I did not much like his appearance—glasses, incipient cataracts, full, rosy cheeks, raised eyebrows, cigar in teeth, rosy lips showing gums, benign smile. It almost looks as if my impulse to write had had some relation to a juvenile anti-Semitic bias, to an anger which had to be directed against the Jewish quarter of me that I half-tried to disavow—a project all the more tempting in that "it" did not show.

As if in confirmation of this disagreeable thesis, memory suddenly presents me with the roommate—a big-hipped, hook-nosed girl from Montana—whom the school had foisted on me that first fall and whom I had asked to be separated from after two weeks. Maybe we had both asked to be separated. She did not like Annie Wright—and never returned, I think, after what must have been Christmas vacation.

But the reader must not think that our school was anti-Semitic. The position was more delicate than that. Miss Preston would never have tolerated expressions of anti-Semitism in teachers or pupils, any more than she would have accepted anti-Catholicism—we had several Catholic girls at the Seminary, including the little dark-eyed LaGasas, whose mother took me to Mass on Sunday. The little La-Gasas were pets, and this was illustrative of what could happen to an attractive, appealing Jewish girl in our Christian schools. I think of darling Susie Lowenstein, with her dainty retroussé nose and finespun pale red-gold curls; that was at Sacred Heart, but at Annie Wright, after my roommate went, in junior or senior year there came the universally popular Elizabeth Staadecker from Seattle, with her deep voice, blond hair, freckles, and big, amusing teeth. It was as though the Jewish people had always to have two representatives with us, their bad angel and their good angel, and this, I think, applied—and perhaps still does—to any minority in our country. Our country needs two of each, like Noah's Ark, for the sake of fair representation, which will allow us to be tolerant and prejudiced alternately, enable us, that is, to point to examples justifying either set of emotions. I am not sure about blacks and Catholics, but, as far as Jews are concerned, I suspect that there is a bottom layer of hostility, which then can be top-dressed or over-painted to any desired degree. Nobody in this land, certainly no Christian, can accept hating on a full-time basis; it is apt to reflect back on the hater.

So then did my impulse to write come out of my allowed quota of private, unvoiced anti-Semitism? I hope not. If it were true, I ought to quit writing. I prefer the explanation that a fierce dislike of self-deception had something to do with it. Moreover the nicer explanation is more convincing, I am relieved to see, in that self-deception remains, in my book, a major sin or vice whereas any dislike of Jews I had as a girl has been, let us say, pretty well sublimated. But I cannot let it drop there. Where did the hatred of self-deception come from? To have been so violent, it must have contained a fear. Yet, so far as I know, I never harbored such a fear. Nor can I find any grounds for it in my make-up. True, through fear of a monstrous guardian, I had become a terrible liar and I was only now getting over it; the Seminary helped, even though there were many silly rules, such as the prohibition of fountain pens (because the girls, shaking them down, could splatter the walls), that made one impatient to break them and then, when caught, deny it. Yet lying to parents and teachers is a quite different thing from lying to oneself. I suppose the first can lead to the second, but the process, I think, generally begins with the lie told to oneself and goes on to the lie told to the world. And yet, in all honesty, I don't recall lying to myself, ever, though I do recall trying to. On the other hand, if I *had* lied, would I know? How, unless someone else caught me? And who could that be? Unless there is in each of us a *someone else* watching—what used to be called our conscience. I believe that there is: I *know* that other person. But even if I can accept that I am not a dyed-in-the-wool hypocrite, do not habitually lie to myself, it does not resolve the question of what made me so sensitive at the age of fourteen to the perils of self-deception. Perhaps I got it from reading—wasn't Sir Roger de Coverley an example of the vice?—or had been painfully familiar with it in a previous life. I can never know the answer.

Miss Atkinson, I see, was not my only reader in the school. On the back of "What Doth It Profit a Man," to my mortification I come upon a penciled note in my handwriting: "If you don't like this, why all right, neither do I. If you say you do, I *know* you're lying." This may have been addressed to my seat-mate, the proud, tall, languid, bronze-eyed Ellin Watts, from Portland, though I wonder whether I had the courage to take that tone with her. Or Katie Urquhart, pale, with flaring nostrils, another member of Lampie's nightly court? In any case, if there was an answer, it was not written on the back of the story.

It seems reasonable that I sent some of my stories to Mark, but what he said I cannot guess. I *know* that I sent a story about a prostitute (not Gracia, another one, with "eyes like dirty dishwater") to a boy named Ed Bent at the University of Idaho in Moscow. How our correspondence began, I don't know, unless it was through an intermediary, like blind-dating by letter. Perhaps I imagined that still another male correspondent would add to my prestige. However we started writing, before long I sent him that story, and he replied more or less in kind. That is, not being up to fiction, he did the equivalent by mail of "talking dirty" to me. What this consisted of, exactly, I have forgotten; doubtless a censor has been at work. In those days there could have been no question of four-letter words between us, and I doubt whether he dealt very concretely with the subject that was on his mind, i.e., mentioned his member in so many words as excited, inflamed, etc., or gave it a Christian name. But I remember being slightly repelled by what were probably innocent or ignorant male fantasies and by the handwriting (which I can still see, though the words have faded from my memory): sloping, close-set, characterless, like a boneless handshake, running evenly across his embossed fraternity-house paper. Evidently there had been a sad misunderstanding: what had begun, on my side, as a literary encounter of minds had turned into a callow campaign on his part to paw me with smutty language. But since Moscow, Idaho, was hundreds of miles away, I felt safe: sticks and stones could break my bones but words could never hurt me. As they kept getting thicker in their envelopes (requiring extra stamps), far from arousing me, his letters "turned me off," and eventually, when I continued not to answer them, they stopped. It was ironical that by the time my grandmother found a stack of them in my bedroom, and *read* them, they might as well have gone to the dead-letter office.

That happened when I was home on vacation, between sophomore and junior years. I am not sure why I had kept them—as trophies or because already I had a respect for the historical record that would not let me destroy any piece of paper with writing or typing on it. But there is no mystery about why I had brought them home; obviously I could not leave them at school. My grandmother had no hesitation about destroying the whole lot, but not, I think, before she had shown at least a sample to my grandfather and their married son, my uncle Frank, then a young lawyer in my grandfather's firm. I don't suppose any legal action was contemplated (on sending obscene matter through the mails, surely a Federal offense), but the discovery of that trove in one of the drawers of my violet and pale-green bedroom furniture brought on a full-scale family crisis—the first and last I remember in Seattle.

There was talk of taking me out of Annie Wright, but where they thought of sending me, short of a reformatory, I do not know. And it was not just a question of the morals of a minor; a crisis in belief was shaking the Preston family—a credibility gap. My grandmother could not accept that this twisted Ed Bent in a fraternity house in Idaho was someone I had never met. For her, the only sense in such a correspondence would have been familiarity between the two parties: somehow, while I was meant to be safely at the Seminary (my worst crime being possession of a fountain pen), we had met at "a wild party" and "gone the limit." For her, that explanation, while not exactly an excuse, would have been more acceptable than the incredible truth, which was that her granddaughter, barely yet in silk stockings, had written some crazy story about a prostitute and sent it to a total stranger. For her, in fact, poor woman, the improbabilities *began* with my writing a story like that, for no reason (a pity I had not thought to say that I had hoped to sell it to *True Romances*), and what did I know of prostitutes, who had told me about them? That it had all come out of my imagination was almost worse than the thought that somebody had shown me a real "house" in Seattle's red-light district.

Finally I must have been accorded a suspension of disbelief, for I was sent back to the Seminary in September, without a word's passing, thank God, from my grandfather to Miss Adelaide Preston on the need for keeping a watch on my mail. He was too kindly, the dear, upright man, to want me to be spied on. Nor would he have liked to have that stout spinster (with whom he had discovered a common ancestor back in northern England) learn what "Cousin Mary" had been up to while in her care. Also, it seems to me, he was not nearly as upset as my grandmother; I guess because my misstep (if I could be believed) had been a mental sin, linked to a talent for words—the real blame, he probably decided, lay with that fool boy in Idaho. My grandfather was always indulgent where my mind's adventures were concerned. It must have been some time, though, before my grandmother could feel the same about me; I fear it is perfectly likely that she never trusted me again.

Nevertheless she let me have my first evening-dress that summer. It was made for me by her dressmaker, Mrs. Farrell, and I cannot think why, except to have in my closet just in case. . . . I was still not allowed to go out with boys; at Lake Crescent, as she must have known, evening-dresses weren't worn. She could not have been looking ahead to junior prom, in the spring, for I remember my prom dress, which was much more sophisticated: flame-red chiffon, straight cut, with tiers of short ruffles. *This* dress—could it have been for the wedding of a Morgenstern cousin?—was yellow chiffon, with a round neck, a fairly full skirt, and an uneven hemline that finished in picoted points. It had a narrow silver belt and a bunch of red cherries at one hip. I had silver slippers to wear with it. That first, girlish, evening dress lived on in my memory to figure in an essay I wrote on George Orwell in 1969. Orwell, when Eric Blair, aged seventeen, had written to a schoolmate describing the terrors of a night spent outdoors in a farmer's field. That brought back to me the night I spent in the "backyard of a university student I loved," dressed in an evening gown ("a bride of Death was the principle of my costume") and hoping to commit suicide. The student was Mark Sullivan.

I cannot say exactly why I was roaming around his backyard with a bottle of iodine in my hand all dressed up to kill myself. It was a cold night; the house was dark. Either Mark was not home or the whole family was asleep. The time was around midnight. I think I was relieved to find, on edging softly past the garbage cans into the backyard, that the window I imagined was his showed no sign of life inside. Though my plan was to kill myself in serenade posture, so to speak, below his window, he was the last person I desired to see. It would have been awful if he had caught me parading around like a mummer. I was also afraid of waking his parents or some neighbor who might call the police. As I wrote in the Orwell essay: "Though eager to die, I was terribly fearful of being caught trespassing before I could swallow the iodine and be discovered on the premises as a corpse." That was partly true—indeed wholly true except for "eager to die." I no more wanted to die than I was in love with Mark.

It was all theatricals, which I was putting on for my own benefit. I would have "died" had I had any other audience, i.e., if anyone had seen me. Yet something must have put the idea of that charade in my head; there must have been a precipitating cause. I had been crossed in love, all right, but that had been some time back and in any case had nothing to do with Mark. No, it was some trivial chagrin: I had quarreled with my family that evening maybe or a friend had disappointed me or I had nothing to read, having finished my library book. Or—just possibly—Mark had promised to bring me a book that afternoon and had not come. Or had gone up to see Harold without stopping to talk to me. Something like that might account for my wish to lay my death, as tribute or blame, at his door. I knew very well that his feelings for me were kindly but not at all amorous—I was still "the Niece," alas, and my own feelings were adjusted to that. Perhaps what was troubling me was simply general boredom and a sense of the vanity of human wishes.

All of a sudden it strikes me that my main motive for that theatrical suicide was to have an occasion to wear the yellow dress. I see it hanging in my clothes closet—a perfect symbol of deluded expectations. Perhaps actually I never *had* worn it until that night when I stood posing before my cheval glass, cherries dangling on one hip, silver slippers on my feet. Perhaps not having worn it was the entire trouble. So, boldly resolved to kill those two birds with one stone, I took the iodine bottle out of the medicine cabinet, glided down the carpeted stairs, and let myself out the kitchen door, shivering. I had decided against putting on a coat, having no evening wrap of my own and unable, in the circumstances, to borrow one of my grandmother's—my regular cloth coat would have looked horrible with the uneven hemline of the dress sticking out.

In Mark's yard, I tipped the iodine bottle to let a drop or two run down my tongue into my throat. I had been trying it at home a few times already, without mustering enough determination to swallow. At Mark's, contrary to my hopes, though the stage was set, it was no easier, and after half an hour or so of nervous attempts I finally let the burning sensation convince me that I would never succeed in swallowing the whole bottle. Meanwhile the cold was helping me decide to go home, though in the dark, in my pale dress, I felt reluctant to leave that protected enclosure for the open streets. On the way over, I had not even thought to be frightened; doubtless the promise of soon being dead anyway served me as armor. But on the way home, robbed of that assurance, I was full of terrors at every street crossing; doubtless I had gooseflesh along my bare arms, and my thin-soled shoes with Cuban heels made me unsteady on my feet.

I got home. No one had missed me. I let myself in with the kitchen key, which I must have hidden for myself— what a confession!—under the doormat. I tiptoed up the stairs and undressed for bed, first replacing the bottle of iodine in the bathroom medicine cabinet. And in doing so, all at once I felt sadly ashamed of my cowardice. I *ought* to have taken the iodine, having made such a parade of it. There was no excuse. Lack of nerve had stopped me—nothing else. Though a few hours ago I had had no particular reason for ending my days, now I had one, in discovering myself to be such a craven. I went to bed. It was my first encounter with self-knowledge—a very bleak sensation. And, though I cannot truthfully say today that I think a better person would have gone ahead and killed herself, I still feel something of that shame.

Yet as I look back over the episode, so strangely fresh in my memory, down to the grateful feeling of the key in my hand, I am puzzled mainly by the dating of it. It was during a vacation, since I was home from school. If I take into account the coldness of the night, I am inclined to place it at Thanksgiving of my junior year. I would have been nearly fifteen and a half. Yet can that be right? By that time Mark (I think) was no longer writing to me. But couldn't that have been the reason, then? The best, indeed, that I can think of.

Yes, if we set the time of my "attempted suicide" as the fall of 1927 everything will fit. It was rather an unsatisfactory semester. Miss Atkinson was gone, I did not know where, replaced by her antipathetic sister. Lampie had graduated and among this year's seniors, no one I liked reciprocated, except Katie Urquhart and there was always doubt

as to *her*. I was not yet doing Caesar with Miss Mackay; at
Captain Proby's riding-school, they made me ride in the ring,
a stable boy leading me; I had lost my love for French and
had not yet found my vocation for the stage—not till Christmas would I terrify the junior school with my one-man show
of "The Fall of the House of Usher," followed by its encore
"A Cask of Amontillado." By November Katie Urquhart
(whose name I loved) from Chehalis was beginning to show
a double face; she no longer seemed to remember that our
mothers had been Gamma Phi sisters at the U. And, instead of taking Natural Science, I had signed up for Cooking with a pink-cheeked alumna who had gone to Simmons
in Boston and married a man named Claude; to my surprise, I had turned out to be the *cancre* of the class—I can
still see the lumps in my white sauce and Mrs. Morrill
straining them out. The best thing that fall was taking the
three-hour boat trip from Seattle to Tacoma—a practice soon
to be supplanted by car travel. Obviously, it had been in
the previous spring that I wrote those stories about suicide.
The evidence bears it out: Miss Marjorie Atkinson could not
have written "I hope, Mary dear, that this version of suicide isn't your own!" And it was not just those suicidal stories and an essay. I have remembered something else.

I am sitting in an open casement window with my legs
hanging out while I consider throwing myself down. It is a
spring night. The height is great enough, I calculate, for the
fall to kill me even on soft grass. It is after lights out, and I
am in my nightgown. This is the room, across from Miss
Atkinson's, I had sophomore year after the break-up with
my roommate—the same room where I had read Forrest
Crosby's at first regular letters, now tied up in a bundle, as
I no longer pore over them for clues as to why he tired of
his "Di." I have switched to reading sad love poems with a
dark philosophy, which are going to help me decide to end
my life. Not just once; for several nights running I sit there
thinking of doing it—depending, probably, on the weather.
It would not be on a rainy night.

I remember edging my bottom over the iron bar to the

very edge, resting my feet on the gutter and hoping to make myself fall. It reminded me of the attempts to fly we occasionally made as children, standing on a window sill and waving our arms but never taking the plunge. To encourage myself now, I would recite poetry, softly, so as not to attract the night watchman's attention: "But there were dreams to sell,/ Ill didst thou buy./ Life is a dream, they tell,/ Waking to die." Or: "From too much love of living,/ From hope and fear set free . . ." Or: "You might as well be calling yours/ What never will be his/ And one of us be happy./ There's few enough as is." Or: "When I am dead, my dearest." Eventually I would pull my legs in, drop back into the room, and go to bed. This did not last more than a month. Then that summer, probably, Mark did not come with us to Lake Crescent. And the occasion of my "suicide" under his window may have been an announcement that he was getting married. As my "fiancé," he was owed that.

The next year when I sat in an open casement window after lights out, I was up to something more dangerous: smoking. I was teaching myself to inhale, with the slight risk of falling out from dizziness since you had to squat close to the edge to keep the smoke from drifting back into the room and alerting a passing teacher. But smoking out the window was junior year, and suicide out the window was sophomore year. Anyway, whenever the failed drama in the Sullivan backyard took place, Mark never knew of it. *No one* knew or suspected. In my pale-green-and-violet bedroom, I hung my evening dress back in the closet, and that was that. Neither did Mark ever guess—how could he?— that an entire girls' school in Tacoma had heard that he had asked me to marry him when I graduated.

One night, several years afterwards, when I had grown up and was home from Vassar for the summer, I sat in a car on a road that ran above Three Tree Point—a wooded section of "secondary" residences that were often the scene of parties. Hidden in the trees below, a party was going on; somebody, probably my uncle Harold, had brought me to it several hours earlier, and now I wanted to go home. I had made the long climb up the steep log-hewn stairs by myself, hoping that whoever had brought me would follow, but the others were all still down there, drinking and playing music. There was nothing to do but sit in the front seat and wait.

Then Mark appeared out of the darkness, breathless and drunk. He had been at the party, alone (though he was married then, I think), and had decided to come after me. But he had had to toil up a great many of those winding stairs made of logs and grope through discouraging pine woods to find the road and the parked car I was in. He fell into the front seat, put his arms around me, and kissed me. Seeing how drunk he was, I pulled away, sad that it had to be this way *if* it was going to be. I tried to pull away politely, because I liked him, because he was Mark. These woods were reminiscent of Lake Crescent at night, of the times we had walked home Indian file to Singer's Tavern from Rosemary Point.

He did not persist but stayed in the front seat beside me resting his head on my shoulder. When the others finally joined us (the party was breaking up), he explained with owlish precision what he was doing there. "I climbed stairs and stairs . . . stairs and stairs . . . stairs and stairs." His thickened voice was dreamy, and when it stopped I thought he had gone to sleep. But then he raised his head with a jerk from my shoulder and looked me angrily in the eye. "Stairs and stairs. But she was as cold as an onion."

5

Annie Wright, to be truthful, was not an "exclusive" school. That may have been why so many girls left, disappointed, after a year or so. In our class of 1929, for instance, what happened to tall Pauline Paulsen, from Spokane, destined by her height, her bearing, her calm gray eyes and soft rounded cheeks, her prowess with the javelin, her basketball, to be a school leader, almost like the one-and-only Retha Hicks, Class of '25, whom Miss Preston still brought up to us in study hall, wiping her eyes? With Pauline's poise and good looks, she was even able to carry off a Scandinavian surname—otherwise a thing to be lived down at the Seminary, witness poor, pale-eyed Gudrun Larsen, whose father owned the Blue Mouse movie theatre in Seattle.

All honors would have been Pauline's had she stayed with us: May Queen, Field Day champion, salutatorian, choir soloist, president of the senior sorority. She was one of three tall beauties from Spokane: herself, Hattie Connor (black hair, high color, blue eyes "put in with a sooty finger," odd, top-drawer accent that I now place as Canadian), and greenish-eyed Betty Reinhardt (only five eight and not exactly a beauty—skin—but counting as one of them because Nature loves a triad and the three were friends). Attached to them, like a burr, was long-nosed, nosy, dark-eyed Josephine Matthews, who had been in school with them across the mountains in Spokane. When Pauline did not come back for junior year, I felt the deprivation almost like the loss of my parents, although I had never been close to her. None of us had. She was a pillar of the school structure and impersonal, as pillars are meant to be.

The Spokane three kept to themselves; they might have been day pupils, so little did they mingle after school hours with the rest of us boarders. I cannot even remember where their rooms were. Nor did they have anything to do with two other girls from Spokane (besides Dodie Matthews) we had with us: nieces of the poet Vachel Lindsay, one very white and fat, one small and spindly, whose parents were missionaries in China.

I have never been to Spokane, though I used to wake up and peek out at the brilliantly lit station, raising a corner of my lower-birth window shade in the train going east. But I have a magical picture of it, thanks to those three tall Graces: a river running through the center of town and creating two great foaming waterfalls, harnessed to make electricity that glittered all night long; on its bank or nearby, the Davenport Hotel, with a dark paneled lounge, a roaring fire, and leather "davenports" on which tycoons sat with their handsome, well-dressed wives. In addition, the 1911 *Britannica* supplies a Federal building, the Paulsen building (yes!), the *Spokesman Review* building, a Northern Pacific railway depot, a Great Northern depot, Gonzaga College (R.C.) for boys, Spokane College (Lutheran), surely for boys, too, and Brunot Hall (P.E.) for girls, obviously Annie Wright's east-of-the-mountains shadow in which our tall three would have been star day pupils.

That Pauline did not come back was interpreted by me, I guess, as a "rejection" of the Seminary, and Miss Preston must have seen it so, in more practical terms: it was a blow to the school, her life's creation, to lose a pearl like Pauline at the end of the sophomore year. What a relief it would have been to hear that Mr. Paulsen's fortune had been swallowed up in a bank failure, thus forcing dear stalwart Pauline to go to public high. But no reason—or excuse—was ever given us. Perhaps she went east to a finishing-school—the Masters at Dobbs Ferry or the Bennett at Mill-brook, both favored by Northwestern parents. We never heard.

It was the same with Ellin Watts, from Portland—five ten, willowy, silver-bronze "page boy" bob, but she was in the class ahead, not in our class, and her languid, sleepy-lid-ded, disdainful (even when occasionally friendly) manner could have warned of a coming defection. And, as though to refill the Oregon quota, there was a new girl that fall, Ruth Williams, from The Dalles, quite tall, with a knot of dark hair, even white teeth, and a brilliant set of widely spaced dark-blue eyes, who was somehow related to the Agens, a Seattle first family that lived in The Highlands, by the Golf Club—her older sister, Florence, taught in the lower school. Ruth Williams was my friend for a few dazzling weeks of my junior year, sailing into my room like a walking Debrett, telling me who was who in Puget Sound society, holding out the wild hope of introducing me to Jimmy Agen, great golfer and rated the catch of Seattle, still more desirable than Léon Auzias de Turenne, captain (we believed) of Harvard's tennis team and Davis Cup alternate. Never had Annie Wright seemed so full of promise. Yet breathless Ruth stayed with us less than a year and even so outstayed her glory. Possibly she was on a scholarship because of her sister and had been warned to settle down and improve her grades. Anyway, after mid-years or some other marking-period, she, too, disappeared, like a falling star, leaving only the strange place-name, The Dalles, behind her. According to Webster, the word, of French derivation, denotes "rapids above a flat, slablike rock bottom, in a narrow, troughlike part of a river." There are several dalles in the American West, but the dalles of the Columbia River (I learn from the faithful *Britannica,* my life's companion, only one year older than I) were famous for their beauty. Yes, Ruth did say that, and I remember picturing her town as a ford paved with smooth flagstones in a brown transparent river, where speckled trout jumped. But shouldn't it have been salmon? Is it too late for me, I wonder, to make a trip to The Dalles and Spokane? Both could be done, by car from Seattle, in two or three days. I cannot make out whether I am destined to see those places, ringed with fading ink on my life's yellowing map, or destined never to see them.

When Pauline did not come back, it was clear that Hat and Betty would soon be following—we had them on borrowed time. I think of my efforts to "hold" Hat for the Seminary— a hint of how it might feel to try to hold a man who was counting the hours till he was free. We had our Irishry in common and also tone-deafness, the latter much more pronounced (I hope) in her case, making it painful for anyone but another tone-deaf person to be near her in chapel. That horn-voice, octaves below the rest of us, flatted out the hymns like an untuned barrel organ. She was worst on the slow ones—"Fairest Lord Jesus," "Now the day is over," "Jesus calls us," which were the ones I loved best. It was like a halitosis affecting the ear. But I did not mind sitting next to her, even sharing a hymn book with her, for to my mind there was something aristocratic in that brute oblivious blare.

Looking on a hymnal together morning and evening was

a tie of sorts; her daily closeness encouraged me to try, like a courting male bird, to interest her in the daring books I read and the bold ideas I was voicing. But, like a genuine gouty Blimp, she was indifferent to reading. As with C and lower C-flat, she did not "hear" a difference between James Branch Cabell and *Sorrell and Son.* I was mad about acting and reciting, but she could no more impersonate an emotion than carry a tune; I suppose she was too incurious to play a part. Nor did atheism hold any charm for her. She was not a Roman Catholic, which gave believers a good foundation for doubting; she was the only Irish person I had ever met to be a born Protestant. Still, to my satisfaction, if not through my efforts—possibly despite them—she lasted till June. In the fall, then, she did go east to one of those schools. Dobbs Ferry, I guess, because two years later I chanced to see her in Grand Central Station, in a smart tailored suit, with her big feet in smart, mannish shoes, when I was taking the train to Poughkeepsie. I was proud of Vassar and despised all finishing-schools, but it was James Branch Cabell all over again: she was unaware of a change in our relative standings and looked down on me from her superior height with a bluff, forbearing smile. I might as well have been going to visit a relative in Sing Sing—the Ossining stop.

Or could she have been at the Bennett in Millbrook, also served by Grand Central? The thought is tempting, because of the Bennett Greek play, well known at the time. At Vassar our beginning Greek class under Mrs. Ryberg went over in a rented vehicle to see them do *The Trojan Women* in Gilbert Murray's translation. Terrible: picture a bare-armed, bare-legged chorus in purple pepluses swaying and moaning on the grass in the hot Dutchess County sun. I like to think of Hattie being imperturbable in a peplus. But where she really went, after Annie Wright, I suppose I shall never know. In the alumnae notes for the Class of '29, the only Spokane girl whose doings are ever chronicled is, naturally, Dodie Matthews.

Tess against photographer's ocean, 1910, The Breakers, Oregon

Tess in her engagement photo

Tess and her daughter, Mary McCarthy, one and a half months old, Aug. 10, 1912, Seattle

From Roy's desk calendar

Mary Therese McCarthy

Date 1912	Bld oz	Week 4th	5:00 P.M.
FRIDAY.			
June 21	8 8		
28	7 12	1	BORN AT
July 5	8 6	2	MINOR HOSPITAL
" 12	9 4	3	DR. C.W. SHARPLESS
			DR. LIPPINCOTT
" 19	10 5	4	NURSE P. BROGAN.
" 21	10 7		
" 26	10 11	5	BAPTIZED AT
Aug 2	11 -	6	ST. JAMES CATHREDAL
" 4	11 8	7	FR. NOONAN.
" 16	11 9	8	W.F. FINN. GODFATHER..
" 21	11 10		2 IMOGENE GRIEBHER.
" 23	11 5	9 ×	GODMOTHER .
" 30	11 15	10	

Roy in his office, probably in the Hoge Building, Seattle, around 1914

Harold Preston

Roy McCarthy

Four generations, Seattle, around 1916: Mary, Simon Manly Preston (great-grandfather), Kevin, Harold Preston (grandfather), Tess with Preston on her lap

(OPPOSITE): *Kevin at his parents' graves, Minneapolis cemetery*

Kevin, aged five, in Seattle house

(LEFT): *Uncle Harold Preston, possibly at Lake Crescent*

Miss Preston, Annie Wright principal

May Queen photo 1929. Queen (seated) is Jean Eagleson; Mary, standing, is in top row, third from left

Graduating class, Annie Wright Seminary, 1929, with Blanche Ford, class of '28, in front row next to Mary

"Marthe" Simpson, art teacher (1898–1984), in 1932

1929, Seattle.   Leonid Finch photograph

It is no doubt to Annie Wright's credit, to that of all those Episcopal bishops who had a hand in its making, that on the whole we could not keep smart, social girls very long. Probably there was too much emphasis on studying, and the faculty, some of it, was too good. How good they could be as sheer educators I did not fully appreciate till I decided early in my junior year that I wanted to go east to college.

Such an ambition was rare then for a girl from the Northwest (it was commoner among boys, who were divided between Princeton, Harvard, and M.I.T.); normally Stanford, with its quota of one-eighth girls, was the height of Annie Wright aspiration. Among us, the majority who aimed at college at all, rather than at a June wedding, had their sights on the U of Washington and were already worrying about whether to go Kappa, Theta, or Gamma Phi. I was determined not to let the U happen to me, and Stanford, we heard, typed a girl as a grind and homely; if I was doomed to stay in the West, I would almost rather go to Reed, the crazy college in Oregon that did not have marks, so probably no sororities either. . . . But I had let the decision wait too long. I had been taking the wrong courses to prepare for an eastern college (*Cooking*, good Lord, with pretty little Mrs. Morrill, a Simmons graduate!), and junior year was too late to start. Or would have been if the Seminary had not risen to the challenge.

Miss Justine Browne, our vice-principal and the school "brain," had me send for catalogues from Vassar, Bryn Mawr, and Radcliffe—my three choices. When they came, that hawk-beaked Athena with pale oysterish eyes seated me at her table—the top spot in the dining-room, just below Miss Preston's table for two—and the thick catalogues passed from hand to hand for our wondering study. Miss Browne liked Radcliffe best, mainly because it shared some classes with Harvard. But Radcliffe had an entrance requirement of four years of Latin—the catalogue left no doubt of that—while

Bryn Mawr and Vassar, apparently, would accept three. But I was just *starting* Latin that fall with Miss Mackay: junior year plus senior year made two. So unless that requirement could be waived (and Miss Browne said it couldn't), it looked as though I could forget about studying for the College Boards. If Providence did not intervene, in its Providential way, I was sunk.

Providence entered in the form—dark, thin, knobby—of Miss Ethel Mackay (pronounced "McEye"), a Scot in her late thirties, a product of Girton and Edinburgh and the strictest teacher in the school. In an earlier memoir I have called her "Miss Gowrie." Now she decided that I could do three years of Latin in two if I read Caesar with her in private lessons while having Cicero next year in class. If we started this spring, then during the coming summer in Seattle, where she would have a furnished room with a screened porch in the University district, we could fit in the campaign against the Germans (Book IV) and the famous bridge across the Rhine. Luckily Latin came easy to me thanks to my Catholic background; from *agricola, agricolae* (first declension)—I felt as if I had known it in a previous life. And not only *"Gallia est omnis divisa in partis tris,"* but *"Horum omnium fortissimi sunt Belgae"*—the war and brave little Belgium had taught us all *that* lesson from the start of Book I.

Yet not even Miss Mackay and my cradle Catholicism could have squeezed a fourth year (Virgil) into me, with the result that I never had the *Aeneid*. So I am unfinished in my Latin, like the little prince in my father's fairy story who, when changed into bird form, lacked a wing because his little sister failed to complete one sleeve of his enchanted sweater.

At Vassar that was an oddity that set me apart from eastern girls, who had all done the *Aeneid* in their fourth year of high school. And that, in turn, may have led to my taking Virgil's *Bucolics* and *Georgics* in college—something that ordinarily only a Latin major (which I was not) would have done. So oddity compounded oddity, as often happens. Indeed, my curious and slightly excessive Latinity at Vassar may have been compensation for the hole in my language credits that Miss Mackay and I had patched over at Annie Wright during our tutorial "hours." In Vassar's Latin Department, headed by stately white-haired Elizabeth Hazelton Haight, author of *Horace and His Art of Enjoyment*, not only did I, an English major, take the *Bucolics* and *Georgics*, Horace's *Odes* and *Epodes*, Horace's *Satires* and *Epistles*, the course titled "Catullus, Tibullus, Propertius, and Ovid," the course titled "Juvenal, Martial, and Pliny," but also a half-year course in advanced Caesar *(De Bello Civile)*, a half-year one-hour course in a late Latin figure called Aulus Gellius, another in Roman comedy, and half-year three-hour courses in Medieval and Renaissance Latin. Some of this (not Aulus Gellius, who was taught by a handsome young widower) was explained by the fact that my field was English Renaissance, with its strong classical tinge; some of it (Catullus and Juvenal) answered to real passions, and some consisted of what are now called ploys. But ploys are seldom idle. The basis must have been the deficiencies, as I felt them, of a Northwestern education, which I sought to correct by additives, as riboflavin is mixed into "enriched" bread. Somewhere in the course of it, I missed Tacitus, which always shocked Edmund Wilson.

Of course the Seminary (like Garfield High School, probably) offered four years of Latin; some of my friends were taking Virgil, though they never used him afterwards, as at Vassar I really could have—my prosody was always weak. One of those bishops, who came west in 1900—the school had been founded by another bishop in 1884, when Washington was still a territory—wanted the Seminary "to be the Wellesley, the Smith, the Vassar of the west." But though Annie Wright, being only a prep school, could scarcely achieve that, it *was* equipped to prepare any girl who wanted it for admission to those colleges. When I took the College Boards, in a university classroom in Seattle, I had had plenty of French (taught by native French-speakers), I had had one year of "hard" science—Physics—three years of math, stopping short of calculus; if I had desired German, there was old Madame Haynes, the Austrian the girls made pie-beds for, to teach it. In English, after the two Vassar-trained Miss Atkinsons, we had Miss Clare Hayward, who gave us English literature from *Beowulf* onward. Under the two Miss Atkinsons, we had learned "Tomorrow and tomorrow," "We have scotch'd the snake not killed it," "Muling and puking in its nurse's arms," "The quality of mercy," besides having Sir Roger de Coverley, Burke, *Silas Marner*, the "Disertation upon Roast Pig"—the standard offerings guaranteed to turn the standard young person against English literature for up to twenty years.

In fact, Miss Hayward did not come to us until we were seniors, at the same time as Miss Marthe Simpson, who was young and half-French and taught Art and made amusing floppy puppets. But junior year we had Mrs. Hiatt, with her eyeglasses on a chain, a wit and the widow of a clergyman; we had had Miss Dorothy Atkinson with *her* eyeglasses on a ribbon and her fondness for Mencken, and throughout there were timid little Miss Helen McKay, and shy, stiff Miss Mackay herself.

On the whole our teachers were greatly superior to our girls, and that was a large part of Miss Preston's dilemma. A Dorothy Atkinson was wasted on a De Vere Utter or a Voynne Setzer or on a chronic case of boredom such as Ellin Watts. The girls could not use what the star teachers had to give. Besides, the star teachers, like Miss Mackay, were almost all hard markers and likely also, when it could not be avoided, to report infractions of the rules. Our school could not maintain an elite status socially while offering anything like a serious education. In the East no doubt it could have; you could point to Saint Tim's, Walnut Hill, and, at that time, Madeira, as well as day schools like Chapin and Brearley in New York. But the real problem facing Miss Preston was the Northwest itself. Washington, Oregon, Montana, Idaho, Alaska constituted the reservoir she had to draw from, with occasional girls appearing from Hawaii and British Columbia. And though it happened that girls went east to be "finished," not only at the Masters and Bennett but even at places like the House of the Pines, the opposite was unthinkable. To induce an eastern girl to come west, the Seminary would have had to turn into a ranch, with cowboys.

Moreover, in our own state of Washington, girls were more likely to come to us not so much from Seattle (which had its day school, St. Nicholas, for the upper crust) as from places with names like Cle Elum and Hoquiam and Chehalis. In Montana it would be Kalispell (Clover Rath) and White Sulphur Springs (the Ford girls), not Butte, which I think had a kind of real society that had evolved from its primitive days as a wild copper-mining town. This human material that came to us for processing was unclassifiable socially; it was, so to speak, too fresh, like meat that has not been hung.

In Seattle (and in Spokane and Tacoma) stratification had developed, a layering considerably aided by the society column of Colonel Blethen's Seattle *Times*, which told who lunched with whom at the Olympic Hotel on Mondays— the day when it counted to be seen there—and this was a service not only to those who had a table every Monday (including an old Sacred Heart girl like Mary Fordyce Blake) but to many who would never have one, such as my friend "Ted" Rosenberg and her sister Till. It was best, evidently, to *be* somebody, with one's name in the paper every Tuesday, but next best was to know who *were* the somebodies. It may seem strange that Jewish intellectuals were interested in the society column (Ted and Till read *Vogue*, too, I guess, besides *Vanity Fair*), but that may have been a healthy sign: *nihil humanum mihi alienum puto*. Eventually I, too, would be "seen lunching" at the Olympic Hotel, though more often than not "with Mrs. Harold Preston and Mrs. M. A. Gottstein," in other words my grandmother and Aunt Rosie.

It may be that the first families of Seattle, so clearly identifiable to themselves, feared to expose their daughters to the contagion of rooming with the daughters of the first families of Wenatchee and Walla Walla—site of the penitentiary—and Chehalis. Why, a parent from there could be *anybody* with the price of the tuition, a Federal judge or state senator but equally well a druggist or feedstore owner. The miscellaneousness of the school's boarders (typified by fanciful or just plain misspelled first names such as "Hermoine," "Rocena," "De Vere," "Voynne," "Betye") had been there from the start, it seems. An account (1884) by the first Bishop of Spokane, whose wife was the first principal, describes a girl who came from Alaska by wagon train, camping out at night and taking almost a month on the way, girls who came from the Hawaiian Islands, girls who went to bed in their clothes, girls who had never been taught to say their prayers. "But most of the girls were nice and well-behaved."

With the day girls it was different. For Tacoma, Annie Wright equaled Seattle's St. Nicholas socially and gave a good education besides; it was the school to go to. Accordingly, our day girls were more glamorous than our boarders. Inevitably there were a few freaks among them, but mostly they were pretty and came from old families—the two Henrys, Elizabeth and Edith, "Baby" Griggs—or had a rich, important father—"El" Perkins', for instance, a real rough diamond who owned the Tacoma newspaper—or were striking and exotic, like Wilhelmina and Marie-Louise Quevli, who looked like South Sea Islands beauties but whose father was a doctor and Danish. There were poetry-reading Elizabeth Hosmer, who was going to Stanford to study premed, and brainy, horsey Dorothy Walker, whose father was an army doctor at Fort Lewis. It was lucky we had the day girls to raise the social tone, even the darling little Catholic LaGasas in the lower school, whose stout mother wearing a vast mink coat took me to eleven o'clock Mass on Sunday—their father was a doctor, too.

That the Tacoma girls appeared to have more interesting

parents than most of the others may have been related to the fact that Tacoma, the fief of the Weyerhauser timber family, was not only a lumber town but a port. Liners left for Japan and China and the Philippines and even for Liverpool and Glasgow, via the Suez Canal. The Seminary, which looked down on an arm of Puget Sound, was close to the railroad tracks (occasionally on our walks we saw hoboes) and to a paper mill smelling of rotten eggs (H_2S, little Miss McKay said) when the wind was wrong. In comparison with Seattle, Tacoma was in decline, and this helped to give it an aristocratic air, as though it were the older city. Fort Lewis probably contributed, too, to the Old World feeling of Tacoma, and the fort, which still had some cavalry, no doubt explained the good riding-horses and delightful trails a short distance from the city. Our girls signed up for riding lessons (an extra) at Captain Proby's riding-academy, but rough Captain Proby fell out of Miss Preston's favor, and instead we went on Friday afternoons and Saturday mornings to the stables of Major Mathews, a gentler English officer who had settled with his short-haired wife in our Northwest. They gave us tea and let us smoke when no chaperon accompanied us. Unlike Captain Proby, Major Mathews did not force us to ride in the ring. He let us explore the woodlands, passing by the shores of a little lake, where violets grew in the spring and where along the bank we sometimes saw iridescent water snakes that scared the horses. Once he dismounted and cut me a branch of flowering dogwood and once he used his hat to hold violets.

He taught us to post—we used an English saddle—and how to keep our mounts to a trot. Breaking from a trot into a canter was against the rules of horsemanship and showed that you were not in control of your animal. The right way was to go from a walk to a canter. You should take care not to let the horse have his head; sensing your inexperience, he could bolt. Sometimes a canter would turn into a gallop, but a riding-horse was not supposed to gallop—that was for cowboys on the plains. If a girl's horse ran away with her, she was to throw the reins over his neck, but Major Mathews could be counted on to head him off if necessary.

One of the horses I rode—a bay—was a single-footer; according to Major Mathews, quite a few of our Northwestern horses were. It was a different gait, more like a rocking-horse. Another, a dappled gray named Bluebell, was a retired race horse, who neither trotted nor cantered but ran. If I recall right, Major Mathews said that was characteristic of a race horse—a long flying stride. I was never a very sure rider, although I loved it with passion, and he was careful of what horses he gave me. The Ford girls, coming from Montana, could be trusted on anything. But one of my horses had a mouth so tender that you could ride him on the snaffle, not using the curb at all.

The Mathewses themselves were mild English people fond of tea and reading. My hours of purest, most intense happiness at the Seminary were concentrated in Saturday-morning spring rides through the woods with another girl and Major Mathews: white-flowering dogwood, violets in thick carpets—purple and white—dark low-branching pines snatching at one's hair ("Hyd Absalon thy gilte tresse clere"), and water snakes, blue, glossy green, and velvet black straight out of "The Ancient Mariner" slithering along the swampy edge of the little lake while the neighing horses reared. I cannot explain why no one was afraid. On the way back to school in the automobile (depending on the chaperon), Major or Mrs. Mathews would let us stop at a take-out place on the highway and have hot barbecue rolls.

There were a number of English influences playing on the Seminary, modifying the social climate, just as the Japanese current brought us mild winters. Not just Miss Hayward and the Mathewses and Miss Mackay. Of the two gardeners, who also tended the furnaces, as I said, one was a Yorkshireman, and the other, even more strangely spoken, a Lancashireman. I do not know whether this was policy on Miss Preston's part, to promote a classy image of the Seminary or whether it merely corresponded to a demographic fact: in 1900, I see in the *Britannica*, the foreign-born population of Tacoma (11,032 out of a total of 37,714) included 1,534 English-Canadians and 1,323 English. The proximity of Vancouver and Victoria, in British Columbia, added a note of Englishness, too, audible in the speech of Puget Sound people, who have been spared the furry California accent (a contamination from the Middle West; my grandmother and great-aunts, born in San Francisco, were too old to have caught it). Our school library took *Punch* and *The Illustrated London News*. Our reading lists for English had no American classics that I remember—no *Moby-Dick* or *Scarlet Letter*—though maybe American literature would not have been found on any private secondary-school list then. Well, yes, there was Poe, but he was not considered to be classwork, and, for some reason, Ambrose Bierce—I remember Miss Hayward's giving us "An Occurrence at Owl Creek Bridge."

Certainly, on my own, I had started reading American poetry: T. S. Eliot, Ezra Pound ("The Ballad of the Goodly Fere"), Edna Millay, Conrad Aiken, E. A. Robinson, even Louis Untermeyer ("Jig to be Danced on the Grave of an Enemy"). But in class, until senior year, it was *The Idylls of the King* all the way. All this was a far cry from the true American taste evinced in my grandfather's library. Of course it contained Dickens and Dumas and the Russians and Bulwer-Lytton, but for my grandfather, apart from these classics, good reading consisted of *Tom Sawyer*, a set of Frank Stockton, Bret Harte (a great favorite), and maybe Booth Tarkington. I doubt that he ever read Galsworthy or Bennett or Wells. To him *The Bridge of San Luis Rey* (1927) was my grandmother's library book.

The "Englishness" of Annie Wright was like a whiff of well-used Yardley's lavender. You would not have found anything like it, I think, in the eastern schools of that time. Yet surely there was no intention on Miss Preston's part to make snobs of us; she was strong on tradition, which she believed was vital to the morale of a school, and possibly to her mind a Yorkshire gardener and *Punch* were part of the school's ivied personality, something for the girls to remember, like the Sunday-night sings in the Great Hall and macaroni-and-cheese (good) for Friday lunch and Wednesdays in Lent.

But the faculty, insofar as it was superior, was surely a wasteful luxury, however badly paid. The average Annie Wright parent was in no position to appreciate a Miss Ethel Mackay with her whistling false teeth. My grandfather, being a lawyer, and my friend Jean Eagleson's father, an orthopedic surgeon, were exceptional—you had to have some education to practice those professions. But the average father, even when he had gone to the U and graduated (thanks to Spanish and business courses) belonged to the great mass of illiterates that knows how to read and write. That was why girls who got bored, like the heavy-lidded Ellin Watts, found a sympathetic ear at home.

Money and culture rarely mix. That was not a peculiarity of the recently settled Pacific Northwest. There is a universal law requiring (truly!) that 99% of the rich be retarded culturally. By and large, Seattle, as I remember it, was not a more uncultivated city than Waterbury, Connecticut (brass), but there was not so much *old* money in Seattle as in a comparable town back east. Old money is fully as moronic as new money but it has inherited an appearance of cultivation. It buys and subscribes to magazines, which it does not read, supports symphony orchestras and art museums, sends its children to good schools, where they will make poor grades. That is all there is to it. As in Toqueville's time, the brains of our country are located in the professional class—doctors, lawyers, teachers. Today that class has grown much bigger, but the increase in numbers has only made its members less distinct from the surrounding business society. In any case, poor Miss Preston. Even with the Episcopal Church behind her, she could not make superior education a marketable commodity in the state of Washington.

Our class shrank, like a wasting body, as it made its way

through the classrooms up to graduation. One by one or in droves they left us: the tall trio from Spokane, Vachel Lindsay's fat older niece, Ruth Williams of The Dalles, Hazel Trethewey, Scheilda Mae Libby, Imogene Brubaker, Bernice Galt. . . . Roughly the best and the worst. And we gained only a roommate for me senior year—red-cheeked Marie Althen of Tacoma, adopted daughter of German-speaking Alsatian parents.

As our class ranks thinned after sophomore year and the glamorous seniors of the Class of '27 graduated, I adapted myself to the thin rewards of reality. I became a success in the school while remaining darkly aware of how little that meant. Hopeless as an athlete (except for swimming and riding, which were neither of them team sports), I won fame as an actress. It turned out that I had a talent for being scary that was greatly relished by the lower school: my deep contralto recitation, with gestures, of "The Fall of the House of Usher" had the little ones shrieking and cowering in their seats in the gymnasium; a week or so later, as an encore, I gave them "A Cask of Amontillado." Soon I was being cast as the star of any play our crazed elocution teacher (let go the next year) decided to put on. I remember best *The Son-Daughter*, an ancient David Belasco hit in which I played the motherless daughter of a "rejecting" Chinese mandarin (Dr. Dong Tong, acted by the impassive Hattie Connor) who had wanted a son. Togged out in a red watered-silk blouse with frogs (rented from a costume house) and black, Chinese-style trousers, I had an old amah for my confidante, and I can still hear my ecstatic final lines as I stood stage center on my dainty maimed feet: "Toy Yah! Toy Yah! He have call me his *son*-daughter!" Without wanting to be too sure of it, I guessed that the play was bad, whereas I knew, without having to be told by a teacher, without even thinking about it, that a Goldoni we did later was good. How? Was it because it was slightly boring in comparison?

I don't remember what we did about my hair in *The Son-Daughter*. In other plays it was powdered with cornstarch to make it gray and tucked behind my ears if I was playing a male part. With my straight dark hair and severe profile, I made a rather convincing man, above all because I could deepen my voice. Normally I preferred to be the heroine, but I did not mind being cast as that great swaggerer Catiline when the Latin Club did Miss Mackay's *Marcus Tullius*. I would not have wished to be Cicero's pretty daughter, Tullia, still less Terentia, his wife. But all that was senior year and yet to come.

Junior year I threw myself into school politics. The big event was the election of a May Queen, in theory the most beautiful senior. In practice, beauty was not really the issue or not always. The whole school voted, except the primary grades and the teachers, and often it became a popularity contest, complicated by crushes and by feuding. It had not been a good idea of Miss Preston's to divide the school into Blues and Greens, as in ancient Byzantium, for purposes of basketball rooting; in our junior year, the factions spilled over into the May Queen voting. The middle grades, it had been discovered, i.e., the sixth, seventh, and eighth, were the "swing vote," so after lunch the girls from the upper school went to the lower classrooms to canvass for one candidate or the other—as in real politics, the choice had been narrowed to two.

That year (1928) in the outside world, adults were divided between Hoover and Al Smith—feelings were hot on both sides. My grandfather became very angry with Harold, who would be casting his first vote: "You mean to tell me that in *a national election* you plan to take the word of a sixteen-year-old girl against mine?" As a political veteran, leader of the liberal Republicans in the state senate, he was outraged all that summer that Harold was lending an ear to my anti-Hoover arguments. In our school May Queen tumult, naturally I had been a leading agitator. Indeed, without me, there would have been no tumult: Katie Urquhart, from Chehalis, would have had a vast majority. Her opponent, Margaret Carpenter, was my creature.

In beauty, they were evenly matched: neither had much

claim. Maggie, who came from Cle Elum, had thick white, slightly pitted skin, dark-red hair, and a placid look. Katie was a thin, strange-looking girl with big flaring nostrils like those of a hungry animal on the scent of prey. We had been friends; it was I who had pushed her for May Queen, drawing converts to what was basically an unlikely cause. I had loved the "qu" in her name, which spoke to me of Highland blood, and I had looked up the Urquhart plaid (squares of dark green and pale green crossed by a bright red line) in the school library and may even have found Thomas Urquhart, translator of Rabelais. Her mother had been a Gamma Phi at the University with my mother and remembered beautiful, sweet Tess Preston. Then something happened, I have no idea what. But I turned on that girl with a vengeance and never forgave whatever it was she said or did. It was my idea to put up Maggie Carpenter against her, and every day as the campaign heated up I was in the middle-school classrooms, haranguing the sixth and seventh grades (the eighth was already won over) on how repellent Katie Urquhart really was—that sallow skin, those yellow eyes, those avid nose-holes, almost scary. I was boldly drawing on the capital of my Poe recitations. And our side won! I had discovered in myself a gift for politics and electioneering and tasted the thrill of power.

The benefits were a friendship with Margaret Carpenter that lasted intermittently through her years at Whitman, in Walla Walla, and mine at Vassar but also, more immediately, a "man" for junior prom that spring: Donnie Fisher, Margaret's cousin, Tacoma's answer to Jimmy Agen in Seattle. Every Seminary girl knew about Donnie Fisher. The surprise was that he was Margaret Carpenter's cousin. With him as my partner, my dance program was full, and she had told him to send me gardenias for my flame-red chiffon dress with tiers of picoted ruffles. Above, on the balcony, sophomores and freshmen and the middle school were allowed, before bedtime, to watch the dancers in the Great Hall below.

If it had not been for those May Queen politics, I would

have been among them. There was nobody I could ask. Mark Sullivan had got married, and because of my grandparents' absurd attitude I never met any other boys. I would have been ashamed to ask my uncle. No; if it had not been for this miracle constituted by Donnie Fisher, I could see myself on the balcony looking over the oak railing with the eighth grade. I would have been almost like that poor Naomi Elmendorf last year, whose "man" never came and who sat her senior prom out in a matronly green silk dress with three-quarters sleeves waiting for at least a message, which never came either. A teacher sat with her on the balcony, holding her big hand. Why couldn't she have been allowed to wait in her room? Anyway, this year *I* was spared. I could have fallen in love with Margaret's charming cousin if common sense had not told me that he would remain impervious, however alluring I tried to be. Since I did not get my hopes up, it did not hurt too much when I never saw him again.

Junior year, I suppose, marked the furthest point in my absorption by the Seminary. I was not exactly happy; after Ruth Williams left, I had no real friends. But I had learned how to exercise power over my circumstances, which was like mastering the over-arm carry in lifesaving. I could hardly have been accused of having "school spirit," yet a note from that time kept for all these years by our class Maid of Honor to the victorious May Queen shows me cheering fiercely for the juniors in a basketball game against the seniors, in which Hattie Connor, no less, had refereed, along with the addressee of my note:

I don't want you to think that I meant anything of what I said about you—didn't. But just the same Molstad had 7 [fouls] and Stimpson 3 personal and 1 tech. What does Hattie Connor know about basketball to suit her for the job of keeping score? My God, on Field Day the juniors are going to have something to say about the referees. No crushes! There were four Molstad crushes keeping score or time. Oh, I'm mad.

Better than basketball I remember our Saturday shopping trips, with a chaperon, to downtown Tacoma. We had our own bank accounts, to teach us to handle money, which we mostly spent on Christmas Night perfume and Guerlain bath powder. Then we would have tea at the Old Tacoma Hotel, which had white-haired black waiters, like a Pullman dining-car, and wonderful thin sandwiches. Or we would go to the Puss 'N Boots (or was it the Pig 'N' Whistle?) for "sweetheart" sundaes. We saw John Barrymore and Dolores Costello and the first talking movie—Al Jolson in *The Jazz Singer*, which I hated.

But the best was when the Stratford-on-Avon players came to Tacoma, and Miss Preston let us go; she may even have let us go on two different nights. Despite the name, they were not a Shakespearean troupe; they were specialists in Shavian comedy and they were not English but Canadian. And Tacoma—not Seattle!—was the town they chose to visit. This was my first real theatre, nothing to do with the Henry Duffy stock company in Seattle, who were specialists in *The Cat and the Canary* and *The Bat*. I remember the philosophical old hotel waiter, played by Balliol Holoway, in *You Never Can Tell*, and a dazzled overall impression of perfect finish. We had had the brilliant idea of inviting Miss Preston herself to be our chaperon; she wore a low-necked dress, and the evening was a riot of pleasure. Though I had never seen highly skilled actors perform before, I had a sense of recognition—the same as with Latin—as though I had met the theatre in a previous incarnation. Miss Preston's next venture into the theatre arts was a projection she arranged in the gymnasium of a silent Swedish film based on *Jerusalem* by Selma Lagerlöf—first woman to win a Nobel Prize, in 1909. The sub-titles were in Swedish and the action seemed to take place in the Holy Land, inhabited, peculiarly, by gaunt, mad-looking Swedish farmers—was it a story of an emigration or was it some modern religious parable? Nobody could guess.

With the departure of Miss Dorothy Atkinson at the end of sophomore year, I lost my audience for the stories about

133

prostitutes and housewives with "eyes like dirty dishwater" that she had encouraged me (once) to send to H. L. Mencken. Now I wanted to be an actress, rather than a writer, whereas my grandfather thought I had the makings of a lawyer. At the same time my screen idols changed: Pola Negri and Barbara Lamarr gave way to straight-browed Eleanor Boardman; Ricardo Cortez was replaced by Ronald Colman. And when in English class we read *The Idylls of the King* with Miss Atkinson's sister, Miss Marjorie Atkinson, I encountered in literature and immediately recognized my fatal type of man. King Arthur's nephew, Sir Gawain. Not the mighty giant-fighter of *Syr Gawayne and the Grene Knighte* (a fourteenth-century alliterative poem unknown to me even by name), but a Tennysonian figure, debonair and disabused.

He won my heart once and for all during his visit to the countrified castle of Astolat seeking an unknown knight—in reality Sir Lancelot—who had won a tourney at Camelot and then disappeared, covered with wounds. Unaware of his identity, the Lily Maid and her father are nursing him. Gawain is quite taken with the Lily Maid—"well, if I bide, lo! this wild flower for me"—till he shrewdly senses the lie of the land: she loves the wounded knight. So he entrusts her with the diamond he is carrying to confer on the winner of the tourney and dryly tells her good-bye.

For if you love, it will be sweet to give it;
And if he love, it will be sweet to have it from your own
    hand;
And whether he love or not,
A diamond is a diamond. Fare you well. . . .

Being Sir Gawain, he cannot forgo a final trenchant hint: "Yet, if he love, and his love hold,/ We two may meet at court hereafter . . ." Having guessed that it is Lancelot, he is wondering of course what Queen Guinevere will say. Saying nothing further himself, he "Leapt on his horse, and carolling as he went/ A true love ballad, lightly rode away."

Cool and dry was Sir Gawain. The faithful Sir Bedivere pronounced a fitting elegy on him after he was slain in the great battle of the west against his brother Modred, the horridest name in literature: "Light was Gawain in life and light in death was Gawain."

It strikes me now, nearly sixty years too late, that Sir Gawain, whose name was seldom paired with a lady's, was the perfect type of homosexual. But the thought could not have crossed my mind then. I liked everything about Sir Gawain, even the pronunciation of his name (not "Gawáyne," but "Gów-wain," the first syllable accented and rhyming with "cow"); he reminded me of Ronald Colman and vice versa. To prefer Gawain, an accessory lord, to the great and somber Lancelot ("His honour rooted in dishonour stood,/ And faith unfaithful kept him falsely true") may seem like preferring Horatio to Hamlet. Yet it was not a ploy. Far from seeking to be different through my foible, I kept trying to get others to share my craze for him, just as I had tried to get my grandmother to like Ricardo Cortez, while she remained true to Adolphe Menjou. I always sought to proselytize.

What I thrilled to in Sir Gawain must have been his sophistication. In that he resembled "the wise youth Adrian" of *Richard Feverel*, another who enchanted me with his disabused ways—it has taken me most of a lifetime (see earlier) to perceive that Meredith intended him, obviously, as a caricature. Later, more nobly, there came Berowne and, best of all, Mercutio (" 'tis not so deep as a well, nor so wide as a church door, but 'tis enough, 'twill serve"—*dies*). I ask myself now whether these blasé young men (leaving out Mercutio) were not second-raters. Could I have fallen in love, in real life, with Sir Gawain in a red two-seater? Certainly he could have been my seducer with no trouble whatever. I wonder about love, though. Does one fall in love with an appalling second-rater? A lot of literature suggests that one does, but I do not believe it. I agree with Plato that one loves the good.

But let me leave the discussion of love for a later chapter.

Sticking to the spring of 1928, when I was still fifteen, I wonder whether Sir Gawain was less a light of love, really, than an alter ego—a projection of some nutty image of myself. Myself as a sophisticate and highly skilled renouncer (Gawain, seeing it is hopeless, *renounces* the conquest of Elaine). I was infatuated with the person I wanted to be like.

But why a man, then? Among my own sex, Elaine the Lily Maid was not to be thought of—too pastel. But even in *King Arthur*, there was a fair choice of sinners: Guinevere, Iseult. . . . Yet their lack of freedom, their passiveness, indeed their married state discouraged identification. The exceptions to that seemed to be either witches (Vivien, Queen Morgana le Fay) or women *nobody* would want to resemble, such as (let's forget the dames and damsels of King Arthur's court) Messalina, on the one hand, Carrie Nation, on the other.

Well, there was the Maid of Orleans, but I did not want to dress in men's clothes or have visions. For me, the attractive person in that story was Dunois, Bastard of Orleans, her brave, dissipated captain—again my fatal type. I thought I might have been Eleanor of Aquitaine, despite her slightly masculine personality. There was the rub. Though I identified myself in my reading with a certain kind of man (tending toward the rotter), I never in real life wanted to be a man or even a mannish woman.

That was the moment when I was nearing my zenith at the Seminary. I had power; I rode Bluebell and the bay; Major and Mrs. Mathews liked me; my application had gone to Vassar with my grandfather's check; sitting beside Miss Mackay, alone in her classroom, I was reading about the Veneti and their long boat-hooks; I had made Miss Marjorie Atkinson cry in class with my well-aimed satirical shafts; I had been invited by the Ford sisters to visit them in Montana; I had found "Sister Helen" by Rossetti in Manly's *English Poetry* and recited it, changing voices the way the choir did between King Wenceslas and the page in the Christmas carol. Then, all of a sudden, the whole house of bright face-cards tumbled; I was suspended from school and could count myself lucky not to be expelled.

One day with another girl I went A.W.O.L. For no reason; just to have something to do. Probably it was in the doldrums after Easter. I remember the two of us in a streetcar; perhaps we were aiming at Point Defiance, which had an amusement park, or at any rate rides—closed, though, for the winter. Having discovered that, we might have taken the streetcar back to school and got some light penalty for the escapade. But unaccountably we didn't. Maybe my partner in crime was running away from a promised interview with Miss Preston. Or simply we were dissatisfied with the tame result, so far, of our deed. In the streetcar, I remember, we passed a file of Annie Wright girls hatted and gloved on a walk with a teacher, and the sight somehow encouraged us, as we laughed and jeered, to maintain our distance from them. I was afraid that they might see us, whereas Molly, my associate, seemed to want them to.

She was a strange girl, that Molly Haynes, one of the several Hayneses in the school, all very blonde, almost albino, with long, double-jointed legs, beak noses, big protruding teeth, receding chins, dark eyes, and dead-white skins, like circus clowns'. Their father, who had the funny first name of Ancil and was said to be *very* self-made, had determined to put his girls in the Seminary right in the middle of a term. Molly was the oldest and had been assigned to the sophomore class; she was the only one I got to know. All the Hayneses were sloppy; there were spots on their uniforms, and the school's black cotton stockings hung in wrinkles on their long legs. A little one, with the funny name of Ancil also, had a long, skinny, tow-colored braid, like a piece of fraying white rope. Because of the dark eyes, the suspicion arose that the whole sisterhood had dipped their bony heads in peroxide.

Viewed on her own, apart from those weird sisters, Molly

was a droll, entertaining girl. She was rather intelligent, I discovered, though you might not guess it from her grammar and pronunciation; I don't think any of the Hayneses had ever read a book outside of school. But Molly visibly thought (tapping her teeth was the sign) and had her own wry philosophy of life.

Before we ran away, there had been a strange episode in her room one Sunday afternoon during "quiet hour." Visits back and forth between mid-day dinner and supper were allowed on Sunday, when many of the girls were out with their parents; you had to sign up ahead of time and not more than three to a room. Anyway, that Sunday Molly decided to show me her clothes. She had a whole closetful of them—very extreme, in design and cut—which she could not wear at the Seminary: at dinner we put on dress uniforms made of crepe-de-chine in three different solid colors—blue, deep pink, and green—with white collars and cuffs—and in the daytime we had our middies, skirts, and ties. Maybe Molly had been burning to model her own clothes to someone. I sat on her bed, not much interested, while she paraded them. But I could not help noticing that her underwear, slightly dirty, showed in the low-necked ones and the big raw bones of her upper chest stood out. Unable to praise, no doubt I grew uncomfortable. She must have been aware of it, for suddenly her mood changed. She turned on the dress she had been modeling—a satiny affair in zebra stripes—ripped it from her back and proceeded to attack it with a pair of pinking shears. She went at it, bare-shouldered, in her bra and slip, wildly laughing till her wastebasket was full to overflowing with ribbons of shiny black-and-white material, notched by the teeth of the pinking shears. Gasping and heaving, she explained that she had done it to satisfy me, because I had not liked the dress.

I do not know whether it was this episode—a creeping fear, that is, of being punished for it, she as perpetrator and I as accomplice—that inspired us to run away. I do not even remember how soon the one followed on the other. And after all what rule had she broken? The dress was her own property, so that she ought to have been free to hack it to pieces. And yet it had been a sort of murder; I felt it myself then, silently watching her. Probably it was the first sign of an attack of hysteria that would come to a pitch, for her at least, in our leaving.

For years I forgot about Molly and the dress. Then, fifty years later, the cut-up dress and the pinking shears surfaced, as if regurgitated, in a novel I was writing. In *Cannibals and Missionaries* one young woman remembers of another that in school on a Sunday afternoon she had cut up her clothes "in a fit of misery and boredom while her roommate looked on." In the novel the school is Putney.

I think we finally took the interurban to Seattle. By the time we reached there, we had been missing all day. I doubt that Molly was still with me when I arrived at 712 35th Avenue. Maybe we had telephoned from downtown. My grandfather was home from the office, and I learned that our cases had already been separated administratively. Harold Preston and Adelaide B. Preston (who considered themselves cousins, descended from a pair of brothers who had emigrated in the eighteenth century, one to western Massachusetts and the other, my grandfather's forebear, to what is now Vermont) had been conferring by long distance and agreed that Molly, when found, was to be expelled forthwith. But I was suspended "till I could get a better attitude."

To the family, I managed a pert little laugh and "How am I supposed to do *that*?" but privately I estimated that it would take me three days, sleeping late in my own room and eating Lavinia's cooking. More than that would be boring. On the fourth morning I could announce a change of attitude and be driven back to school. I reflected on what fools older people were. But it occurs to me as I write this that Miss Preston, who probably knew girls better than I knew adults, had counted on my absence to last just that length of time, not so long as to affect my schoolwork and not so short as to let my classmates feel that I was getting off too easy. "Well, Cousin Mary!" she said approvingly, on the prodigal's return, taking me onto her slippery lap.

At home, during my "suspension," I was not scolded or lectured. If my grandmother did not take me with her on her daily prowls through Frederick's and Magnin's, it must have been to avoid questions as to why I wasn't in school. She was ashamed for me, I guess, while I was feeling—or acting—boastful. It must have been aggravating, as people said then, for her to hear me repeat that sentence about my attitude and follow it with that short, sarcastic laugh. But I did show one sign of repentance or at least of a sense of the fitting: I did not ask to go to the movies.

In the long run my exile and rapid restoration did teach me a lesson, if not the one intended. I learned the utility of high marks. Wild horses, needless to say, could not have got Miss Preston to expel a junior with a straight A and A+ record (I had not yet hit Advanced Algebra and the binominal theorem) who was going to go east to college carrying Annie Wright's name with her. I had not realized that when I "ran away." I had thought that except for a miracle I would be kicked out. Now I knew, and knew, too, that I was getting a first real taste of unfairness. I was glad not to be expelled and sorry as well—nobody really likes to be the beneficiary of a flagrant injustice. Miss Preston doubtless argued that I had been led astray by the Haynes girl, and it was true that the idea had been hers. But it was unlike me, as Miss Preston herself pointed out, shifting my weight on her lap, to have followed Molly's lead. I don't know the reason. Simple boredom maybe. Maybe, weary of my successes, I really wanted to get kicked out of school for a change and so was disappointed when instead they killed the fatted calf—one wonders about the Prodigal Son's true feelings. Still, even if I was tired of school and myself in it, could I actually have wished to try being a wild, crazy person like Molly? Most likely, I was just being companionable, which was a good side of my character.

I never saw Molly again. I never knew whether her remaining clothes were packed up by the house-mother and sent to her or whether her family came and got them. Before long, all the Hayneses were quietly withdrawn, and no further word was heard of them. The "pool" from which the Seminary drew was so large geographically and socially that it was common for girls who left (even a Pauline Paulsen!) to drop totally out of sight.

At any rate Molly's fate was sad to think about. It was evident that she was a white blackbird at the Seminary and so, one way or another, would have managed to get herself expelled; in school, character *is* fate. Still, I did not like what the episode showed me. Although a rebel, I did not care to picture authority as weak, putty in my hands, and so on. For self-realization, a rebel demands a strong authority, a worthy opponent, God to his Lucifer. I preferred to see Miss Preston as fair and just rather than as a principal who could be bought with good marks. I would find the same problem with Dean Thompson at Vassar.

At the time we ran away, Molly and I may in fact have been the least of Miss Preston's worries. Every girl in the boarding department was uncomfortably aware of Miss Preston's sister, a person totally unlike Miss Preston who had appeared in our midst in the fall of junior year. Her name was Mrs. Blanche P. Johnson, and she was a widow, grass or sod. The school function assigned to her was vague, mainly connected with the infirmary, but at times she was given the duties of house-mother.

Except for a large bust, Mrs. Johnson was a most unmotherly person—a tall fat painted overdressed woman decked out in trailing chiffons, large swaying bobbles of "costume" earrings, bracelets, rings, beads, small handkerchiefs drenched in Toujours Moi perfume. Everything about her joggled and jiggled, even the pouches under her eyes when she laughed.

She was the opposite of Miss Preston in her structure and in almost every other respect. Mrs. Johnson was highly talkative, too confidential with some of the seniors; Miss Preston was terse. Mrs. Johnson was tall; Miss Preston was short, and the fat she carried, unlike her sister's, was solid and corseted. In Miss Preston's broad, compact face, the long nose and level dark eyes rather suggested a piglet; Mrs. Johnson was a "cow." Despite her garrulous tongue Mrs. Johnson gave us the impression of being loaded with secrets, like a chocolate box with a false bottom, while, behind the hedge of her taciturnity, Miss Preston, I think, consistently tried to be open and aboveboard with girls and parents. Her tastes and prejudices were all known to us; indeed, they were buckled onto her personality like old-fashioned jet ornaments. Her disapproval of fountain pens, her favorite hymn (117 in the hymnal, Bunyan's "He who would valiant be," posted on most Fridays), her favorite carol ("A Virgin Unspotted," distributed in hectograph, not in the hymnal), her favorite anthem ("For he cometh, for he cometh to judge the earth"). We knew that she was partial to whole-wheat-bread sandwiches and to a macaroni-and-cheese casserole and that the dessert she thought girls liked best was chocolate ice-cream with marshmallow sauce.

She had a deep, vibrant voice, and to hear her intone the General Confession night after night ("We have left undone . . . And we have done . . . And there is no health in us") struck responsive chords throughout the still chapel. She was an emotional woman, and her sentimental history was an open book to more than a decade of Annie Wright girls: she had obviously been in love with Bishop Keator, whose large portrait, seated, in white lawn and episcopal purple— rochet and chimer—hung over the big stone fireplace in the Great Hall. If she wept on Fridays when we sang 117, it was because Bunyan's hymn had been his favorite, too.

From his demi-profile portrait, he must have been a handsome man, dark-eyed, ruddy, dynamic, graying, with a Celtic look about him. He and Miss Preston had created the Seminary almost *ab ovo*. He had found her, teaching, somewhere in the East and brought her out west to be principal when the school was still in the gaunt old firetrap building, full of rats, that went back to Bishop Paddock. He and Miss Preston had dreamed the new school together, choosing the site (in Old Tacoma, high over Commencement Bay), studying blueprints, finding the architect, the landscape gardener, picking the hedge material and the creeper to festoon the Tudor-style buildings, getting advice on swimming pools. In those days Tacoma was diocesan headquarters, and the magnetic bishop had his office in the old school, down the hall from Miss Preston's obviously, all through the time of building. When the new school finally opened, in 1924, they had been together eleven years.

In my time, his widow, a tall sweet-voiced, gray-eyed woman, taught us Sacred Study and led the choir. Whenever in the course of a homily Miss Preston at the lectern mentioned Bishop Keator's name, out would come her handkerchief to mop up the tears running down her broad cheeks. Sometimes, as she continued to sniff, we girls stole looks at Mrs. Keator dry-eyed in her place in the choir; there was never a sign of emotion on her beautiful calm face. It was hard to know what to make of this. Did Miss Preston cry because he had been her lover or because he hadn't? Either way, she certainly gave the appearance of grieving for him as if she were his widow and the Seminary their child.

Like so many things at the Seminary, Miss Preston's tears were *unfailing* at the mention of the bishop's name. In our class we had a girl by the name of Frances Ankeny who was exactly the same; only what set *her* waterworks going was the song "Juanita." As it happened, that was one of Miss Preston's favorites for the Sunday-evening sings we often had after high tea in the Great Hall. But our principal had not noticed that whenever the piano tuned up with "Far o'er the fountain," Frances would start crying. Like other mischievous and observant girls, I *had*, and if, on some particular evening, it looked as if Miss Preston were going to forget "Juanita" or had decided that "Santa Lucia" sufficed, I would ask if we couldn't have it, please. I believe it was pure, disinterested cruelty that prompted me—a vivisectionist inclination such as causes boys to tear the wings off flies. The fact that this girl's grandfather, Levi P. Ankeny of Walla Walla, had defeated my grandfather early in the century in a race for the U.S. Senate would not have played any part.

"Gladly the cross I bear"—Mrs. Johnson was Miss Preston's. What caused her to bear it gladly, or at least to dourly embrace it, we had no way of knowing. It appeared as if Mrs. J. had fallen on evil days—all her jewelry was costume—while a number of things about her suggested that she had once been a nurse. Her large, soft, somewhat pendulous body looked at home in the white nurse's uniform she wore when for a few weeks she actually took over the infirmary. She was conversant with a great many diseases and their remedies. And, at least in our part of the world, the nursing profession was not made up of Florence Nightingales—at fifteen, thanks to Harold and his friends, I was well aware of the reputation nurses had. But if Mrs. Johnson was down on her luck and Miss Preston was "tiding her over," the motive remained obscure. Given Miss Preston's upright and open character, it would hardly have been blackmail. The two ate together at the small round table where Miss Preston had once throned it alone, but our poor principal spoke charily. They seemed to have no history in common beyond a surname that lingered as a vestigial trace in the "P." of "Mrs. Blanche P. Johnston," so listed—note the "t" suddenly materializing—in the school catalogue.

Of course it was wrong to infer that she had been a loose woman. We had never even seen her smoke a cigarette or smelled liquor on her breath. The most we could be sure of was that her hair was tinted; you could tell by the gray at the roots. But just watching the pair of them in the diningroom made us feel that the difference between them was more striking than it should have been. It told against her. The verdict on which all could agree was that Mrs. "Johnston" was common. Among a little circle of Annie Wright girls of that time a snobby game was played to decide who was common and who was vulgar. Somebody (I suspect myself) thought you could make it more interesting by decreeing that vulgar (e.g., Al Smith) was better than common (e.g., Mrs. William Randolph Hearst). Vulgar was frankly plebeian, and common was cheap middle class. So if we had pronounced Mrs. J. vulgar, she would have scored higher in our books.

I thought Mrs. Blanche "Johnston" was awful, starting with her name. But the subject did not much interest me. If asked, I might have said that it was common to discuss her so often. Obviously Miss Preston had brought her to the school from a sense of duty, and we were making it harder for her by our attitude. Our watchful eyes were fixed on them in the dining-room, especially when Miss Preston was entertaining some diocesan dignitary. In the infirmary, we noted Mrs. Johnson's white nurse's shoes. It went without saying that parents coming to visit the school at Founder's Day or Field Day would make a point of looking her over, remarking the tinted hair and matching gold-rimmed glasses, the jiggling earrings and the cleft too visible in her flouncy chiffon neckline. And on her side, naturally, Mrs. J. would talk an arm off them. Not that our parents, by and large, were in a position to judge. Many of them had huge beams in their own eyes, even in the matter of dress. But all the more reason, then, for our principal's sister to be above reproach. A judicious parent like my grandfather, a true admirer of Miss Preston as woman and educator, might well have advised her to "space" her sister's visits to the school.

To have opened the subject with a teacher was unthinkable unless we wanted to get a reprimand. Most of us, seeing Miss Preston's tight lips and set jaw as she sat facing her sister at table, expected that somehow she would manage so that Mrs. J. would not return in the fall. Like the Haynes clan, like Vachel Lindsay's other niece, and, alas, like Hattie Connor, she would be leaving us, and nobody would be discussing her any more. So convinced was I of this thesis that I ventured to name her that summer to Miss Mackay while we did Caesar in Seattle. But Miss Mackay denied any knowledge of Mrs. Johnson's plans and redirected my attention to our text. And sure enough, when school reopened in September, and the entry hall was full of new girls, returning girls, parents, the first sight that met our eyes was Mrs. Johnson herself on the staircase, effusive, with bells on, a reception committee in one person offering her rouged cheek to be kissed. This fall, she told us with a broad wink, we seniors would be coming to her to be excused from athletics. In other words, when we had the curse. By good luck the allusion passed over the head of my grandfather, who probably had forgotten that girls had periods. With a handshake for Miss Preston and a nod to my friend Jean Eagleson, my grandmother gave me her own rouged cheek; we said good-bye.

6

Seattle is often compared to San Francisco. It is spread out on hills (First Hill, Capitol Hill, Second Hill, Queen Anne Hill, all told the Roman seven, though some have been leveled) and ringed almost entirely by water (Elliott Bay, Lake Union, Green Lake, Lake Washington, the canal). It has cable cars, Orientals, a skid row, and a Bohemia. The University district, across the canal from the city proper, matches Berkeley, across the Bay Bridge. Both cities grew rich on a gold rush (my grandmother's father, described as a "broker," was a forty-niner in San Francisco); the Klondike came in 1897, when my grandmother and her sisters were already matrons in Seattle.

Both were ports trading with Japan, China, the Philippines, Hawaii; both harbored a White Russian population, mainly from Harbin in Siberia. Each had had a famous fire. The climates are similar, mild, without a real winter but with plenty of rain—good for the complexion. As a natural wonder San Francisco has the Golden Gate. Seattle has Mount Rainier. Both have good things to eat, in restaurants and on home tables. Seattle's are Dungeness crabs and little Olympia oysters and Columbia River salmon; San Francisco's are sourdough bread and abalone. Both are "wide open" towns—ships in the harbor, sailors in the streets; in my time Seattle had loggers and trappers, too. Both had smart shops, jewelers, furriers, well-dressed women. My grandmother, well off but not rich, owned six fur coats: a mink, a squirrel, a broadtail, a caracul, a moleskin, a Persian lamb, besides a skunk jacket and a suit with copious monkey trim.

Compared to San Francisco, Seattle was hardly cosmopolitan. Yet we had our own new smart hotel, the Olympic, with a palm court and violins playing at tea-time; we had theatres besides the Henry Duffy stock company—at the Moore, in 1907, Laurette Taylor had got her start, playing regular leads. We had the Ladies' Musical Club (with Aunt Rosie as its dynamo), the Seattle Symphony, and, soon to come, "Symphonies under the Stars" in the University stadium (copying the Lewisohn in New York), with Michel Piastro, concertmaster of the New York Philharmonic, conducting. My grandmother, who played the piano but liked her comfort, objected to the cold nights and stone seats. I went with a new friend named Evelyn Younggren (Swedish father, Italian mother, fair silky hair, dark-brown eyes, cloak of soft gray wool buttoning up to the small chin, whose poetic looks I never forgot and borrowed for the heroine of a novel). Under the brilliantly lit skies, I first heard the words "Scarlatti," "saraband," "Couperin," and classical music became romantic to my tone-deaf ear. It was a change from "Valencia," played over and over on the family phonograph, even though I did not follow a single sound the orchestra made, apart from an occasional resemblance to the Gregorian chant I remembered from church. For that rea-

son, surely, I liked early music better than the three B's—
"You're in modality, not in tonality," a musician friend told
me later, at Vassar.

Our city also had the Cornish School, run by old Miss
Nellie Cornish, where Mark Tobey taught painting and
Maurice Browne and his wife, Ellen Van Volkenburgh, pi-
oneers of "serious" drama, directed the theatre. Like San
Francisco, we had a Chinese Opera. We had the Pike Street
Market, with stalls of Japanese truck-gardeners and bright
colored stands of fish from river, lake, and sea, and open-
air shops of Far Eastern merchandise—crystals, kimonos,
incense-burners, fans. And we had more Jews (a "cosmopolitan element," *vide* Hitler and Stalin) than you would find
in South Bend, Indiana. Yet our only poet, as far as I knew,
was a child prodigy named Audrey Wurdeman, the daughter (I think) of an army colonel; this girl, no older than I,
was *published*, with her picture (not bad-looking) in the paper.

In my mind, Seattle's Bohemia was identified geographically with Queen Anne Hill, the highest part of the city,
formerly a "good" neighborhood with large old frame houses
painted in dark colors and looming up from overgrown yards.
It looked down on Elliott Bay. My grandparents' pale-gray
house was in Madrona, between Cherry and Columbia,
looking out across the Lake toward Fuji-like Mount Rainier.
In front we still had a carriage block engraved "1893," where
the horses used to be drawn up to the curb. On the street
side, to the left of the front door a narrow porch wound
around toward the rear, and on the right there was a swell-
ing bay window two stories high containing on the ground
floor an étagère full of Tiffany glass. In back there were a
wide porch and two grass terraces going past the rose beds
and corn and peas and asparagus and artichokes down to
where the red currants grew. Despite my tenure in this paradise, where ice-cream was churned every Sunday morning
on the kitchen porch, where my grandmother's pearl-gray
electric was charged every night in the stately garage (until
she got the Chrysler), where you could watch the crew races

on the lake from the third-floor sleeping-porch outside the maid's bathroom, restlessness had set me to exploring, by foot, streetcar, and cable car all the far-flung districts of Seattle, from Alki Point to Laurelhurst to Seward Park. And I longed to "come from" Queen Anne Hill.

Not Mount Baker, where my grandfather's partner Mr. Thorgrimson had a new house and a lot of tulips, not Broadmoor, a development centered on a new golf club attractive to successful automobile dealers among the "young marrieds," not The Highlands (Jimmy Agen) next to the Seattle Golf Club, not even that green point of land near the Tennis Club—the old Alexander place, they called it— where, beside a tall poplar, a weeping willow bent over the Lake. No; Queen Anne Hill. A few "early settler" girls from the Sacred Heart (was one of them Eugenia McClellan?) had their houses there, I remembered, but I did not know where. On a dismal afternoon, procuring a transfer, I would take the long streetcar ride up the steep grade just to look at the secretive, half-run-down neighborhood, which had scarcely a soul on the sidewalks; you could not see in the windows, boarded up or with drawn shades or set back behind rambling porches, vines, once-ornamental shrubbery. They said that it was up here that the White Russians lived, but I am not sure it was true.

It was through Ted Rosenberg, herself very much a plains-dweller, that I penetrated this terrain. She had managed to get herself introduced to a person who lived there, the fabled Czerna Wilson, known to all Seattle by rumor, Ted assured me. She was married to Carl Wilson, a classmate at the University of my uncle Frank and owner of the Archway Bookstore, a big dusty downtown place that I turned up my nose at but that had belonged to his father and was probably the oldest in town. Ted thought that Carl might be a fraternity brother of Frank's. Frank would certainly have heard of Czerna and so would my aunt Rosie, as an intellectual. She was not sure about my grandmother, since Czerna was hard to meet unless she had a reason for wanting to know the person. You would never see her, it seemed, in a place like Frederick's tea-room; she never went out—people were brought to her, just like in a European capital. In fact, Czerna was Czech, or believed to be. But no one really knew how or when she had come to Seattle or where little Carl Wilson had found her. There was a feeling that she had had a profession, such as dancer, before. As a young officer, Carl (unlike my uncle Frank, who never got out of training-camp) might have made it overseas and found her at the end of the war, when the Austrian Empire was falling to pieces—she might have danced or sung in a night club.

By the time I met her, I already knew a good deal about her, thanks to Ted, who was excited by her. According to Ted, she did nothing but read advanced books and lie on the floor of her living-room when "receiving," which was morning, noon, and night. It was the equivalent, for Seattle, of a salon—the first time, I think, that I had heard that notion aired; we would not have got that far yet in French. For some reason, even before meeting Czerna, I was slightly curious about her husband. Ted said that he stayed away from home generally when she received, implying, I supposed, disapproval of something. Still, as a bookstore owner, he must have had one foot in Bohemia, the other being in textbooks.

Let me describe how she appeared to a sixteen-year-old girl. I wrote a description of her, I remember, for my English class that fall. She had thick, almost negroid lips, ashy skin, green eyes, and bronze-colored hair that she wore in a heavy pigtail going down her back to her hips. She was not beautiful but she looked erotic and dangerous. It was her slow, lazy movements, matching a slow, lazy voice, which, I now realize, had no Central Europe in its accent. Could she have been an octoroon, I wonder, and "Czerna" an assumed name, drawn, say, from Czerny piano exercises, which every beginner knows about?

Lying on her cushions on her floor, with her bronze pigtail beside her or under her strong, straight spine, she was not fat but she was solid; her waist was thick, like her lips, like her braid. From my present perspective, I cannot guess her age, but probably she was "old"—thirty, if she was contemporary with my uncle. The marriage with Carl was not new, although they had no children.

The first time Ted took me to see her, it was in the morning, the summer after junior year at Annie Wright. I never learned what qualifications Ted had offered on my behalf—possibly my "story," orphanhood, my beautiful mother, my grandmother, and the rest. It was ten or eleven o'clock, but Czerna was still in bed, a low, wide, couch-like affair, in a big living-room like a studio, rather bare but containing scatter rugs, throws, and books. Volumes on thick paper of Pierre Loüys—*The Songs of Bilitis* and doubtless *Aphrodite*—with appropriate nude lithographs were lying about. I failed to realize how daring that was, confusing the turn-of-the-century male Sapphic with the author of *Pêcheur d'Islande* (Pierre Loti) whom we had just been having in French at the Seminary.

Next to Czerna in the bed was a pale, sharp-nosed, blue-eyed Jewish girl, thin and quite a lot younger and named, as I remember, Florence. After a little while, this Florence, a University student, apparently, who had a rather acid personality, got up without a word and went into a smaller room. If I recall right, she had nothing on and was flat-chested. As she dressed in the smaller room (sweater and skirt?), she kept throwing ironical remarks into our conversation. I had the impression that she disliked me, but maybe it was Ted. Perhaps she merely disliked our intrusion. Czerna, on the contrary, who now rose and put on a bathrobe, seemed amused by being "caught" with Florence or by having Florence "caught" with her; she was the indolent, experienced woman, and Florence was the thin-bodied boy, with eyes like ice.

Without Ted's actually telling me, I had understood with promptitude that these women were lesbians. We had a case like that in the class below ours in school. At sixteen or nearly, unlike Ted, who was thrilled, I think, by the evidence we saw, I retained my cool. I was not interested in being a lesbian myself, having been groped more than once by hairy girls who had had me to stay the night. My heart was set on men and boys. Sex and love and social conquest were inseparably wedded in my mind with men, even though the male organs were far from beauteous in my eyes. But I was attracted to Czerna aesthetically, as a superb foreign object, as a possibility of what one might become, with resolution.

She was the most sophisticated person I had yet been exposed to. Yet there was no sign of pose or forcing. My memory of her is made up of a few strong, central images, without much detail to fill them out. I see curls of smoke lazily exhaled by her broad nostrils, but I cannot remember what cigarettes she smoked, whether she used a holder, or whether in fact they were small cigars she puffed at, like Amy Lowell. In school that spring, after lights out, sitting on my window sill, I had been trying to teach myself to inhale and would get so dizzy in the process that I feared I would fall out. At the same time I was trying to settle on "my" brand of cigarette. When I eventually hit, that fall, on Marlboros, the ivory-tipped kind, was I copying Czerna? Looking back, I would say that she was more a Melanchrino type. I was forming my persona with such little touches, like the Greek "e"s and tall, scroll-like capital "M"s of my handwriting, which I still have. But what personalizing touches, if any, I took from Czerna I now forget. It was her insouciance, above all, that I would have wanted to imitate. I certainly did not want to have a man like little Carl Wilson for my husband; it was too high a price to pay for a free hand.

I do not know how many times I went with Ted to Czerna Wilson's house on Queen Anne Hill. Enough to have seen her in several changes of costume. There was a long close-fitting garment of the kind later called a hostess-gown, maybe several of these, and then I remember at least once finding her dressed to go out—in a soft beige suit with a flaring back that resembled a lady's riding-habit; her braid was done up in a chignon under a small hat, and there was a frilled blouse. The conversation was always about books and art: Aubrey Beardsley, Pierre Loüys, Robinson Jeffers. Yes, Jeffers, above all: *Tamar, Roan Stallion, The Tower Beyond Tragedy*. Though the author in his picture did not look much like an "urning," his themes were phallic, elemental, incestuous, sodomitical, and he lived in a tower in Carmel. For me, he was a taste, like olives, gladly shed a few years later when Edmund Wilson told me that he was a false prophet. Whatever else I may have learned from Czerna I have banished from my mind except the interesting word "cunnilingus."

She made no advances to me, and I never went there without Ted till one day toward the end of the summer when she told me that she would like me to come to a party, by myself, as Ted could not make it. Her reasons were probably those of any other hostess: the need at a party where there would be single men of a new nice-looking girl. I had just let my hair grow into a knot at the nape of my neck, and my prayers were being answered—I was finally getting pretty. Not as beautiful as my mother, "the most beautiful woman in Seattle," but not bad, let us say winsome, because of my Irish blood.

Anyway she asked me. Since it was an evening party, I had to invent some lie for my family, of course. Then, doubtless using a transfer from the Madrona streetcar, I went, with beating heart and no idea, I suppose, of how I was going to get home. I remember that there were drinks and that the big, long living-room was full of people, all of them, except Czerna, strangers to me. But they proved to be easy to talk to; particularly some of the men: Kenneth Callahan, for instance, a young painter with a blond moustache, who eventually would be counted Seattle's third-best painter (after Mark Tobey and Morris Graves); besides him, a White Russian, somewhat older, called Baron Elshin, who had a greeting-card business upstairs in an office-building near the Olympic Hotel—he had a small brown clipped moustache. I think I talked, too, to a young man from one of the papers. The only person who in a sense knew *me* was Czerna's husband; exceptionally, he was present that evening, and he took an interest in me, behaving in fact rather protectively, as though Frank's niece needed to be shielded from Czerna's crowd. Probably he curtailed my liquor consumption, and it must have been he who drove me home, complete with my alibi, when the streetcars had stopped running. Needless to say, I did not pass on his greetings to Frank.

In Czerna's crowded living-room that night I sensed that I was "launched." To a certain extent this proved to be true; it was my coming-out party—the only one I would have. Both Kenneth Callahan and Baron Elshin were soon after me, despite my age. Callahan had no difficulty in persuading me to come to his studio, on First Hill; it was a sort of shed raised on stilts and set back from the street. To reach it you crossed an unsteady wooden bridge—a common feature in poor sections of our hilly town—that ran teetering from the sidewalk across an overgrown ravine to the door. He had invited me to pose, and it was no problem to "sit" for him in the afternoons: I did not have to account for my doings in the daytime, and nobody in the family was likely to be in that neighborhood and spot me hurrying along the shaky approach to his door. He did not invite me to pose nude, but naturally we "went the limit" when he set down his brushes—he mostly did oils. Even after several times (and horseback riding at school), it still hurt; my defloration two years before had not been complete.

On the whole, I was relieved late that fall when Kenneth, having sold almost no paintings, decided to go to sea to earn a living (writing me many letters with little drawings in the margins to Annie Wright). He bored me; he was weak; he lisped slightly, and his studio was squalid. The best thing about it was the companionway-like approach. And some of the things he did in bed made me cringe with shame to think of afterwards.

It was those sexual practices of his—now common, cf. John Updike—that taught me while still a senior at Annie Wright how to deal with shame and guilt. When you have committed an action that you cannot bear to think about, that causes you to writhe in retrospect, do not seek to evade the memory: *make* yourself relive it, confront it repeatedly over and over, till finally, you will discover, through sheer repetition it loses its power to pain you. It works, I guarantee you, this sure-fire guilt-eradicator, like a homeopathic medicine—like in small doses applied to like. It works, but I am not sure that it is a good thing. Perhaps I did something to my immortal soul in my narrow bed in the room I shared with Marie Althen on the senior corridor. As I forced revolting memories to surge up before my closed eyes, almost burning the closed lids with fiery self-disgust, did I kill a moral nerve? To flinch from such memories, simply suppress them, might have been healthier. Is it right to overcome self-disgust? Well, in any case I learned the trick of it. Nobody told me; I found out the recipe for myself. If sexual guilt is bad for you, what I did was good. But suppose that the act I shrank from remembering had not been something I let a little blond-moustached man do to me but something worse, such as cowardice? Would it be good to force myself to contemplate it over and over, shutting my eyes to relive the shaming moments, till they lost their power to stab my conscience, their agenbite of inwit? I cannot say, for I never tried that. Perhaps sex—certain forms—was the only thing I did or was induced to do that shocked me badly for myself.

So I was a true girl of my generation, bent on taking the last trace of sin out of sex. According to our current belief, in sex everything is permitted (as Raskolnikov said in another context): one must just conquer a "natural" revulsion. But if, as Raskolnikov learned, the inhibition was really a deep-lying instinct, part of my interior warning system, hence necessary to my animal safety, what stupid thing was I doing? All I knew at the time was that I had devised a method that let me live with myself. It was a bit like the exercise of teaching myself to inhale, as I had been doing last year on my window sill. I was getting myself in training for my adult "career of crime."

Mr. Elshin was quite another pair of gloves. He was too old-fashioned to do me any harm. One of his absurdities was to call on me at school on a Sunday afternoon, wearing a pair of cream or pale-yellow gloves and carrying a stick. He must have come all the way from Seattle on the interurban. He arrived during visiting hours but of course he was not on the list of approved visitors each girl was meant to be supplied with by her parents. Nevertheless Miss Preston or the vice-principal must have taken pity, for I was sent for to come down to the school parlor, across from Miss Browne's office. It was quite an embarrassing interview we had, sitting on two straight chairs. No Humbert Humbert, he seemed taken aback by my uniform, and for my part I died at the thought that anybody glancing through the open door could see how crazy my poor old suitor looked, with those gloves and the stick and possibly a pair of spats, too. Before or after this, he took me to the movies in Seattle one afternoon, probably during Thanksgiving vacation, where he held my hand in the dark and embarrassed me then as well.

It was better to visit him in his little gift-card gallery, which had a showroom window on the corridor, fortunately, so that anybody could see in, and, behind, only a cubbyhole for the telephone. One of my visits inspired him to use the idea of me in a Christmas card, which he then (I suddenly recall) sold to me, as though it had been a commissioned order—two dozen examples, with envelopes to match. The colored drawing he had done showed a thin, prettyish girl with a "cubic" face and angular arms and legs who was wearing a cloak and carrying a pile of Christmas packages; inside was a printed text: "There was a cubic maiden,/ Who

157

had a cubic smile." This is all I remember of those verses of his except that there was a rhyming line about the cubic maiden walking a cubic mile. Again an embarrassment— how could I send out a likeness of myself as a Christmas card, for even then, I guess, I was said to have a "crooked smile," which the artist had caught in his drawing? Finding the money from my allowance to pay for them was another difficulty. And how explain to my grandmother what on earth had prompted me to order them? She had no idea of my knowing a "Mr. Elshin" (not a real baron, someone finally told me, but a Russian Jew from Harbin), and I could not invent a plausible circumstance in which I might legitimately have met him. In the whole causal chain that led to the pile of "Cubic Maiden" Christmas cards being hidden, unused, in a bottom drawer in my bedroom, the sole element my grandmother was aware of was my friendship with Ted and her sister, Till.

I think she was vaguely aware, also, of their mother, as someone who went regularly to Aunt Rosie's reformed synagogue. Like Mrs. S. Aronson (Aunt Eva) and Mrs. M. A. Gottstein (Aunt Rosie), Ted and Till's mother must have been a contributor to the *Famous Cook-book of the Ladies Auxiliary to Temple de Hirsch*, third edition, 1925—a book I still own. Could she have been the "Mrs. Flora Rosenberg" of "SPANISH SOUP" (p. 21), "CREAM OF POTATO SOUP" (p. 26), and "LENTIL SOUP" (p. 27)? "Mrs. E. Rosenberg," of "NO-EGG MAYONNAISE DRESSING" was somebody else. As one of my husbands said, this was the "Take a pound of caviar" cookbook. No bagels and lox. In any case, my grandmother saw no harm in that friendship, possibly because the girls were Jewish, like her, though she herself did not go to the Temple, did not even have a recipe ("Mrs. Harold Preston's SWEETBREADS POULETTE"?) in the wondrous book. If the girls' being Jewish warmed her to them, it would have been because that constituted a familiar quantity—she was able to "place" them, as she comfortably placed the Rupps, the Gerbers, Dr. Raymond and his daughter, Louise Owen—

families who lived on our block on 35th Avenue. That their father was a tailor, that they did not have an automobile and Till worked in a doctor's office, she did not hold against them; with her diamonds, rubies, and sapphires, her mink, broadtail, and monkey-fur, her "Louis" heels and safe in the bedroom closet, my grandmother was far too peculiar to be snobbish.

Czerna Wilson got back at me for something, but what I do not know—for not being a lesbian, for having attracted some single men? Most likely, her husband had chided her for luring the niece of his fraternity brother to one of her soirees. At any rate, it was through Frank that she struck. The following summer, when I no longer saw her, she consulted my uncle as a client. It was a will, I think, that she asked him to write for her, and in the course of the sessions in his office, she let him find out that she knew me—what an interesting young girl, how amusing to have her come so often to the house, Carl was quite taken. . . . My uncle, naturally, concealed his stupefaction. But at once, that very night, my grandmother was told. Though a virtual recluse, she was fully aware of Czerna's reputation. Again I floundered in a nasty morass of deception.

I don't know what fresh lies I told to minimize Czerna's delation. For some reason, though, the storm at home this time passed rather rapidly. It was bad enough that I had gone to her house on the quiet, but they supposed it had been in the daytime and with Ted. And they may have been slightly impressed by my "making time" with an undeniable celebrity. It was around that time that my grandmother and my aunt Rosie read *The Well of Loneliness* (1928). In the back seat of the Chrysler, with my grandmother at the wheel, I heard them discussing what those women "did." They could not figure out. All at once, Aunt Rosie, lively as a bird, turned around: "I'll bet she knows." I told them, but they would not believe it. "In the lowest depths of Montmartre I've *heard*," murmured my grandmother. "But not among anyone we would ever meet, Mary." She let the sentence hang, till it turned into a question. Possibly she and Aunt Rosie were considering Czerna Wilson as, still disbelieving, they shook their coal-black heads in their straw hats and eyeglasses.

I never saw Czerna Wilson again and do not know what happened to her. At some point, I gather, she and Carl Wilson were divorced and at some later point he became a millionaire, through a monopoly he established in the circulating-library business in the Northwest. In my day, unless I am mistaken, the Archway Bookstore did not even *have* a circulating library—my grandmother got her Bromfields and Hergesheimers from Frederick's and a lady named Mrs. Evans, and I took out my own advanced fiction from the blind Harry Hartmann's pace-setting bookshop.

No one in Seattle, that I'm aware of, remembers Mr. Elshin. Kenneth Callahan became the program director of the Seattle Art Museum, as well as a high-ranking local painter. He married, and I think his wife was some kind of artist, too. I never saw him again either. I was in Tacoma when he shipped out on that freighter—on the Hawaii run—from which he wrote me so many letters that I answered in study hall. Then I stopped; I got tired of hearing from him. A reference book places that trip of his in 1927, which would have been junior year, but that must be a mistake. Unless he shipped out twice?

It was not the last time that letters completed my disillusionment with a man. In that respect, being literary has been a lifesaver for me; put to the test of correspondence, few infatuations, on my side, survive. Even a great passion cannot survive a series of long, "wet" letters. The men I have clung to, all of them, including my son, Reuel, have "written a good letter."

But to think back, once more, to Kenneth Callahan, it seems to me that these pages are the first I have ever "let on" about him. Unless I told Ted something, though certainly not *all*, when the "sittings" were going on. Occasionally I have asked myself whether the same applied to him.

Did he never talk about me, to his wife, his painter friends, other people in Seattle's small Bohemia? It would have been natural for him to do so, since I had written about myself in books and widely circulated magazines and thus made myself, if not public property, at least an interesting topic for reminiscence. Yet if he "told" people, no word of it, no repercussion, has ever reached me on my subsequent visits to Seattle, when I went to see my grandmother and more recently my uncle Frank.

Now and then, coming upon his name in a feature in a newspaper on the art of the Northwest, I would wonder what he had done with those oils he painted of me. In short, having become "Kenneth Callahan," did he realize that I had become "I"? If so, probably too late. Like any poor artist, like the young Picasso, for example, he must have used the canvas of old work to paint new work on top of. Canvas cost a lot. So I, who was not yet "I," had been painted over or given a coat of whitewash, maybe two or three times, till I was only a bumpiness, an extra thickness of the canvas. Somewhere not long ago I read or heard that he had died.

As I make myself look back with older eyes on that time in my life, another question occurs to me. Have I done Czerna Wilson an injustice? When she let the cat out of the bag to my uncle, is it possible that she did it innocently, not intending me any harm? In other words, is it conceivable that she had no inkling of what a bombshell she deposited on Frank Preston's desk? That would imply, of course, that she had no inkling of having a bad name. The answer is no. She knew very well the picture she presented to the community, of a veritable temple harlot. If she did not deliberately promote the impression, she lazily let it shape itself around her, like those drifting curls of smoke. I am reminded, not exactly of the Nita Naldi of Cecil De Mille's *The Ten Commandments*, then the screen's own thick-lipped, heavy-hipped embodiment of every Thou Shalt Not—Czerna was less coarse and fleshy than that—but of the tribe of Astarte, or Ishtor, or Ashtoreth, icons of venery for those awe-struck decades, icons, I suspect, of her own indolent self-worship. *She* knew what she was doing, even though I do not. I leave her, then, in my uncle's office in the Northern Life Tower, prompted to consult him by who knows what amused whim, wearing the severe suit with the flare at the skirt of the jacket and a smart pair of oxfords; she leans forward, looking up at him from under her felt hat brim out of those sultry green eyes, as he lights her cigarette for her. A Melanchrino, a Sobranie? "Kind of a chāracter, that Czerna," he now remembers, making the "r"s very western.

Looking back on these people for the last time, I see that none of them had much effect on me and—what until now I have failed to notice—that I did not really like any of them, with the exception of Ted and her sister. Though I regarded Annie Wright as a more or less unworthy place of confinement for my rebellious spirit, it was school that was the predominant, the most powerful influence.

So let me put Czerna Wilson behind me, leaving her to figure only as the subject of an exercise in "Description" in Miss Clare Hayward's English course senior year, and turn back to Annie Wright. Senior year in some ways was the best of the Annie Wright years, having something of the serenity attributed to old age—*Oedipus at Colonus* and the late plays of Shakespeare.

If our grades were good, we could study downstairs, unsupervised, in the senior "sorority" room rather than in study hall. There were the changes I have mentioned in the faculty. Amusing, unconventional Miss Marthe Simpson, who made puppets, came to be our art teacher and taught us some innocently naughty French songs, such as *"Il était une bergère."* And, in English, replacing the pop-eyed Miss Marjorie Atkinson, we had the Viking beauty from Oxford with the perfect blue-eyed profile which she often turned to the window, looking dreamily out to nowhere.

Her every vocable was exquisite, too. Miss Clare Hayward could have taught us Urdu without any protest, but she actually gave us a survey of English literature, starting before *Beowulf*, the official point of departure. We learned of a figure called the Venerable Bede (673–735), author of the *Ecclesiastical History of the English People*, and listened while she read us his famous extended simile of the sparrow that flew through the king's banqueting hall and signified the transience of mortal life: "Like the swift flight of a single sparrow through the banqueting hall when you are sitting at dinner on a winter's day with your thanes and counsellors. In the midst there is a comforting fire to warm the hall; outside, the storms of winter snow or rain are raging. This sparrow flies swiftly in through one door of the hall and out through another. . . . Even so, man appears on earth for a little while; but of what went before this life or of what follows, we know nothing."

She took us back beyond Bede, to the wonderful Caedmon (fl. 670, at Whitby), whose strong, alliterative hymn, quoted in Bede, Miss Hayward said aloud to us in her beautiful, measured voice.

> Come, let us hymn the Master of Heaven,
> The might of the Maker, the deeds of the Father,
> He, holy Creator, he *hung* the bright heavens,
> He, Lord Everlasting, omnipotent God.

I wish I knew whether she said it to us first in the Northumbrian version (a West Saxon one exists, too) or gave it to us directly in English translation. But, hearing it, the dullest of us grasped that this was the genius of English, our wonderful language.

She gave us Chaucer, with the rules for how to pronounce him, which have stayed with me for life. It was never as well taught by poor Miss Foster at Vassar. We memorized quite a lot of the prologue to *The Canterbury Tales*: "Aprill with his shoures soote," of course, and "the hooly blisful martir for to seke,/ That hem hath holpen whan that they were seeke," but not overlooking the Prioress with her coral beads "gauded" with green, her little arm from which hung the gold brooch saying *Amor vincit omnia*.

Other parts of the survey I remember less well. The Pre-

Raphaelites, certainly, but what about "The Rape of the Lock"? Did we have it with her or the previous year? She gave us Thomson's *The Seasons* and Thompson's *The Hound of Heaven*. Our last assignment was Galsworthy's *Justice*—an odd choice.

In French we must have been having *Aucassin et Nicolette*; in Latin, after Cicero, we had Sallust's *Catiline Conspiracy*. And I had plenty of activities to keep me busy: president of the French Club, secretary of the Latin Club, playing Catiline in Miss Mackay's play *Marcus Tullius*, playing the heroine of Goldoni's *The Fan*, preparing for the College Boards, riding with Major Mathews and having Miss Mackay as chaperon, reading Swinburne and Ernest Dowson and Thomas Lovell Beddoes in study hall and Sir Hall Caine and Mrs. Belloc Lowndes and Marie Corelli, memorizing early Ezra Pound, Edwin Arlington Robinson, Edna St. Vincent Millay. Writing poems of my own in study hall (". . . Feet, feet tapping/ Up and down the stairs/ French heels rapping/ Of amorous affairs") and knowing they were trashy. There was an idyllic picnic of our Physics class, only five of us, when little Miss McKay, our teacher, took us to see the Cushman Dam and first we had our basket lunch by a rushing brook—strawberries brought by a day girl, the daughter of an army surgeon, and white-meat-of-chicken sandwiches. Did Miss McKay let us wade in the clear, cold water?

This was possibly the happiest day of my young life. I loved gentle Miss McKay, Jean Eagleson, Dorothy Walker, Barbara Dole, maybe even four-eyed Mary Ellen Warner. And Dorothy Walker's mother—wasn't she with us, too, driving us in her car, in fact? Yet in those same spring days I was meeting a one-legged boy after supper in the woods behind the athletic field and—again—nearly got myself expelled when someone, probably Miss Mackay, caught me after lights out coming in a gym window. I have told that story elsewhere and quoted the verses I wrote about the delinquent boy, whose name was Rex Watson. He was a younger brother of one of Miss Preston's favorites of the Class of '25 and had been sent to the reformatory after losing a leg in a hunting accident—perhaps he had got the drug habit. He and his gang used to roam through the district called Old Town, where the school and the pulp mill and railroad tracks were; I was induced to sneak out to meet him several times in the still-daylight evenings, and we smoked, he lying on the ground beside me with his crutch next to him. That was all. I have described how I lied—or at any rate practiced *suppressio veri*—when, until I did, Miss Preston was left with the prospect of having to expel me on the eve of graduation. There was no denying that I had been caught coming in after hours through a window.

The other change was that senior year I had a roommate, assigned me by the school. Marie Althen had come to Annie Wright for just the final year; she was the adopted daughter, as I have told, of elderly Alsatians and was already engaged to a Herbie Wetmore, who was in the insurance business. Maybe her parents, who lived in Tacoma, wanted to give her a little "finish" before she got married. She was a slim, pretty, bright-cheeked girl, undemanding and with no mental interests. We got along quite well. She did not mind if I left my bed at four in the morning to write a story before breakfast. On my side, I did not make her listen to it or to any of my elocution. I had just discovered Maurice Hewlett; even more than the better-known *The Forest Lovers*, I loved *The Life and Death of Richard Yea-and-Nay*, about King Richard the Lion-hearted, published in 1900 and so crabbed and allusive as to be almost impenetrable today. The medieval romances I was writing at top speed on an empty stomach were meant to be in his manner. I cannot remember whether I showed any of them to Miss Hayward or kept them to read aloud to myself.

On Sunday afternoons, you may remember, parents were permitted to take girls out during the long "quiet hour" that stretched from mid-day dinner to supper. Marie's parents, instead of taking her out themselves, arranged for her to go out with Herbie Wetmore—she already had her engagement ring. Marie was generous about inviting me, too, and we usually made up a foursome, with a friend of Herbie's called Evans Buckley. Most of the time we took Buckley's car, so that Herbie and Marie could use the back seat for their version of going the limit (on top of her but not inside her) while Evans drove and I sat beside him, endeavoring not to listen. But occasionally he parked, and I had to struggle hard to keep his insistent hand from going above my knee or down my neck while we hotly kissed. It turned out that his father was an undertaker, and there was one Sunday when he took me out all by myself somehow in the hearse. I think that the struggle that day was because he wanted me to lie down with him in the back, where the coffin went and where nobody could look in. I would not do it, and that was the end of Evans Buckley—sad, because he was good-looking and sophisticated and said funny things. I might have truly liked him except for the hearse. I did not go out with Marie and Herbie any more on Sundays.

Totally different was our senior prom. My grandmother got me a pink moiré dress with a big deep-red velvet bow on one hip and an uneven hemline, shorter on one side—skirts were about to go down. My uncle Harold, who was twenty-one then and still in college (he was an Art major), found a friend of his to be my date—a dark, small-featured young man named Frank Reno. His full name was Benjamin Franklin Reno, and Harold maintained that he was the nephew of President Eliot of Harvard. If that was so (which I wondered about), he was T. S. Eliot's cousin. He sent me a corsage of deep-pink camellias, to go with my dress, and this was a decided score for him, utterly outclassing the banal orchid. The lowest a boy could get was sweet peas, then roses, then orchids, and, best of all, gardenias (which the divine Donnie Fisher had sent me the year before), but camellias were something no other girl had.

My relation with Harold had been warming up; he liked my friend Blanche Ford, from Montana, the daughter of a

Federal judge, and had given up trained nurses for the time being. He came to the prom with Blanche (juniors took part, too), who wore an ice-blue satin dress—I forget what flowers Harold sent her. We ate supper as a foursome in the sacred precincts (opened for the occasion) of Miss Preston's Cottage, which was attached to the Great Hall. I do not know why—Frank Reno was a good dancer, he was not hard to talk to, he had even read books—but that prom for me was a strained charade. I think it was mainly that I did not like his name, which belonged, I felt, to a place, not a person, and hence sounded "common." Almost like an Italian name. The only bright spots were my dress and the camellias.

Can it have been the same in the East, at the schools my Vassar friends went to—Walnut Hill, Miss Madeira's, Abbott Academy (where Edmund Wilson's mother had gone)? It does not sound so; nothing like the jumble of incompatibles I floundered in that frightens me now just to think back on: today I would not have the stamina to keep my head in that tangle of contradictions. Perhaps it was not the Northwest; perhaps it was me. My classmates Jean Eagleson and Barbara Dole—I know for a fact—did not have to spend their Sunday afternoons, before high tea in the Great Hall, in a parked car with a Herbie and a Marie in the back seat heaving and panting while they in the front seat fought to keep their thighs pressed together. When *they* were taken out of school during quiet hour, it was by their parents, who came bringing oranges and cookies. On the other hand, they did not have my advantages, that is, they did not read "Sohrab and Rustum" or *Diana of the Crossways*. Even the little bit of the Seminary we had in common consisting of Miss Hayward's pure profile, chaperons, dance cards, senior lifesaving tests was itself made up of inconsistent elements. Senior prom was an intrusion of unreality both on their innocent pursuits and on my guilty ones. It was a goofy fiction we were made to live through, like those visitors' lists, like supervision of our mail (I think of Miss Preston in her office opening the copy I had ordered of *Point Counter Point* on the scene of Burlap taking a bath with his mistress and hastily closing it, to let me keep the book anyway), a borrowing from some place and time other than Tacoma, Washington, spring 1929, when skirts were about to fall. Perhaps the most glaring discrepancy between school fact and school convention came at my graduation that June.

Two days before Commencement, my uncle Harold with a friend—maybe again Frank Reno—drove over to Tacoma to take Blanche and me out. It was a Sunday (Commencement being on a Tuesday); classes were over. Anyway there was no problem about getting permission, because of his being my uncle. The next day—Class Day—I was going to be valedictorian in a white cap and gown, and my grandparents would come. Having signed out with Miss Browne, the four of us went for a ride.

They had brought some liquor with them. Blanche was an accomplished drinker, but I, as I had already learned when staying with the Ford girls in Montana, was very far from it. We sat on the ground in the woods somewhere, having a sort of drinking picnic of which I remember nothing except that when I stood up, teetering, I fell into a bed of nettles. No. I fell, bare-bottomed, because I had chosen to urinate, out of sight in a thicket, and then tipped over.

My punishment came the next morning. In the dining-room, the sight of a sugar-bowl caused me to feel violently sick, and I just made it, gagging, to a wash-basin or toilet. All morning I retched and vomited. My white wool cap and gown were waiting for me on my bed, but I was too sick to put them on. The frightened Marie concluded that I had better send to tell Miss Preston that I could not pronounce the valedictory—I could not even stand up. But I thought of my grandparents, who must have already arrived, and made up my mind to try. I knew my speech by heart, having written it myself and practiced it in our school auditorium. And in case the worst should happen in the middle of it, Marie and I would put a pail backstage.

Moreover time was on my side. The valedictorian *followed*

168

the salutatorian, and that would be Beth Griffith, who could be counted on to give a long harangue while the aromatic spirits of ammonia (which had just been procured, no doubt from the infirmary) got a chance to work in me. After Beth Griffith, there would be "On from Strength to Strength," our school song, to the tune of "High above Cayuga's waters." I put on the white gown and set the white mortarboard on my trembling head. By the time we were on the stage, seated behind the podium, the waves of nausea were subsiding a bit. It was going to be all right. But when I rose to speak, noting my grandparents in the audience, a new sensation seized me—under my robes, in the seat of my pants. The nettles! An intolerable itching. And I could not scratch *there*, publicly.

Not to leave you in suspense, Reader, I gave the valedictory. Palely, I finished; someone put roses in my arms, like St. Elizabeth of Hungary—there must be a photo in some archive. The strange fact was that the moment I began speaking the memorized words, the itching abated. When I stopped, it was completely gone. The nausea went, too. I suppose it was a question of my nervous system: the words forming on my lips acted like leeches, drawing sensation from the rest of my body. It was odd, and even while it was happening I felt that I had learned something—a new law: you can only pay attention to one part of the body at a time.

So our queer class graduated. In June, in Seattle, I took the College Boards, and on June 20, from her furnished room in Seattle, Miss Mackay wrote on my behalf to Vassar—a letter that stayed in the files of the Committee on Admissions unknown to me for fifty years.

Mary McCarthy is a student of quite unusual intelligence. She has studied Latin with me for two years, and in my opinion has a remarkable aptitude for languages. I have always found her industrious and pleasant to deal with in the class-room.

Mary also has considerable dramatic ability, and played

169

the leading part in the senior play this year. She was president of our school French club and secretary of the classical society, and in both capacities proved very efficient, and showed the qualities necessary for leadership. She has a strong will and plenty of ambition, and a magnetic and charming personality.

E. Mackay, M.A. Edin.
Instructor in Latin, The Annie Wright Seminary

Reading that, how can I fail to feel like a worm? Noble Ethel Mackay! The kindly upright woman was greatly deceived in me. In her worst nightmares that dear Latinist could not have pictured my frequentations: Rex Watson in the woods, Evans Buckley in the hearse, Kenneth Callahan in that eyrie reached by a cat-walk, to say nothing of Forrie Crosby in the Marmon roadster sophomore year, before I even *knew* her, *when I was fourteen*. Worst of all, Pelion on Ossa, the mountains of lies. Nonetheless I wonder. Invincible in her ignorance, she may have known me better than I knew myself. That is, *I* was deceived by the will-less, passive self I seemed to be living with, and Miss Mackay was not.

An old program tells me that on the evening of Class Day, opposite Jean Eagleson, I played in Goldoni's *The Fan*. Though this must have been a repeat performance, one would imagine that under the circumstances—post-throwing-up, post-nettles—it would have been memorable as an ordeal. Yet I don't recall it in the least; nothing comes back to me until the next day—Commencement—with all of us in the chapel in our white caps and gowns and the bishop giving out the rolled-up diplomas. That was when the thunderbolt struck; no wonder I forgot everything between the valedictory and then. Miss Preston was leaving! She was not coming back next year. The reason she gave in making the announcement was that she had been asked to open a school in Arizona.

No one believed that. Most of us, I think, supposed that the sad decision had something to do with her sister. According to one theory, Mrs. Johnson had TB, and Miss Preston was taking her to Arizona to cure it, opening a school to support the two of them. (There were two obvious objections to this: that TB victims dramatically lost weight; that a conscientious school principal would scarcely harbor a person suffering from a communicable disease—and in the infirmary, of all places!). Another suggestion was that Mrs. Johnson had cancer, which however did not explain Arizona. More plausibly there were conjectures that the trustees had given Miss Preston six months to get rid of her sister, and Miss Preston had refused. Or else, still more plausibly—forgetting Mrs. Johnson—it had to do with the drop in the enrollment, to which our pitifully shrunken class bore witness. Miss Preston was the responsible party, so she had to go. Whatever the reason, it was evident from Miss Preston's tears, which for once she tried to master, that the choice had not been her own. Unbelievably, after sixteen years, Miss Preston had been asked to leave, like a student found cheating. That was how it looked and how it probably was. In her office, after the exercises, she took us in her arms one by one—here the fact that we were a small class was lucky—and wept without saying a word.

In fact, Miss Preston did open a school near Phoenix, but I never heard how it fared, nor what happened to her sister. Once again it was the way of the Far West, possibly attributable to the vast expanses of geography: one did not "keep up" once the train whistle blew. Still, it seems to me now that once, after I had published something—a magazine piece—she wrote me a friendly letter, enclosing a photo of her school, and I hope I answered. Nothing further. I have heard twice from gentle little Miss McKay, our Physics teacher, but never from any of the others. Miss McKay wrote that Miss Mackay had married—a surprising piece of news.

The Seminary is still there, more thickly ivied, or, rather, Virginia-creepered, than it was in my day. Bishop Keator's likeness still hangs in the Great Hall. But now they call it the Annie Wright *School*, and graduates (oh, dear) are called "Annies." In the photos they use in fund-raising pamphlets the school looks quite "prestigious." Maybe there are fewer desertions from the boarding department at the end of sophomore year. In the publicity material there is hardly any mention of faculty, and in a letter I received a few years ago from the headmaster, inviting me to visit, there was one awful mistake in grammar.

Yes, a head*master*. The whole story of the social evolution of our Pacific Northwest is hinted at there. Starting out with a "principal," Mrs. Lemuel Wells, 1884, and continuing in that forthright style through to Miss Preston, we sank (aping eastern schools) to a "headmistress" with Miss Ruth Jenkins and her several successors till we have finally arrived at a "headmaster" with the incumbent and his grammarless predecessor. It is the story of a loss of regional identity, and I doubt that anyone else feels the shame of it as keenly as I do, I who left the Northwest at twenty and never came back, who only half-live in the United States, who have not attended a single school reunion. Weep with me, Reader, for all those resolute bishops, starting with Bishop Paddock, for all those widows of clergymen (Mrs. Hiatt, Mrs. Constance Aylwin, Mrs. Keator) doubling as teachers of Sacred Study, for the Vassar-trained Miss Atkinsons, both of them, and every old-maid teacher of Burke and Addison, for bath schedules, gym bloomers, pen nibs and inkwells, for clog dancing and "quiet hour," Puss 'N Boots, and Pig 'N' Whistle, for macaroni-and-cheese and chocolate ice-cream with marshmallow sauce, for deep-voiced "Papa" Wallace, our choir conductor, and "Good King Wenceslas," "He who would valiant be," and the red camellia tree by the cloister steps—for what *was*, ineluctably, and on whose like no "Annie" will ever look.

7

N ow, to tell what happened next, after graduation, I must go back a whole year to the summer of 1928, when the American Bar Association held its convention in Seattle. It was in the month of August. In honor of the occasion, the local chapter was staging a pageant on the signing of the Magna Carta. As a former president (1896–97) of the State Bar Association and of the City Bar Association (1909–10), my grandfather of course had tickets for the event, scheduled to take place in the Outdoor Theatre at the U.

Not only did he have to go; he wanted to go. He was hooked on the theatre. When he had taken my grandmother to New York the previous winter—her first trip—on his way to Washington to hear testimony in a case of the government against a shipping company, they had opened every theatre, she complained, because of his habit of arriving an hour before curtain-time, ahead of the ushers—he was the same way about trains. That was when they had seen *The Green Hat* and my grandmother had found a dressmaker to copy Katharine Cornell's second-act ensemble of thin kasha-colored wool and beige caracul trim—the elegant dress and matching jacket that now hung in her crowded clothes closet above rows of "Louis"-heeled shoes. Anyway, my grandfather was hell-bent on being at that pageant and determined, on account of his leading position in the legal community, that the rest of his family should be on hand, too.

I resisted. I loathed being seen at any function with my family, for it exposed the fact that I was still treated as a child. Every Thursday night (the maid's night off), I died of mortification when we went to dinner at my grandfather's club and he greeted us, coming in from the men's side, by clapping his hands and kissing my painted grandmother on both cheeks.

A Magna Carta pageant, moreover, was the type of event—middle-class, boosterish, "educational"—that I spurned in any circumstances. More "Lincoln apple sauce," as Mark Sullivan had written of the native variant; more boloney. While I was not actually on the side of bad King John, the hallowed civic character of the Great Charter was enough to turn me against it, especially when touted by a bunch of corporation lawyers.

We quarreled. My grandfather refused to hear of my staying home, called me "Young lady," doubtless swore— "Hell and damnation," his only oath. Finally I submitted, planning to sulk tight-lipped through the evening. After dinner we all got into the car and drove to the University district, with my uncle Harold—probably glowering, too— at the wheel. Frank, who as a lawyer had to go anyway, would have come in his own car, with Isabel and maybe her brother Dell, who was in the electrical-supply business but was writing a book illustrated with his own drawings on Paul Bunyan and his ox.

To start with, I imagine, I refused to look at the grassy stage. But at some point my attention must have been caught, by a voice that made my eyes turn to seek the figure it belonged to. It was the leader of a group of knights. He wore a helmet and a suit of chain mail with a red cross on the breast—the whole no doubt made of dishrags as in our plays at the Seminary. It was still light, and I could consult the program: "*The Red Cross Knight*, Harold Johnsrud." The name meant nothing to me. He had a crisp voice and very pure diction, a slender waist and a fairly tall figure, taller at any rate than his followers, ranged behind him in a wedge. You could not see much of his head and face because of the side pieces of his helmet, but he was dark, and there was something oddly compressed about his features—a broken nose, it turned out.

Above all, he had "presence"; he was arresting. And this quality in him was often remarked on; it was not just a young girl's notion that he "stood out" under the lights on the greensward representing Runnymede. I cannot explain why that should have been. His part, of the Red Cross Knight, was not important historically, unless he was meant to be Robert Fitz-Walter, leader of the barons, but Fitz-Walter, as I dimly remember, was a different character in the pageant, played by a different actor. No Red Cross Knight figures in the *Britannica* account of the day; he must have been someone very minor. Did Johnsrud covet the part of the wicked King John, which would have suited him well—"ablest and most ruthless of the Angevins," the *Britannica* says? Perhaps the author of the pageant, finding a gifted mummer on his hands, had *invented* the character for Johnsrud. Whatever it was, there was a theatricality in him that commanded attention—that was why he got jobs rather easily. That night, in the Outdoor Theatre my grandmother and I exchanged glances; maybe my grandfather, too, gave a forcible nod of approval.

The reader has guessed that this Red Cross Knight is going to be my husband. Yet for a while that summer in Seattle I could not even find out who "Harold Johnsrud" was. I might have forgotten about him had it not occurred to me that a person to ask was Ted Rosenberg. As I feared, Ted knew nothing of the Bar Association pageant, but her brother Dan did, the tall older brother who was in the Speech Department at the University and who was the family's real intellectual, played the jazz violin, and in later years, under the name Van Dragen, went to Hollywood and became a speech coach for big film stars. Not only did he know about the pageant; he knew Harold Johnsrud.

Dan said that he had come to Seattle from New York to help his friends Burton and Florence James start the Seattle Repertory Theatre—real repertory (as opposed to stock), our first. Mrs. James would be directing, and Burton James and Harold Johnsrud would share the principal male parts. Right now they were looking for a theatre, with the idea of eventually building one in the University district. I don't recall what else I heard, but probably the Magna Carta pageant had been entrusted to the Jameses by the local bar association.

Ted promised to introduce me to Johnsrud the next time he came to their house. In her program for my intellectual development, introductions—to people as well as to books—played a big role always. She had already engineered my admission to Czerna Wilson's "salon" (her idea) and now (my idea) she would bring me together with a real actor from New York. The introduction to Czerna in the long run did not lead far, even in its side effects, except that it deepened my grandmother's suspicions of my truthfulness. But the meeting with Dan's friend was deeply consequential: so many long roads in my life lead back to it. Indeed, if anybody ever played the Fates to me, it was the Rosenberg family in their little frame house not far from the Madison Avenue streetcar line. My own grander house, with its carriage block incised "1893" and its view of Mount Rainier, was ten minutes walk farther along, above the Lake.

So Ted got her hospitable mother to invite me to lunch. It was a Sunday, and Johnsrud had been invited to lunch by Dan. For me the great problem, naturally, was what to wear. The August weather decided me to put on my new dress. It was a tennis dress, sleeveless, in soft white cotton with a big green V inset in the front, at the décolleté, which made a V of its own against the bare skin of my chest. I pictured it, except for the green V, as something Helen Wills or Helen Jacobs might wear on the courts. My grandmother and I had sent in for the pattern from *Vogue*, and I had cut the dress out with her help, and sewed it on the machine, not counting the hem, which of course was hand-sewn. It had only just been finished, the first dress I ever made.

There was only one slight drawback. It was a bit short, showing half of my kneecaps at a time when this was not "in." But I persuaded myself to wear it anyway; it was the only new thing I had. Unfortunately, my grandmother, absorbed in the rituals of her own toilet, did not see me before I left for the Rosenbergs'; otherwise, she would have made me change. As I walked along the sidewalks, the dress got shorter, or so it felt: cut rather close to the body as far down as the hips, it was twisting around and hiking up. My entire knee was now showing. At the Rosenberg house, they were too kind to make any comment. And if they had, what could we have done? Little Mrs. Rosenberg could hardly have let it down for me while cooking lunch.

Out the window on the landing leading up to her room, Ted and I could see Johnsrud and Dan in the backyard below; they were fencing. Tall, big-boned Dan, with his owly glasses and buck teeth bared, looked a little ungainly. But Johnsrud was lissome, with a perfect fencer's body; only his bald head, seen from above, like a skull fitted on for a fancy-dress party, appeared incongruous—I had not been prepared to find him bald on top, with that slender figure. Ted and I did not know enough about fencing to tell who was winning.

I have the sense that I talked a lot at the lunch table, to cover my shame about the dress. The whole family was there: Dan and little Jess, who was two years behind Ted at Garfield High School and would grow up to be a lawyer, Mother and Father, Till and Ted. While I talked, Johnsrud's eyes came to rest on me curiously from time to time, as though he could not put me together. Something I said made him smile to himself and glance quizzically at Dan. There could be no doubt that he had observed my too-short dress. Misled by my bare knees, he was treating me as a child, and the books I knowledgeably mentioned—wasn't that the summer I was trying to read *Zarathustra*?—in order to seem *older* than I was, far from correcting the visual impression, only confirmed it, making me sound weirdly precocious, I guess. Though I was still forbidden to wear real lipstick, starting on my sixteenth birthday this last June 21, I was allowed Tangee, a stick of colorless salve supposedly good for chapping, that turned a brilliant orange when you applied it to your mouth; no doubt I had applied it as thickly as possible that morning. Needless to say, my Helen-Wills, Helen-Jacobs dress, apart from its shortness, must have looked crudely home-made.

It was the pits, as people say now, a fierce humiliation of all my pretenses. There was a quality in Johnsrud that, together with Dan's lofty manner, made my brave performance more painful than it might have been with a different young man as witness. His was a mocking nature, as was shown by the quizzing wrinkles around the eyes and the habitual lilt of one dark eyebrow. If he understood (as I feared he might) that I had come here especially to meet him and was doing my utmost to make an impression on him, that ironical look of his twitted me for my girlish folly. Sympathy with failure was not a strong point with Johnsrud. In short, he was cruel, like so many young men of the period (a debt they owed to Nietzsche or, more directly, to Shaw). When they were kind, it was condescension.

The next time I saw him was at the Metropolitan Theatre, when he played in *The Wild Duck* in the late autumn, probably during Thanksgiving vacation. Ted and I went to a matinee and afterwards she took me backstage to his dressing-room. It was a production that I still clearly remember, the best Ibsen I have seen to this day. Burton James played the photographer Hjalmar Ekdal, and Johnsrud was his friend and evil genius, Gregers Werle, intruding on the Ekdals' semi-bohemian and self-deceived family life with "the claim of the ideal." Immersed in that performance, from Mrs. Sorby's tinkling laugh in the first scene to the gunshot at the end, I came to understand Ibsen, at least as fully as I ever shall. Johnsrud as the baleful Gregers (often thought to be based on Kierkegaard, with his thirst for the absolute, but why not on Ibsen himself, the Ibsen of *The Enemy of the People* and *Pillars of Society*?) wore a tightly fitting gray suit of an old-fashioned cut that brought out something knife-like in his appearance; I remember his Gregers always in profile, with that bald skull and mended broken nose, while Hjalmar was mostly full face to the audience, soliloquizing even when speaking dialogue. This effect—the relation of a knife and a spoon must have been carefully studied by Florence James, the director, possibly seeing a dramatic use for a narrow, two-dimensional quality in the character of Johnsrud himself. There was a lot of Gregers in him, of the pontificator, the home-truth teller; maybe it is a Scandinavian type of being. In any case, when it was over, Ted took me to his dressing-room. He met us in the doorway, and as he talked to Ted and listened to our praises, he glanced at me and appeared to search his memory. "Ah. So this is the child Mary." That was all. I heard the amusement in his voice, the Standard-English accent drawing my name out to ´mɛari—the correct pronunciation, as I learned the following summer when studying the Daniel Jones phonetic system.

I saw him play once more at the Metropolitan Theatre—the Seattle Repertory still did not have its own house—when he and Burton James were doing *The Jest*, a John and Lionel Barrymore vehicle that had played on Broadway in 1919. It was adapted from a play by the Italian Sem Benelli that Sarah Bernhardt (in the John Barrymore part) had staged and toured in before the war. The story, a florid melodrama set in Renaissance Florence, had to do with two bitter enemies, one a moody artist and the other a brutal mercenary. In Seattle, the John Barrymore part (the artist) was played by Burton James, and Johnsrud took Lionel's. Of his performance, not much comes back to me—chiefly the use he made of his shoulders to suggest primitive strength. They were high and surprisingly broad, as if built out by pads, like those in football uniforms, in contrast with his lithe slender frame and tapering waist; in fact, he had played football in college and owed his broken nose to it. I thrilled to *The Jest*, so baroque and violent, though it did not move me as deeply as *The Wild Duck* had done, but I don't recall visiting him backstage in his dressing-room this time. Perhaps I had gone in the evening with Grandma and Grandpa rather than to a matinee with Ted.

I did not see him again till late the following summer, after I had graduated from Annie Wright. But I began to hear his name spoken at the Cornish School, where I was taking a summer course with Ellen Van Volkenburgh Browne, before going to Vassar in September. Ted and Till were impressed to know that I was studying theatre under her at Cornish, and I was impressed myself. She had great prestige as a director, though I could never quite find out why, unless it was that she and her husband, Maurice Browne, the inventor of the term "little theatre," were in some way connected with the Elmhirsts, who owned Dartington Hall in England—a famous Devonshire property that had an experimental school and an arts center—and the Elmhirsts were in some way connected with the Whitneys. In fact, Dorothy Whitney, who first married Willard Strait, founder (with Croly) of *The New Republic*, after his death married Leonard Elmhirst, an Englishman, and started the Dartington Hall complex with some more of her Whitney money. But I did not know that then, though doubtless Johnsrud did; it was the type of information he was master of. All I knew or, rather, learned was that studying theatre—which to me meant acting—under Mrs. Browne really meant *under*: one was supposed to be content to look up to her.

At Cornish, I did not study acting, let alone act; with the rest of the enrollees, I was put to doing eurhythmics, which were taught by Miss Louise Soelberg, a pale young woman in gray dancing tights with a bun. Our class took place in an exercise room; to the music of a piano, we pranced about, girls and gangling boys, in a long line that formed an ill-shapen circle. Sometimes we extended our arms and waved them; at other times we skipped. The one accomplishment I learned at Cornish was skipping, which I still do quite well, bounding springily through the air. The idea, of course, was that we were training our bodies to be expressive on the stage. We also took phonetics with a Mrs. Lois Hodgson to purify our diction. I acquired the Daniel Jones phonetics' dictionary and learned how to write my name in phonetic symbols: ´mεari máka: thε. But wild horses could not have got me to pronounce it that way.

Finally, at the end of the summer, the school staged a theatrical event, with parts for everybody. Mrs. Browne directed; it was a fantasy with a good deal of miming and perhaps had to do with a voyage of exploration. We summer-school students were assigned the role of pirates in a corps-de-ballet interlude that was imagined as happening under water, in Davy Jones's locker, at the bottom of the sea—our pirate ship had been sunk. Obviously none of us had lines to speak; the sub-aqueous illusion demanded that we not open our mouths. During rehearsals, dark-eyed, gracious, twinkling Mrs. Browne (she was Medea, Burns Mantle tells me, in a 1920 Broadway production of the Euripides) waxed eloquent to the cast on the subject of illusion in the theatre, using our band of pirates to illustrate the principle. We were to move so as to create the illusion of a resistance offered to us by the water, that is, slowly, heavily, with groping hands extended against a counter-force—veering, twisting, turning, drunkenly reeling when a current swayed us. We wore black caps with the Jolly Roger emblem and loose black trousers, carried cardboard knives and cutlasses, which we were meant to wave in murderous style, always bearing in mind, though, the resistance of the water in those lower depths. And we were supposed to undulate as a single body acted on by the watery force, as a whole rather than as individuals—no one was to stand out.

In Maurice Browne's autobiography, *Too Late to Lament*, I find the explanation. The play, called *The Princess Who Wouldn't Say Die*, had already been put on by the Brownes in Carmel and was repeated—I'm not sure when—in London. It was one of their workhorses. Here is his word-picture of the scene (*our* scene) in the watery depths: ". . . passengers and crew, sunk to the bottom of the sea with Davy Jones and all his pirates, wavered rhythmically but not realistically with teetering arms and legs. . . . Enchanted audiences grew helpless with laughter. We had learned to apply to comedy those lessons which *The Trojan Women* had taught us in tragic dance, *Medea* in lighting," etc.

I do not know what my grandparents made of this performance, my grandfather, in particular, who was used to applauding me in the leading part in school plays: "Toy Yah, Toy Yah, he have call me his *son*-daughter!" "And I shall extinguish the flames of my own ruin in the conflagration of all Rome!" Watching me sway and reel with a dozen others, he may have dryly regretted his investment in the Cornish School training. Or he may have been indignant, quite simply, at what he felt was a misuse of my talent.

I understand now what a sad cheat it all was, almost necessarily so. Any summer theatre, calling itself a school or not, takes on groups of fees-paying students or "apprentices" with the unspoken reservation that none of these aspirants will ever set foot on the stage in a speaking part. Actually, in most summer theatres, the apprentices never get to tread the boards even as walk-ons. Today's domestic farces and "situation comedies" have no parts for spear-carriers. Instead they are put to work building and painting scenery and are grateful for the privilege of being physically close to "names." Summer theatres are in business, and audiences come to see professionals; the principle applies wherever tickets are sold.

Today, as a professional myself (though in a different trade), I tend to share Mrs. Browne's view or, rather, that of Miss Nelly Cornish, who must have faced the problem in every department of her school, each art student, for example, wanting personal attention paid to his or her work by Mark Tobey or Morris Graves. Somehow that must have been better in Rembrandt's time: Rembrandt (like a summer theatre) at least got some work out of his pupils, who pitched in and did the journeyman work on commissions and that way could benefit from the master's corrections. Anyhow, if I was cheated, I deserved to be. I would have wrecked any play they had let me open my mouth in, with or without phonetics. If I hold something against Mrs. Browne, with her deeply musical voice and soft gray marcel wave (and it sounds as if I do), it is simply that she went too far in "including" us in her production: those pirates, those ridiculous pirates! That was the real fraud. There was no need beyond dreadful gentility to cast us in anything. This was not real work, like painting flats, which has to be done, but "made" work given us to *seem* to repay our (quite high) tuition. It was a version of feather-bedding. It was not just my ego that resented being a pirate; it was my common sense. I felt silly—absurd.

Yet let me try to be just. Mrs. Browne did have a lesson for us, namely, that illusion in the theatre is tied to the imagining of a "counter-force" (here represented by the specific gravity of fluids): the actor playing a drunken man depicts not staggers but the effort to walk straight. But if that was what she was trying to demonstrate, she misread her audience. We were too young and avid for fame to catch on. We wanted Cornish to let us *act*, rather than to teach us the principles of acting.

It would be wrong to say that I got nothing out of Cornish. Quite a bit less, certainly, than I got out of the summer I spent at typing school one year later, on my grandfather's recommendation. But not only did I learn to skip correctly at Cornish, I met a girl wonderfully named Marmion Connor whom I liked, and I became conscious of Bach. One night in the Cornish auditorium, our teacher Louise Soelberg did a kind of solo dance (eurhythmics, I suppose) to the music of a Bach cantata, *Liebster Herr Jesu*. Later, at Vassar, we saw Mary Wigman (I hated her), but the Cornish evening was my first experience of modern dance, as well as of Bach—we did not get him in our "Symphonies under the Stars" with Michel Piastro in the stadium. Miss Soelberg stood stage center in her gray ballet dress, moving only her head, white arms, long neck, and torso in accord with a voice and with notes struck by an offstage instrument. Her legs and feet and her rather expressionless flat Scandinavian features remained utterly still, giving an impression of exquisite control. That evening cast a spell on me—I even decided to add German to the languages I was promising myself to learn at Vassar, starting with Persian. "*Liebster Herr Jesu*," "Dearest Lord Jesus"—it did not sound too hard. I loved the bare stage, the solitary, barely moving figure, the single unseen instrument (a clavichord?), the voice. I must have felt something like what others were feeling on first seeing Martha Graham.

No, I am not forgetting Johnsrud. He was Louise Soelberg's "friend." That was why I was hearing his name, it turned out; Ted Rosenberg, as usual, knew. And as usual she was right: on the last night of the summer-school term, the school had a dance in the big upstairs practice room, and Johnsrud came with Miss Soelberg. They danced with each other, both very straight and tall. I did not think he would notice me in the crowd of watchers, but he did. When someone else claimed Miss Soelberg, he came over. Nothing this time about the child Mary; instead, without preamble, he asked me to dance. I was not a very good dancer; like so many boarding-school girls, I tried to lead. But with his hand on my back I followed, not thinking about my feet. I must have talked a blue streak, for he learned that I had been accepted at Vassar and was going east next month, which prompted him to tell me that he, too, was going east in September, to New York, to look for a part in the fall season on Broadway—the producers were already casting. I may have told him that I had to stop over in Minneapolis on the way, to see my other grandmother, which may have prompted him to tell me that he, too, had Minnesota in his background—he was born there, delivered by Sinclair Lewis' brother, Dr. Claude Lewis, the local doctor, and he had gone to Carleton College, whose president was still his friend. A strain of boastfulness was already evident in his character, though maybe not to me. In any case, he said, it was the end of Seattle for him; he had done all he could. I wondered about Miss Soelberg but of course did not ask. (In reality, as I have learned, from that autobiography of Maurice Browne's, she followed "Nellie Van" and himself to Dartington Hall and then joined the Joos Ballet as a prima ballerina.) Instead, we talked about a freckled boy in the eurhythmics class who was going to the Carnegie Playhouse in Pittsburgh: Clarrie Kavanaugh. When our dance ended, I think Johnsrud told me, lightly, to look him up in New York, but I did not take that seriously, for how would I find him when I went there with my grandmother and Isabel—assuming that I would have the daring to try? Yet I was happy to know that we were both bound for New York next month; it was a sort of bond.

We stayed at the Roosevelt Hotel, my grandmother and Isabel and I; it was where my grandmother had stayed with my grandfather on her earlier visit, when they had seen Katharine Cornell in *The Green Hat*. Just above the Biltmore, on Madison Avenue, between 45th and 46th Streets, very convenient to the theatres. We would have three days of theatre-going in New York before they took me up to Poughkeepsie for registration.

I did not see the need of that, and especially of the tiresome increment of Isabel. After all, I had just traveled alone from Seattle to Minneapolis in a lower berth and then changed trains by myself in Chicago. Grandpa had been firm about my making the Minneapolis stopover, so as to see my brothers, who were living with Uncle Louis that fall. I stayed at my grandmother McCarthy's; Grandpa McCarthy had died, leaving a trust fund for our education (which, Grandpa Preston said, did not begin to cover the Annie Wright bills), but *she* was unchanged, still wearing those improbable feathered hats. This time, she was intent on buying me an electric doughnut-baker for my college room—in her understanding, today's equivalent of the chafing-dish. At Donaldson's department store, I managed to discourage the thought: if she had made me accept it, it would have been an embarrassment to me at college. I knew perfectly well that Vassar freshmen today did not go in for midnight "spreads." Besides, she would probably have charged it to my trust account, as she did with her Christmas remembrances to my brothers—a fact, however, that I was not yet aware of. In the end, the old lady did not get me any present. Instead, she had the parish priest in to her sun-parlor to warn me that Vassar was "a den of iniquity." But the priest, too, was uncooperative. After a stiff evening with my brothers at Uncle Louis', I was relieved to leave for Chicago, where I had the excitement of changing stations to board a New York Central train for New York. In the club car I met my first Vassar girl—a tough, deep-voiced blonde senior called Flea (for Frances) Lee from California, who "filled me in" on the real Vassar in a rather alarming way, warning me, above all, what and whom to avoid. Davison Hall, where I was going to live, on the Quad, was not the worst, she said, of those houses; I was lucky not to be in Lathrop or Raymond. If I had wanted to ride, perish the thought; the horses were no good; better not get roped in to signing up for an "activity"; skip the "J" dances; expect no help from my senior adviser. I forget all the other steers she gave me, this hard, friendly Californian with a heavily made-up full-lipped mouth; I looked forward to seeing more of such an interesting person. But I was disappointed; she never noticed me again. After graduation, she went to work for the new *Mademoiselle* in the college department, blazing a vocational trail. Class of '30, she was a real jazz-age person, perhaps the last of the breed, a survival.

In any case, I did not need Isabel to show me my way around. My uncle Frank's wife—like my mother, a Gamma Phi at the University—must have been thirty-seven in 1929. With me, at seventeen, she took a bright, assured, young-married tone. She and Frank lived directly across from us in a small new frame house, and she was pretty in a high-colored, dark-haired, Scotch-Irish way despite a wobbly chin and slightly goiterous neck. I would have loved her if she had let me when I had first arrived in Seattle six years before. But she could not resist making fun of my poetry-recitations, pretending to want to hear "The Inchcape Rock," so that a roomful of her friends could be amused. And she would not let me get close to her literally or otherwise. Once I sought to bury my head between her breasts (I was trying to determine how big they were) and was pushed away with one of her sharp laughs. She repeatedly interfered with my grandmother's guidance to me on the subject of nail polish, lipstick, silk stockings, and so on, but never in the direction of a greater permissiveness. Despite being a younger person and rather clothes-loving, she would not take my part. Her dry, "amused" chatter seemed to parry any intimacy; it was impossible to imagine her and Frank in the conjugal act (easier my ancient grandparents!), which may have explained their lack of children. She called my grandfather "the Honorable" (from the official form of address we found on envelopes addressed to him), which did not displease him, but she had failed to find a teasing little sobriquet for my grandmother, whom no daughter-in-law could have called "Mama" or "Mother." Speaking *about* her, Isabel said "Your mother," "Frank's mother," "Your grandmother."

Of me, she had evidently made a considerable study. I remember her thoughtful comment offered to the world at large one Sunday evening after we had finished one of our maid's-night-out suppers and were putting the ice-cream goblets into the pass-through to the kitchen: "If she assimilated all she ate, she'd be a mountain."

I suppose she was never comfortable about the Jewish half of Frank; there were no Jews among the couples who made up their set, mostly lawyers and business executives and their peppy wives, who gave "progressive" dinners, going from house to house and from first course to pineapple upside-down cake, and who named their children "Sara" and "Sheila." Her own father, who died of cancer of the throat, had been a doctor, and her mother, poor dumpy Mrs. McCormick, was a nondescript gray bundle of polka-dotted clothes, whom Isabel was nervously gay about, doubtless feeling just as ashamed of her socially as she was of Mrs. Moses A. Gottstein and Mrs. Sigismund A. Aronson, who had a good deal more to offer. The sons and daughters of doctors, I have noticed, are often mortified by their mothers, that is, by the women their fathers have married before becoming successful practitioners.

I am sorry now for Isabel, who eventually tried to be friends with me, sorry for her childlessness, her insuperable shallowness, which could not be remedied by travel, by incessant "keeping up" with art, music, architecture, gardening, gourmet cooking—all the known deepeners and broadeners except, I guess, sex. I do not think she wanted to be what she was—a person short on true emotion. She was a clever housewife; she was economical, could sew her own curtains and hang them; she taught me how to do fringed tablecloths and matching napkins for bridge tables by pulling out threads from the raveling edge of the material. She also showed me how to make a "sandwich loaf" with little sandwiches inside, though I was too clumsy to follow her instructions. She was onto icebox cookies early. She knew how to cut bread and spread colored fillings on the bias to produce a rainbow effect. Naturally she was one of the first, after the Second War, to catch onto drip-dry, *so* useful for travel. Today, if she were alive, she would have a Cuisinart and one of those sets of little wheels for her suitcases. Her temper was invariably cheerful. All this should have made her an ideal daughter-in-law, if not an ideal wife. My grandfather liked her—she played cribbage with him— but about my grandmother I never could tell. She gave Isabel enviable presents every Christmas—last year a beautiful gray squirrel coat, when I did not even have an ocelot. But maybe fur coats did not mean much to my grandmother, who had so many of her own; eventually, one Christmas, she gave our maid, Lavinia, a very stylish, well-cut muskrat. Not by a look or a sound would she divulge her private thoughts about Isabel, despite the opportunities I put in her way. Nobody in our family (excepting me) ever let his private feelings be seen. The only thing I was sure of in respect to my grandmother and the McCormicks was that she was crazy about Isabel's handsome brother, Dell. She bloomed whenever he came to the house; it was the one time you could count on her to be willing to tell stories of early days. But Isabel bloomed herself when Dell came, even after he married Mabel. And so, very likely, did I.

To get back, however, to the fall of 1929, when we were all three staying at the Roosevelt, I was sad that my grandmother, for whatever inscrutable reason, had seen fit to bring Isabel along. She was everything in Seattle that I wanted to get away from. Anything I thought of doing she would be bound to oppose. Actually, on our first night, it was my grandmother who had picked out the play we went to see— *Let Us Be Gay*, with Francine Larrimore, a Rachel Crothers comedy that was still running from the previous season— and we had all agreed on a restaurant, the Lobster, which was on our way from the hotel to the theatre.

The next morning we planned to go to the Metropolitan Museum. There, at the top of the great staircase, our differences came to a head. On our left were Italian paintings, which was where I wanted to go—I loved Botticelli and thought I could glimpse one around the corner, in the first room—but my grandmother and Isabel were determined to see the American Wing, which was in another part of the museum and whose very name offended my ears—I imagined "Paul Revere" silver, spinning wheels, "testers," butter crocks. In other words, they wanted to look at antiques, and I wanted to look at art. We quarreled. With a final furious word, I pulled myself, half-weeping, from Isabel's grip, which sought to propel me in *their* direction, but instead of turning, as I should have, into the first Italian room, where I might have found calm and Titians, I flung myself at the staircase. And fell. All the way down, bouncing from marble step to marble step; if I recall right, there are no landings to interrupt the long flight of stairs from top to bottom. At the bottom, winded and tearful, I picked myself up. It was a wonder I was not hurt. Evidently my relatives had not witnessed the prolonged epic fall (like that baby-carriage in the film *Potemkin*, of which I was not yet cognizant); they were already on their way to the Paul Revere silver and the butter crocks. I was too shaken to try to go back upstairs. Instead I walked out to Fifth Avenue and got on a double-decker bus, which, I reasoned, was going in the right direction. New York looked easy to find your way around in. If I got off at 46th Street and turned left, after one long block I would be at the hotel.

On the downtown side of 46th Street between Fifth and Madison I met him, coming toward me, the only person I knew in all New York. He seemed pleased to meet me. I told him about my fight with the Preston ladies, and naturally he was on my side. Then he made a suggestion: if I still wanted to see some art today, a few blocks off there was a show by Archipenko, the modernist sculptor, which he had been thinking of going to. It was on the top floor of a smart department store, Saks Fifth Avenue—to me that seemed a bit strange. We went through aisles of gloves and stockings and costume jewelry and then we were in the elevator. I was too much excited as my savior guided me through the evidently very advanced, non-representative exhibits to be anything but confused. Archipenko, I gathered, was a Russian and an extremist. He believed in pure forms. I did not quite grasp it, but that did not bother me. For me, the marvel was simply in being there, as though by a miracle. And it had happened so swiftly, as things did in New York: an hour before, I had never heard of Archipenko and now I was gazing at curious metal shapes of his making. In my hand was a catalogue; Johnsrud had taken one for me from a stack on a desk.

He walked me home to the Roosevelt, which he seemed to regard as a droll choice of hotel, fairly expensive but not classy, I guessed. Yet, as we stood in front of the hotel saying good-bye, he suddenly offered to take me to a matinee the next afternoon, down in Greenwich Village. If my grandmother agreed, he would come to get me around noon. I dared not ask him up to our little suite of rooms (anyway he had an appointment), but I was wild with joy. To think this had happened on *my first day in New York*. When I went upstairs, my grandmother and Isabel were there, and, to do them justice, as astounded as I was by the remarkable event that had befallen me. Not finding me on their return, they had worried; now they were relieved of guilt pangs by the statistically wondrous chance that had brought this man to 46th Street at the very moment that I, thanks to our fight in the museum, was coming along it without a friend in the world. At first they could not take in that this was the Red Cross Knight in the Magna Carta pageant—what a tale to tell Grandpa! If my grandmother finally remembered the Knight (and now I am not sure whether she did or not), it might well be in some typically derogatory way ("the one with the crooked nose in the armor"). Yet in the hotel room, to complete the miracle, she was all smiles; perhaps she was sorry for having given in to Isabel on the American Wing.

Because of Johnsrud, we made peace with each other.

Though I was brimming over with triumph, I managed not to gloat over Archipenko and Saks Fifth Avenue; I let *them* marvel at the catalogue. On their side, no difficulty was made about his taking me to the play the next day; he would bring me home before dark, in plenty of time for us to have dinner and see another play—Elmer Rice's *Street Scene*, I think it was, or *Journey's End*, with an all-male English cast (produced, though I did not know it, by the husband of Ellen Van Volkenburgh Browne). The oddest part was that they were letting me go out not with a boy but a *man*, who was losing some of his hair. In fact, he was only twenty-six, nine years older than I. Still they knew nothing about him; I suspect Isabel told herself that he was someone I had met at the Cornish School. It occurs to me that the explanation lay in a place where I would not have thought to look for it—myself. With the prospect of me on their hands for several days and especially after this morning's dispute, they may have *welcomed* Johnsrud: he came to those two women as a savior too.

It was a play by Mike Gold that he took me to see. Somehow I must have known—or did he have to tell me?—that Mike Gold was a Communist writer who had a regular column in the *Daily Worker*. The play, laid in Mexico, was called *Fiesta*; I suppose it had a connection with the Mexican revolution of a few years back. I did not find it very good but I enjoyed it and enjoyed being with him in the old Provincetown Theatre, where the early O'Neill plays had been done. We rode downtown on the subway—my first subway ride—and he put me in a seat against the wall, at the end of a bench, and then sat himself down beside me. So I would not have to sit next to a Negro, he explained, with his raised eyebrow. I understood the joke, which was not against Negroes but against people like Isabel, who would certainly take that precaution if she had to ride in the subway. We also took the subway back.

I cannot remember whether I saw him again before we went up to Vassar. It may have been the next day—or was it weeks later?—that he took me to see the Georgia O'Keeffes at the Stieglitz gallery and made me look at the Fuller Building on 57th Street and at Bonwit Teller as the best examples of modern design New York had to show. And when did we do the Staten Island ferry ride? In any case, whenever we said good-bye, he instructed me to write to him.

My grandmother and Isabel were certainly not shocked that he had taken me to a play by Mike Gold—the name would not have meant anything to them. I doubt that either of them had heard of the *Daily Worker*. Communism was not one of our family bogeys. That may have been a result of my grandfather's radical Republicanism in his days in the legislature. Unlike the McCarthys, though occasionally hot-tempered, he was tolerant. I never heard him fulminate against the IWW or even mention Communism, pro or con. It was true that he did not like Al Smith.

As for Johnsrud, I do not know why he took me to see a play by Mike Gold. Possibly as a jape or he knew somebody in the company and had free tickets—or both. He was certainly not attracted to Communism; he had his own brand of radicalism—the populist streak. As for me, I find I have forgotten where I stood on Communists in 1929 and what I knew about them. I was aware that there had been a revolution in Russia; my picture of it must have been formed in Minneapolis by the Sunday-magazine section of the paper, where I would have seen pictures of the murdered Tsar's family, the girls in their long white summer dresses and the boy in something like the sailor suits my brothers had had in Seattle. With my interest in royalty, I would have studied those faces and maybe known some of their names. Still, though I surely knew the name of Rasputin (as well as those of the Austrian Archduke Rudolf and poor Maria Vetsera and, for that matter, of the Emperor Maximilian of Mexico, cruelly executed, and his spouse, Carlotta), I feel doubtful about the names Lenin and Trotsky: when did they enter my consciousness? I think back to driving through Taylor Gate in a station taxi with my grandmother and Isabel and

ask myself whether I could have been aware, as a register-
ing freshman, that Lenin had died five years before and
that Trotsky, already expelled from the Party, had just been
exiled. Surely not. Those events, momentous for my personal history, had not counted among Current Events at
Annie Wright—rather, we got the Kellogg-Briand pact. I no
longer saw Mark Sullivan, who might have told me something, and the Rosenberg girls, although Democrats, were
not really interested in politics. I was matriculating at Vassar in the dawn of what I later knew as "third-period Stalin-
ism," and it would take me eight years and a failed marriage
to find out what that was.

Having seen me installed in my room, which shocked my
grandmother by its lack of amenities, she and Isabel left,
with assurances from the house warden that a lamp, a rug,
bedcover, and so on, could be bought downtown at a store
called Luckey Platt. I was alone (no roommate!) in Davison
Hall on the Quad, probably still wearing the smart new Oxford gray suit I had traveled in, with a royal-blue silk blouse
and matching cloche hat, the whole utterly out of keeping
with my campus circumstances. Soon I would have to eat
in the dining-hall with perfect strangers. The outlook was
as friendless as New York had been until I saw Johnsrud
coming briskly toward me on East 46th Street. It would be
better when classes started, but on that first night I did not
know a soul at Vassar, unless you counted Flea Lee, which
I was wise enough not to do.

Actually, there was a girl from Seattle in our entering class.
My grandmother had found out her name—Glee Jamison;
she was the granddaughter of Mr. Skinner of Skinner and
Eddy, shipbuilders, the defendants in the case for over-
charging brought by the government that my grandfather,
appointed Master in Chancery, had gone to Washington the
winter before last to take evidence in. That was when my
grandmother, who stayed in New York, had got her kasha-
colored suit like Katharine Cornell's.

He had decided against Skinner and Eddy but in doing

so seemed to have gained the respect of Mr. Skinner, who told me that he was "the only honest lawyer in Seattle"—it was not the first time I had heard that said. The Skinners, thinking obviously of the Vassar-bound granddaughter, had invited me to dinner at their Seattle house, and my grandfather, with some misgivings, had decided that I could accept. They were the first plutocrats I had met, and though he disapproved of the class they belonged to (and maybe specifically of their trying to cheat the government), he let me go with the stipulation that I take no more than two (!) cocktails—Bacardis, they turned out to be, in a silver shaker. These were the first cocktails, though not the first drinks, I had tasted, proof of Mr. Skinner's wealth and power. At dinner, that night, he had spoken expansively of inviting me to their suite at the Savoy Plaza when they came to New York in October—that was where they always stayed. Nevertheless, once at Vassar, I made no effort to find Glee. When we finally met—she was fattish and blonde and blue-eyed—we saw we had nothing beyond Seattle in common. She did not like Vassar, I gather, and left before the end of freshman year. My grandfather never asked about her, as if to illustrate his lack of interest in the class of businessmen and their progeny. Some time in the fall I did go to that suite in the Savoy Plaza, and the day afterwards the Skinners' son-in-law and business partner, Bill Edris, took me to lunch at a restaurant called L'Aiglon and made a rough pass at me, which I never spoke about.

Anyway I could not count Glee as a person I knew. And I could expect no social help from my senior adviser, a soap-and-water Christian by the name of Hope Slade, who probably did not take to me in my royal-blue blouse. As Flea Lee may well have warned me, the senior adviser routine was a formality, honored only on Registration Day, while the parents were still there.

As it turned out, it was not hard to meet other girls in my dormitory. Indeed it was easy. That was the trouble. I was soon trying to shake the first friends I made. The queerest of these was the girl across the hall, a poor little plucked chicken by the name of Jane Westermann, who had a collection of lariats and bridles and a sister named Helen, known as "Peter." It was Peter who picked me up in the hall before dinner the first night, to introduce me to Jane, her little sister. This amounted to a kind of pimping (for which she doubtless deserved credit; not every older sister would do it) and was effective at the outset: Peter, a knowing junior with hard blue eyes and blond hair cut like a man's, was attractive, positively alluring to a literary freshman; she belonged to an intellectual set that lived in Josselyn and had arcane standards of judgment that terrified noninitiates. Such brilliant, glittery upperclassmen were a vanishing species, dating back maybe to the era of Edna Millay; there were none in the class that followed and emphatically none in mine. Possibly the species of college wits went out with the onset of the depression.

In any case, though I was flattered to be singled out by Peter and even dazzled for a time, the price—friendship with poor Janie—soon began to seem too high, especially as the pitying smiles of Peter and her friends for some of my literary tastes, for my interest in "activities" (such as the freshman debating squad) were all too intimidating. Dropping sad Janie with her absurd lariats was fairly forgivable if only it could lose me the frightening attentions of her older sister. Within a few weeks the Westermanns and I were barely speaking. I think I felt slightly guilty, though, when Jane left college at the end of freshman year, taking her horsey gear with her. She went out west to a ranch, we heard, and that was not surprising; she was surely happier there. What was odd was to learn, from an advertisement in some college publication, that her sister, after graduation, had joined her in running the ranch—a peculiar career choice for a literary intellectual. In the Fiftieth Year Bulletin of the Class of '33, Jane's address is a box number in Bozeman, Montana; maybe Peter is still with her (no address is given for her in the Register of Living Alumnae); I remember hearing years ago that they had both married cowboys.

Though I rapidly shook the Westermanns, Peter may have left an imprint. It may have been from her that I learned to scorn college sings, tree ceremonies, "Vassar devils" (a fudgey mixture of devil's food cake, chocolate sauce, and, I guess, ice-cream), the Outing Cabin, the Cider Mill. In the fall of 1929, all that Vassar folk lore seemed to me as corny as my grandmother McCarthy's electric doughnut-maker. In my four years at Vassar I went maybe twice to the Cider Mill, a nice walk through Dutchess County apple country, but I never had a "devil," which is why I am not sure of what goes into them. But were those aversions spontaneous? I can see them now as partly a contagion from Peter Westermann.

The next friends I made lived in Davison Hall, too. They were Alice Butler from New Haven, Virginia Johnston from Waterbury, Helen Edmundson from Pittsburgh, Elinor Coleman from New York, and Betty Brereton (a navy daughter) from Washington, D.C. Alice had gone to Abbott Academy, Helen to Madeira, Elly to a day school, Horace Mann, in New York; the rest I don't remember.

There were also in Davison, among the freshmen, some New York society girls, mainly from Chapin, whose deaf-sounding voices were constantly calling to each other in corridors, out the windows, across the dining-hall. "Cum-cum!" they called, for Comfort Parker, "Rosil-l-la!" for Rosilla Hornblower, "A-lye-dah!" for Alida Davis. A whole bevy of them, trilling and cawing, lived in Davison and behaved as if no one else did. As it turned out, most of those detested New York girls left Vassar (no more "A-lye-dah," no more "Cum-cum"), and those who stayed were the nucleus of what, by senior year, became my "group." Yet the aversion they inspired that first year in corridors and dining-hall served to draw me together with Alice Butler, Helen Edmundson, and so on, most of whom would soon leave Vassar, too. Our resentment of the bird-chorus of New York debutantes must have made us stick together in sheer self-protection; otherwise we had nothing in common, though of course we never admitted that. We thought we liked each other. The only one I truly liked, though, was Virginia Johnston, from Waterbury and Baltimore, a cool beautiful math major; we had got to be friends through sitting near each other in Durant Drake's Philosophy 105. Sophomore year, when the others except Betty Brereton mercifully left, Ginny and I became roommates after a fashion, turning my single room into our bedroom and hers, across the hall, into our study. It was not a very practical arrangement. I kept her awake at night, talking, and we soon reverted to two singles. At the end of the year, Ginny left to get married to Dick Goss of Scovill Brass, Waterbury. When I moved to Cushing at the beginning of junior year, again I was all by myself.

Johnsrud had given me his address: 50 Garden Place, Brooklyn. Not to seem too eager, maybe I let a week elapse before writing. My letters to him are lost—if he kept them, like me, he probably failed to pay the storage bill on old trunks he sent to the warehouse when we broke up—so I cannot cite what I told him. But I can *guess*, from my word-perfect recollection of a sentence in his reply. "I thought you would find Vassar brittle, smart, and a little empty," he wrote.

"Brittle, smart, and a little empty"—wow! The words ravished me. I kept saying them over and over. But did I believe them? I cannot tell. Maybe they described Flea Lee and Peter Westermann, but they certainly did not apply to my gang in Davison; none of whom with the exception of Ginny could remotely pass for smart, let alone the rest of those things. And hearty, outspoken Miss Kitchel, my faculty adviser, whom I had in freshman composition (English 105)? Or the seniors I admired—tall, serene, beautiful, blue-eyed Elizabeth Beers, for instance, who had just been elected chief justice.

I would think that my letter to him recounting my first impressions had simply been telling him what I thought he

198

would like to hear, feeding him his own idea of Vassar; I would think that if I did not have copies of letters I wrote that same year to Ted Rosenberg in Seattle and that her family thoughtfully saved. There Johnsrud's phrasing (without attribution) recurs as my own observation. On November 1: "But there is too much smart talk, too many labels for things, too much pseudo-cleverness. I suppose I'll get that way, too, though I'm doing my best to avoid it. The scenery is nice in a way, but it's much too pastoral, if you see what I mean. Nice little rounded hills and shorn fat trees. It looks like an English countryside. It is too domesticated. I am homesick for geometric lines, points, and angles." Again, after Christmas: "As for me, I do nothing but bewail my fate for being in this damned assured stupid college and write letters even more assured and stupid than the college. What the hell?"

I wonder how much of this can have been sincere. The only thing I remember is the feeling about the scenery. The gently rolling Hudson River countryside was so like the landscapes in English literature that I *recognized* it in a way. And this was a sort of coming home—pleasurable, though perhaps at first I really did miss the "geometric" firs and spruces of the Puget Sound country. In other words, the feelings I remember, of rapturous discovery that was like a rediscovery, are almost the *opposite* of those I wrote down.

This is alarming, above all to one who has set out to write her autobiography. It raises the awful question of whether there can be multiple truths or just one. About truth I have always been monotheistic. It has been an article of faith with me, going back to college days, that there is a truth and that it is knowable. Thus Vassar either repelled me on the whole by "cleverness" or it didn't. Even allowing for variance of moods, both cannot be true. I see only one way out of the dilemma I am placed in by my own letters. It is an Einsteinian solution, basing itself on the premise that time fatally intervenes between what is seen and the seer. What I foresaw in the first letter—"I suppose I'll get that way, too"—

has in fact happened: I have changed; I have become like Vassar or, better, Vassar changed me while I was not looking, making me more like itself. If I can no longer feel what I felt about the college when I wrote to Ted, it is because I, too, the product of a Vassar education, am now brittle, smart, and a little empty. And oblivious of it.

But no, I do not believe that. I don't mean about myself—how can I judge?—but about how Vassar struck me when I was seventeen, a bright wild girl from Seattle. What the letters seem to hint at is something I have forgotten: that I was not very happy during my first term before I got close to cool, beautiful, glamorous Ginny and warmed to Miss Kitchel's course. Yet already I was impressed by what I still see as the spirit of the college at the time, the gay and tolerant empiricism, the love of reality, the rejection of what I called "labels" in my first letter. If anybody was guilty of sticking labels on things, surely it was Johnsrud. That is not a Vassar habit, and it has never been one of my own faults, congenital or acquired. What I must have been doing in those letters to Ted was a bit of mourning plus a bit of impersonation, speaking to her in a soprano rendition of the Johnsrud voice. Or, more simply, I was trying to speak a language that he would approve of. And the courting of approval, I am sorry to say, *is* in my character. So it fits.

Johnsrud, or "John," as I began to call him, was rehearsing in a play called *The Channel Road*, an adaptation by George S. Kaufman and Alexander Woollcott of a Maupassant story, "Boule de Suif." Arthur Hopkins was the producer—the same who had done *The Jest*—and it was going to open, as most of his plays did, at the Plymouth Theatre. So at Johnsrud's invitation, in the middle of October, I took my first weekend and went down to see him in it, staying at the Vassar Club in the Allerton House, an all-women's hotel.

The story had to do with a group of French aristocrats and rich business people trying to reach the coast by diligence during the War of 1870, when the northern part of the country had been taken by the Germans. The party has

200

a *laisser-passer* from the German commander in Rouen, which they trust to see them through. A last-minute addition to the party is a high-class prostitute with her bountiful hamper of provisions. On this fat girl's virtue, or, rather, on her sacrifice of it, the fate of her companions depends: a German officer in whose power they find themselves demands that she sleep with him, but to the horror of the French respectable people she is too patriotic to want to. John played the count, an aristocratic figure in a redingote who was the spokesman of the French group—the villain, you might say. It was a good part, but the best male part was the German's, played by Siegfried Rumann, a Hopkins discovery of that year—and later a popular movie villain—who became a great friend of John's. The play was witty, with well-written lines, well staged and well acted, and was counted among the three best of the season, or so I wrote to Ted. But it did not last long.

Sixty performances. Whether the poor business they did was connected with the stock-market crash, which had taken place in late October, I cannot guess now. At Vassar that fall news of the crash did not reach me or not for some time. Insofar as the public world impinged on us freshman year, it was mainly in the shape of the Oxford pledge (for peace), Moral Rearmament, Buchmanism, none of which was my cup of tea. The phrase "merchants of death" about the armament-manufacturers was pronounced in chapel, and a favorite villain was Sir Basil Zaharoff. Not till sophomore year, I think, were there apple-sellers in the streets of New York and unemployed men sleeping on park benches. At college it was said that a few girls' fathers jumped out of windows; certainly more girls applied for scholarships. And yet for her engagement present, in 1931, the Goss family gave Ginny a silver-gray Pierce-Arrow touring-car with a folding bar and ice-chest in the middle. The gift, one later heard, "ruined" them: when Ginny came home from her honeymoon, she and Dick had to move into what had once been the chauffeur's apartment over the garage.

I remember seeing my first bread-line in New York that second winter. Yet if it had not been for John, I might not have been really conscious that there was a depression. He moved into a cheap apartment on Bank Street with a friend who was a half-employed architect's draftsman. When *The Channel Road* closed, John was out of work till *Uncle Vanya* with Lillian Gish opened in mid-April—Jed Harris gave him a job in it as assistant stage-manager, with a tiny part. Though he did not have a real kitchen, he was doing his own cooking a lot of the time—things like chile con carne and spaghetti and a recipe for meat loaf his mother sent him. He started making an awful milky colored drink out of raw alcohol, water, and oil of anis which he called anisette and said was Italian; he got the recipe from the actor Eduardo Ciannelli, another great friend. Finally in May of freshman year he took the train up to Vassar, where he met Ginny and was driven around the country in her Packard—this was pre-Pierce-Arrow; one of her admirers had brought it over from Waterbury. That winter in the studio-couch bed of the Bank Street furnished apartment I lost my virginity for the third time. John and I were engaged, I told my friends, not knowing for sure whether we were or what it meant.

8

A good deal of education consists of *un*-learning—the breaking of bad habits as with a tennis serve. This was emphatically true of a *Vassar* education: where other colleges aimed at development, bringing out what was already there like a seed waiting to sprout, Vassar remade a girl. Vassar was transformational. No girl, it was felt, could be the same after Kitchel's English or Sandison's Shakespeare, to say nothing of Lockwood's Press.

For example, English 165 swiftly learned that a bowdlerized text would not be tolerated in Miss Sandison's classroom. If one turned up, it was banished with a shudder like a deck of cards removed by fire-tongs from a Baptist home. In our sophomore year, poor Maddie Aldrich (Margaret Chanler Astor Aldrich, later one of "the group") innocently brought an expurgated version of *The Two Gentlemen of Verona* to class, and Miss Sandison spotted it; it was not like the big blue Oxford that most of the rest of us had. Maddie's little book, suede or tooled leather, was probably a family hand-me-down that had already done service with her brother Dickie at Harvard. The Aldriches, who were related to John Jay Chapman and "Sheriff Bob" Chanler (the one that married Lina Cavalieri and got the famous "WHO'S LOONY NOW?" cable from his brother Archie, who had changed his name to Challoner and was doing time in a madhouse for shooting his butler), dear souls, were land-poor and practiced the strictest economy at Rokeby, their Hudson River property, where Mrs. Aldrich (known as "the American Florence Nightingale" and "the Angel of Porto Rico" in the Spanish-American War) distributed home-made pen-wipers for Christmas. Maddie's punishment, to get back to that, was to read aloud, from Miss Sandison's copy, Launce's speech to his dog (Act IV, Scene 4): "He had not been there (bless the mark) a pissing-while, but all the chamber smelt him."

No doubt it taught Maddie some sort of lesson. I can still hear the bad word bravely pronounced in her pretty Saint Tim's voice. And I can still hear Miss Sandison's own delicate light voice—*she* was Bryn Mawr—lecturing us, apropos *The Two Gentlemen* and the sonnets, on the Platonizing tendency—male homosexuality—of the Elizabethan period. I knew about homosexuals, but it woke me up to learn that the subject could be talked about so coolly in the classroom by a small pretty gray-haired full professor with dark eyes and a face like a Johnny-jump-up, which unfortunately had a purple birthmark across one finely boned cheek. It was that, we assumed, which had kept her an old maid; in our senior year a product called Covermark was put on the market, and, though she was quick to use it and it completely hid her disfigurement, I felt almost sad for her because it had come too late, when she was over forty. Well! Darling Miss Sandison, whose scholarly specialty was Sir

Arthur Gorges (pronounced "Gorgeous"), 1557–1625, love poet, translator of Lucan, Ralegh's friend; her edition of his English poems was published in 1953. . . . It was she, I discovered, who had written the college catalogue, so very clear, that had made me at Annie Wright Seminary choose Vassar in preference to the two others. I hope I told her that.

Then there was Lockwood's press course (Contemporary Press), a junior year offering renowned for the un-learning she made girls in it do. According to the course description, the class was taught to read the press critically—doubtless a healthy thing. But it was not just the fine art of reading *behind* the news that the girls learned, sitting around a long table seminar style; they were getting indoctrinated with a potent counter-drug. The class, we heard (I never took it), was the scene, almost like a camp meeting, of many a compulsory transformation as hitherto dutiful Republican daughters turned into Socialists and went forth to spread the gospel. It was said that Miss Lockwood insisted that a girl completely break with her mother as the price of winning her favor. The effect on the girl was a kind of smug piety, typical of the born anew, that could last for years, long after the one-time converts, now alumnae (married, with 2.4 children), had turned back into Republicans.

Needless to say, I was in no danger. Having never been influenced by the politics of my grandparents, I did not require conversion. A young person who disliked certitudes of any kind was proof against the recruiting methods of the "charismatic" Miss Lockwood, who had a moustache and a deep "thrilling" voice. There was instant antagonism between us, which did not come to a head, though, until junior year when the Blake-to-Keats course, which I had been taking with my own dear favorite, Miss Kitchel, was turned over at mid-years to Miss Lockwood. We knew that Miss Kitchel was going on a half-sabbatical to work on George Eliot in the British Museum but we did not expect to be handed over to Miss Lockwood. The Blake-to-Keats course was given in two sections, and most of us in Kitchel's were there because Lockwood taught the other. Even though there had already been ructions—over Wordsworth's "Michael," which we hated—in Miss Kitchel's class, our section felt cheated by the transfer. With me, it was war from the very first day.

Many years later, over an Old-Fashioned in a downtown Poughkeepsie restaurant, Miss Kitchel told me the story, as she had heard it, of a famous passage-at-arms between the dread Miss Lockwood and a very pert me. One morning, it seemed, Miss Lockwood, who was much given to leaning across the professorial desk, chin in hand, and raking the class with her burning dark gaze, had fired an opening question at us in her profoundest bass: "GIRLS, what is poetry?" At which, from a back row, I put up a saucy hand and sweetly recited: "*Coleridge* says it's the best words in the best order." She could have slapped me, I imagine.

Today the portentous Miss Lockwood seems like a grotesque caricature of the Vassar teacher as shaker-up. At the time I hated her too fervently to view her as a simple exaggeration. One day I actually cried during an argument with her after class, and of course that made me hate her all the more. Miss Kitchel and Miss Sandison shook up their girls more gently. They were not at all partial to Helen D. Lockwood but were too high-minded to let us see it when we were students. The idea that English majors were drawn up in hostile camps, one pro-Kitchel (or Sandison), the other pro-Lockwood, was a myth propagated by Lockwood's disciples (cf. Norine in *The Group*). One of the delights of Kitchel and Sandison was that they would never seek to make a disciple of a young person or encourage the formation of any kind of alignment. They were trying to teach us to stand on our own.

I suppose that the "two hostile camps" myth ("You people were the aesthetes. We were the politicals. We eyed each other from across the barricades") included the notion that Kitchel and Sandison were political conservatives. I must have half-believed that myself, for I remember the surprise I felt when a poll of the college taken just before the 1932 election (when Roosevelt, our trustee and Dutchess County neighbor, was voted into the White House) showed the faculty as overwhelmingly pro-Socialist (perhaps 80%) and that Miss Sandison, when I exclaimed on it, seemed surprised by my surprise, which let me understand—correctly—that she and Miss Kitchel belonged to the 80%. It is easy to see now that they were Norman Thomas Socialists, which eventually I, too, became, but the only directly political discussion I remember with either of them (as long as I was an undergraduate; afterwards it was different—we were equals) took place in Sandison's Shakespeare: someone—was it I?—compared King Lear to Woodrow Wilson.

Unlike Sandison and Kitchel, Miss Lockwood was a rich woman, though apparently few had suspected it till she left her fortune to the college on her death. Miss Peebles (Contemporary Prose Fiction) was rich, too, and lived in a well-furnished house of her own off campus, rather than in a spare college dormitory like Miss Sandison and Miss Kitchel, who had apartments opposite each other on the first floor of Williams Hall with a screened porch in the back that they shared. Until recently I had not grasped the fact that they took their meals, with the rest of the Williams women, in a sort of mess-hall.

With all the enmity I felt and possibly still feel for Miss Lockwood, looking back on her, I can now see that she embodied in her aggressive way faculty traits that could be found even in the mildest of teachers such as the retiring, duteous Miss Swenarton, who lived with her mother. Almost twenty years after graduation, coming back to write something about the college, I was amazed to hear Miss Swenarton, now gray-haired, gently teaching English 105 to a docile class of freshmen in the tried-and-true icon-smashing way. Shades of Miss Kitchel; who had retired, suffering from heart disease—evident in her flushed cheeks—only the reading-list was different. Under Miss Kitchel, we had started with Benedetto Croce and Tolstoy's *What Is Art?* Miss Swenarton was giving them *High Wind in Jamaica*. The effect was the same: to disturb the girls' preconceptions. Our class had been told by Tolstoy that Shakespeare was a meretricious author, above all in *King Lear*; this class was hearing that children are moral monsters ("said to have ended the Victorian myth of childhood," the *Oxford Companion to English Literature* observes of the book), and reacting with shock and anger. Miss Swenarton's soft persistent questions were aimed at their unexamined epistemology: how did they know what they thought they knew about children? With a faint smile, she called on a student who had worked as a baby-sitter and had direct experience to contribute.

It was in English 105, writing my weekly "effusion" ("Girls, hand me your effusions") for hearty Anna Kitchel, that I un-learned the ugly habit, picked up at Annie Wright, of putting those circles like fish-eyes, instead of dots, over my "i"s. By May of 1930, in a letter to Ted Rosenberg, the circles, as if on tip-toe, had disappeared. I wonder what other practices under her cheery blue eye folded their tents like the Arabs and silently stole away.

She was our Class Advisor and my faculty adviser, too, and she must have undertaken to reform my taste. It was done so matter-of-factly that I was unaware of any change. It must have been Miss Kitchel's doing that I stopped being crazy about Swinburne. Perhaps that happened during the "fourth hour" I elected with her—a once-a-week session for which she let me write a paper on Turgenev. Or at tea in her apartment as she puffed on her English Ovals, inducing on my part a shift from Marlboros.

She was an expansive woman, big-boned, high-colored, with a shock of fair, graying hair and very light-blue eyes. Smith was her college, but she was a middle-westerner, from Milwaukee, and had a rich middle-western diction. Her graduate work had been done at Wisconsin, considered advanced at the time, and she had an admiration for Alexander Meiklejohn, the educational reformer, who had been at

Madison after she came east. Her usual method of conveying instruction was to find the comical side of the book, person, institution she was seeking to open our eyes to. "Oh, he was a rare bird!" she exclaimed of Wordsworth in Blake-to-Keats, after telling us the whole story (then generally unmentioned) of the French girl Annette Vallon and the illegitimate child the great revolutionary disowned. I loved hearing Miss Kitchel marry the classic *rara avis* to the derisive American "that bird," with a rolling "r" that no Daniel Jones dictionary of phonetics could ever do justice to. Surely she would have chuckled over naughty Algernon Swinburne, both life and works—all those verses too easily memorized occupying valuable space in my brain. "From too much love of living,/ From hope and fear set free . . ." I don't remember when those dearly loved words turned to derision in my ears. I guess I just dumped Swinburne without a backward thought. And Edna Millay? "You might as well be calling yours/ What never will be his,/ And one of us be happy,/ There's few enough as is." Did Anna Kitchel "kill" her for me with a jovial dart of satire? And James Branch Cabell? When did he go?

From his furnished room in Bank Street Johnsrud, too, was taking my reeducation in hand. Like Shaw, he was a born pedagogue. His own father had been a school principal back in northern Minnesota, who had lost his post through the chicanery of local officials and been reduced to selling encyclopedia sets and artificial limbs for a living. John was thinking of writing a play about him, to be called *University*, in which he made him the president of a state university instead of the principal of a high school. He spoke of his parents as "Iver" and "Molly," and I did not think I would like them. Older people were attracted to John— Adrienne Morrison, the agent (mother of Joan Bennett); Jed Harris; Arthur Hopkins; Paul Reynolds, the editor of *Red Book*. . . . But there was one older man that he took me to meet who was a surprising friend for John to have.

That was Albert Parker Fitch, D.D., pastor of the Park

Avenue Presbyterian Church, a handsome white-haired product of Harvard College and Union Theological Seminary, celebrated as a fighting liberal and as a preacher. It seemed that he had taught religion at Carleton College when John was an undergraduate and they had somehow kept up a friendship, partly no doubt because Dr. Fitch loved the theatre. Maybe he had gone to see *The Channel Road* or John had got him tickets, and on Sunday evenings John was often invited to the rectory—I guess it should be "manse" for a Presbyterian—to read poetry aloud with Dr. Fitch and drink a few highballs. One Sunday when I was down from Vassar he took me along and again on other nights. So that when Dr. Fitch came up that winter to preach in chapel, I could boast of actually knowing him, I a "lowly" freshman.

"Known as a university preacher," his obituary in the *Times* said, and I was puffed with pride in him when I went up to speak to him outside after chapel was over. He had shocked the Vassar congregation by SWEARING in the pulpit! Yes, he had thundered "God damn them!" in a wonderful voice; his sermon had been on the munitions-makers, "merchants of death." I am not sure whether he was actually a pacifist; to denounce munitions-makers at that time you did not have to be. But he was some sort of radical; that was clear. I think Miss Kitchel was aware of him; he had been at Amherst, where Meiklejohn had been president. Certainly he knew Durant Drake, whose silly Philosophy course I was taking; "the last of a long line of maiden aunts," Dr. Fitch recalled, and I must have quoted the *mot* to Miss Kitchel. It was a good description, and I have occasionally thought of it since. All the more eerie to find it, applied to quite a different Harvard figure, in a strange, slightly Jamesian novel he published in the twenties and that I have just now come upon. *None So Blind*, Macmillan, 1924, and all about Harvard—you would never guess a Presbyterian minister had written it.

In any case, Dr. Fitch's sermon really upset a lot of people at Vassar. He was not asked to preach there again. I could not understand the attitude. If you were going to pronounce an *anathema sit*, the pulpit was the place to do it: he had only been calling on God to do His rightful job of damnation. But if you said that, few would recognize what an *anathema sit* was. Vassar had a capacity for ignorance that did not suit its style, and I myself was always shocked and startled to see it displayed.

Dr. Fitch well knew what an *anathema sit* was. He knew classics and had a passion for language. He and John shared a weakness for Robinson Jeffers; he loved to have John read *Roan Stallion* aloud. *Tamar*, too, one night, and *The Tower Beyond Tragedy*, and above all a short poem beginning "Shine, perishing republic" that was about the U.S. Both Dr. Fitch and Johnsrud were crazy about that poem (Jeffers' best, said John), which evidently said something to them politically. Today that seems a bit odd, since to modern ears the poem, hymning the decline into the west of our setting republic, sounds slightly fascistic. Neither of them was that, but both may have been Nietzscheans, enamored of the notion of the superior individual—a far cry from Hitler, as it turned out.

"Divine bombast!" pronounced Dr. Fitch when John had finished reading. Or was that what he would say about Marlowe, his great favorite, whom he always read aloud to us himself? In the "manse" I thrilled to his voice intoning *Tamburlaine*, which I was hearing for the first time; "Come live with me and be my love" was all the Marlowe we had had at Annie Wright. He would let his voice linger over the name of the fierce Timur's captive and only love, the Egyptian sultan's daughter: "Ah, fair Zenocrate, divine Zenocrate,/ Fair is too foul an epithet for thee." "Now walk the angels on the walls of heaven,/ As sentinels to warn th'immortal souls,/ To entertain divine Zenocrate." As though he wanted to make the rafters of the paneled clerical study ring with the praises of the sultan's daughter. I do not remember a Mrs. Fitch's being present. Perhaps she had died. The New York *Times* tells me that there was one, and apparently she was English.

I would listen raptly, too, to *The Tragical History of Dr.*

Faustus, especially the end, when Faust is waiting for the devil to come and get him. *"O lente, lente currite noctis equi,"* down to the awful screams for mercy: "See see where Christ's blood streams in the firmament,/ One drop would save my soul, half a drop, ah my Christ."

The connection was obvious with *Don Giovanni*, which Johnsrud took me to that same winter at the Metropolitan, the first opera I ever saw. We were way up in the highest reaches of the gallery, in standing room, but I understood the plot and understood from the way John behaved that he attached importance to this occasion on my behalf, as an initiation. He had chosen the opera with care and not mainly for the singers; there was Rosa Ponselle, I think, and Beniamino Gigli as Don Ottavio, but I cannot even remember who sang Don Giovanni. John saw the piece as theatre certainly (which most operas aren't) and maybe he was fond of the sulphurous ending, as in *Dr. Faustus*: the soul of a great sinner being carried off howling to hell. He was much taken with the devil; his broken nose and raised eyebrow gave him a devil's face, which he treated as a saturnine mask. And possibly one thing he and Dr. Fitch had in common was a certain diabolism, which had come to John through Shaw (who had his own Luciferian set of eyebrows), while Dr. Fitch may have gone straight back to the source—Holy Writ—for an interest in damnation. In his novel, *None So Blind*, there is a clear representation of satanism in an epicurean graduate student (who is also given to secret drinking and reading pornography in the Latin original); he has an intensely Puritan mother and a very Bostonian sister (not badly drawn) who could stand in for Lilith. Flirtations with the prince of darkness are fairly common among religious men, though less so, I would say, among Calvinists; it is more a High Church Episcopalian proclivity. Without a mass, it is harder to have a black mass.

But Dr. Fitch, with his love of the pomp and circumstance of the language, was a strange kind of Presbyterian anyway. Enlarging on the *"O lente, lente currite noctis equi"*

("Run slowly, slowly, ye horses of the night": Faustus, awaiting the hour of his certain damnation), he explained that the quotation was from Ovid's *Amores*; there the licentious Roman poet was begging the night hours, figured as swift horses, to slow down for him while he made love to his Corinna or whoever it was. "Delicious blasphemy" or words to that effect was the minister's appreciative verdict. But Marlowe was an atheist, and Dr. Fitch, I assume, was not.

I remember, too, the soft, reasonable, almost caressing tone of his voice as he read Mephistophiles' "But this is hell, nor am I out of it," shook his white head in awe, and read it again. This whispery sentence was perhaps my first intimation of what hell might be. Of course, like Johnsrud, like many a fine preacher, Dr. Fitch was a histrion.

You may wonder why Johnsrud and I, when it finally came to the point in June 1933, did not ask Dr. Fitch to marry us. Probably John did, and that was how, on telephoning the church, he got the assistant minister, who told him that Dr. Fitch had had a stroke. "The saddest thing," the aide confided, in lowered tones, "is that he can't remember the Lord's Prayer." I used that, forty-six years later, in *Cannibals and Missionaries* for the old Episcopal bishop. In fact, as I have only now learned from *Who Was Who*, Dr. Fitch did not die for eleven more years. Eleven years without the Lord's Prayer—hell for a minister.

Instead of him, for our marriage, we asked the Reverend Karl Reiland, of St. George's Church on Stuyvesant Square, another orator and rebel of the liberal sort (there was a Vassar connection), but John and I were too unimportant to rate Dr. Reiland, and he passed us on to one of his curates. That is pretty much the wedding described in *The Group.*

Ever since I lost my faith, in the convent when I was twelve, I have been an unswerving atheist. Yet I have had good relations with the clergy. There is an attraction on both sides, perhaps there has been something slightly paradoxical, equivocal in the situation. In the case of Dr. Fitch, I

suppose I found it piquant to spend Sunday evenings listening to quasi-erotic (and atheistic!) poetry in the book-lined
study of a minister of the gospel. And the fact that it was
the *Park Avenue* Presbyterian Church (today it is not called
that) could not fail to excite my aspiring Puget Sound soul.
All those mornings spent poring over *Vogue* opposite my
grandmother with her mending in the upstairs bay window
had left their mark. I still yearned for admission into the
New York society I read about but which was forever barred
to me by our position on the map—there was never a word
in *Vogue* about what happened socially in Seattle, scarcely
even about San Francisco unless it happened to a Spreckels.
Dr. Fitch's fashionably located fieldstone church must have
made me feel I was getting warmer. John and I went once
to divine service—or whatever the Presbyterians call it—on
a Sunday morning; it was my only experience of the Presbyterian rite, different from the Episcopalian in that the
minister made up his own prayer—at any rate the main one—
instead of using the set prayers of the prayer book. To
someone of Dr. Fitch's literary gifts, this was a literally
heaven-sent opportunity for rolling sonorous vowels and
consonants off the tongue. I was struck by the amount of
feeling, sounding more deep-dredged than our P.E. General Thanksgiving, that he put into his prayer. Of course,
being a performer, he had seen that John and I were there.

John was initiating me into the mysteries of New York.
Whenever I could come down from college, he showed me
not only the perennial lovers' haunts, such as the Barnard
Cloisters, the Staten Island Ferry, Fifth Avenue bus-tops,
but the new Museum of Modern Art, the Yiddish Café Royal,
the Russian Bear and Romany Marie's, a speakeasy with
sawdust on the floor called Julius's, Barbetta's restaurant.
He got cut-rate tickets at Gray's for the theatre. We saw
Clayton, Jackson, and Durante in a night club called Les
Ambassadeurs.

At Vassar, my Davison friends, Ginny excepted, had rapidly lost interest for me. Even before Thanksgiving, I was

At Vassar,
sophomore year

Main Hall, showing South Tower, on right

Miss Sandison, in the library

Vassar library

Miss Kitchel

Library

Frani Blough

Cushing dining hall

Uncle's Been Dreaming, *adapted from Dostoievsky, Hall Play, 1932.*
Elizabeth Bishop is the little man in black, in front of the fireplace; Mary,
standing, is in profile at right

Elizabeth Bishop, from 1933 yearbook photo
of Vassar Miscellany News *staff*

Main Hall with "soap palace" and South Tower in background

With "Mannie"
Rousuck of the
Carleton Galleries in
Portsmouth, Rhode
Island, 1950

Vassar yearbook photo

Wedding photo, June 21, 1933. Harold Cooper Johnsrud and Mary, at the apartment of Mr. and Mrs. T. R. Sunde

tired of hearing about Alice Butler's boarding-school room-mate, and Betty Brereton's father in the Navy. Yet something had happened between us that condemned us to stick together. It concerned a small, very pretty girl with fine-spun reddish fair hair, green eyes, and a soft childish lisping voice who was literary, like me—her name was Elinor Coleman, and she wrote short stories. She was the only one of us to come from New York, where she had gone to a school called Horace Mann, which she talked about a lot. She was also the only one who had been abroad; last summer she had gone with her mother to Le Touquet, a resort in Normandy, where her mother had made the *gaffe* of announcing in the hotel dining-room, "Every man who makes water here gets a medal for it." We all liked Elly a lot, even though I took exception to the poetic prose of her stories, much too dainty for my taste. But we were still friends, all of us, when one afternoon in the dormitory someone—I no longer know who—came to tell us that Elinor Coleman was Jewish. We laughed. If charming golden snub-nosed sheltered Elly resembled anything, it was a girl straight out of a convent.

You have guessed it; she *was* Jewish. But we were slow to catch on, the slowest being big fair Alice Butler from New Haven, who just could not contain her guffaws when Elly came home and was confronted by chortling Alice and the rest of us expecting her to join in the merriment. "Well, Elly, ha ha, we hear you're Jewish, ha ha." I think I knew almost before she said it, in a quiet voice. "Why, yes, I am." But the disbelieving laughter continued; big Alice's was the last to stop. Finally every face had grown as grave as Elly's. There must have been five of us standing there; Elly had sat down and turned her unsmiling little face up to ours. It was a terrible moment; there was no way we could take those hee-haws back. If I had been the first to believe that she was serious, I was helped by a memory of darling Susie Loewenstein in the convent—red-gold curls, retroussé nose, she had looked quite a lot like Elly. And nobody would have guessed *she* was Jewish, if it had not been for the name.

Out of shame, we were forced to stay friends with her. We never again mentioned her being Jewish. Neither did she. But it came up unavoidably, of its own accord, as we got to know her better, as we met her mother and her grandmother, both of whom did look Jewish, especially the grandmother. At Thanksgiving time Elly invited me to stay with her in their apartment in New York—it was on West End Avenue, which, though I did not know it, was then at the height of its fashion among better-off Jews. And as Elly's house guest, I finally "made it" into New York society—coming-out parties with "name" bands and the young men in dinner jackets, a stag line, and a dining-room of the Hotel Plaza turned into a Childs' at dawn to serve breakfast of scrambled eggs and bacon and flapjacks (flipped before our eyes, just like in a Childs' window) with maple syrup and sausages. Thousands and thousands of dollars spent on glamour in the first winter of the depression—in Seattle we had never even imagined anything like it. I was in high society, no question. The only thing was that it was *Jewish* high society.

The young men I danced with went to Yale and Haverford (no Harvard or Princeton), yet they did not look quite the same as the Yale men Ginny knew who had names like "Huck" Aldrich and Dutton Noble and Dick Goss. These had queer names, some of them, like Justin Bijur, that seemed to go with frizzy hair and pouting lips. Looking back, I am not sure that this was in fact the summit of New York Jewish society; there were no Schiffs or Lewisohns or Seligmanns among my partners. One of the chief beaux of those dances was "Andy" Goodman, whom I later (at second-hand) knew as "Mr. Andrew" at Bergdorf Goodman when my saleslady was sending "upstairs" to the business office to know if I could have a further reduction on the sale price. It was garment money, I guess, and furniture-store money and jewelry money rather than banking money that was clasping me to its shirt front in my long ice-green satin dress. But I was unaware then of all the layers of German-Jewish society and was awed by the heavy spending.

The Coleman ladies, both widows, were not rich, I could tell, but they dressed well and Elly had nice clothes, even if she didn't seem to have any close friends in the world she took me into, or, rather, none among the girls. If she had had, I might have met Florine Klingenstein, who became my friend later, via another route, after I was out of college. But maybe Florine, whose family were English Jews, belonged to a higher reach. It seems to me now that Elly's mother and grandmother were launching her that year all fitted out, like a spruce little privateer, on the trade routes of upper Jewish matrimony. And the reader can rest assured that she secured her prize. She left Vassar at the end of freshman year.

Alice Butler and Helen Edmundson left college themselves at the same time, and Betty Brereton found other friends. It strikes me that Elly's being Jewish was the cause of our break-up. Our mass refusal to believe that she was Jewish made us look like a bunch of anti-Semites; the common memory of that was an embarrassment. Who would not feel the need to separate after such an experience? In any case, that is what happened. By sophomore year, Ginny and I were alone and glad of it.

One question, though. Shouldn't I have mentioned my Jewish grandmother? Apparently the appropriateness of doing so did not enter my mind. I never considered it, not even in the privacy of my thoughts. In fact, I remember noting with interest at one of those big dances that I was the only Gentile present.

It was as though I had forgotten the flock of Morgensterns in my family tree; out of sight, out of mind. By senior year this had changed. Doubtless the rise of Hitler had something to do with it. By senior year I was well aware of having a Jewish grandmother and aware of it—let me be blunt—as something to hide. I excused myself by saying to my conscience that I could not fight on all fronts at once. In Waterbury, whenever I visited Ginny, I had to live down being Irish. To Ginny's admirers, just out of Yale, it was a rich joke that a girl named Mary McCarthy should be drinking cocktails with them at the country club: Irish were mill workers at the Chase and the Scovill and American Brass plants. There was a dirty song, "Mary Anne McCarthy went out to dig some clams," though I never understood what was dirty in it: "All that Mary got was oysters,/ All that Mary got was oysters,/ She didn't get a goddamn clam." . . . Ginny's men deeply chuckled over that name of mine, and their club-mates, driving me off in their touring-cars, loved it, too. It was not so different from that other ha, ha, ha, of "Elly, we hear you're Jewish."

All this had come as such a surprise to me that I could not take it seriously; in Minneapolis and Seattle, to be Irish was to be among the "gentles," entitled to look down on Swedes, Norwegians, and Finns. Nonetheless I did not wish to add another handicap to those I already carried. And concealing it was easier because nobody would think of asking a person named McCarthy if she was Jewish. Seattle, which knew my history, was far away.

Not far enough, however. A bad moment came when my friend Frani Blough from Pittsburgh announced that she was planning to take a trip to Seattle with her mother the autumn after we graduated and, naturally, expected to meet my grandparents. For months before the threatened visit my guilty imagination was tortured by pictures of that meeting. I was unable to decide how Jewish my grandmother looked or didn't look. I reviewed her glinting dark eye, her very slightly hooked, "aquiline," nose, her still-black hair, her rouge. How would that register with Mrs. Blough and her daughter? "Why didn't she *tell* us, Frani?" I could hear the dialogue begin. "As I said to your father, nobody would have thought the worse of her. . . ."

I was too much ashamed of these worries to confide them in anyone—John, for instance, who by that time had met my grandparents and would have been able to give me his objective estimate of whether my grandmother would look Jewish or not to Frani. I could not bring myself to say a word to him. My fears were the more shameful in that Frani,

as I knew, was free of prejudices. That was not the problem. It was simply that if she recognized my grandmother's
Jewish traits—assuming they *were* recognizable—she would
wonder at my never having mentioned that detail in the
whole course of our friendship. And she would be right. It
would be useless to plead that the subject had never happened to come up, that if I had been asked, I would have
told, which was true: I would not have gone so far as to
deny Augusta Preston, or, rather, her Jewishness, outright,
like Peter in the Garden, whom I could never forget—"I
know not the man." Still, that did not make me better, only
less bad than some famously craven apostle.

The worst feature of this story is that I do not know the
ending, not even now. After Frani's return from her Seattle
visit, there was nothing in her conversation or behavior to
show whether she had noticed anything . . . what shall I
say . . . Levantine? Or not. And I had no way of determin-
ing whether her opinion of me had altered. She had made
me the Madonna—beautiful and good—in a Christmas tab-
leau she directed senior year. Would she still do that?

If I asked her now to think back more than fifty years to
that visit, she probably would not remember. Anyway I
would be too shy to bring it up. And, supposing I overcame
that and asked, how would she differentiate at this remote
distance what she knows of my story today, having read
my memoirs, from what she may have made out for herself
sitting opposite my grandmother in the grass-papered living-room of the Seattle house? My punishment, I guess, for
that old sin of mine (a variety of false witness) is that I shall
never find out.

My friendship with Frani Blough, which went back to freshman year in the Chem Lab, was a watershed for me at Vassar. She was the reason Ginny and I were going to move to
Cushing and that I went there on my own when Ginny did
not come back. Frani was my first and for a while my only

literary friend. Both her parents had been teachers. Her father, from Indiana (like Miss Sandison), was a metallurgist when he was recruited by the Aluminum Company of America (Mellon), and her mother had taught high-school English in Iron Mountain, Michigan. There was a lot of that left in small, sandy Frani; I remember hearing her say that the depression had not affected her parents because they lived on the income of their income, that is, rather modestly. They owned what had been the first Mrs. Mellon's little house known as "the Jewel Box" in the East Liberty section of Pittsburgh, not a fashionable neighborhood; Mrs. Blough collected china, including a line of Toby jugs on the mantel-piece in the dining-room, washed her breakfast dishes in a bowl of hot water at the table, which she claimed was an old American custom; she "took in" numerous periodicals such as *The Nineteenth Century and After* (which eventually turned into *Twentieth Century*), and *Life and Letters Today*, English journals mainly that were spread out for reading on a library table as in an English country house; she was interested in the College Boards and in her Scottish ancestors and had been with Mr. Blough "over the sea to Skye" as well as several times to the Lake Country; she taught a class in English for poor girls in the downtown YWCA and had Frani and me give lectures to it when I came to stay in the spring of senior year; both she and Mr. Blough were fond of the theatre and went with a bachelor friend of the family to whatever play John happened to be in that came to Pittsburgh—that had included *Uncle Vanya* with Lillian Gish, whom they took out to supper afterwards. Mr. Blough was short, dark, spry, and humorous; his family name, I believe, was a corruption or re-spelling of a Swiss name, perhaps "Blau"; when prohibition ended, he was fond of serving sparkling Vouvray.

Frani was their only child; her first name was pronounced "Fraynee" and was a Swiss "little name," I think. It was very like her parents (as if Blough were not enough!) to have given the child a baptismal name that was bound to be mispronounced and required erudite footnoting. All my life I have been correcting people—the latest being Vassar's last president—bent on calling her Franny.

Frani had been to Bath and knew Dove Cottage before she reached puberty; she knew Botticelli and Fra Filippo Lippi. Yet she had had time to be sent to various camps, especially a sailing one on Cape Cod, where red-haired Miss Belding, the Vassar Physical Education head, had been a moving spirit, along with "Dr. B.," who taught us Freshman Hygiene. She had gone to the Walnut Hill School, in Natick, Massachusetts, where she and Elizabeth Bishop had studied with a wonderful English teacher named Miss Prentiss. But Bishop, though she was a year older than we were, did not arrive at Vassar until our sophomore year.

By that time I had been to visit Frani at the end of the summer at Osterville, on Cape Cod, where we played golf—the last time, mercifully, I ever would—at the Wianno Golf Club, took Mrs. Blough, who did not drive a car, to the hairdresser, and dropped in on one of Mr. Blough's associates, a first vice-president of the Aluminum Company of America, who had green silk wallpaper in the living-room of his summer house. Soon "E. B.," as his wife always called him, would be a vice-president of Aluminium Ltd. (Canadian) because of some ruling of the Anti-Trust Division that had obliged the Mellon interests to break up their monopoly. Anyway he had bought Frani a nice new little Ford that summer, and we went off in it to visit Pittsburgh friends of hers in Maine, at Biddeford Pool, where they had a cottage.

All this was my first experience of the New England seacoast. I remember a drawbridge—didn't we have them out west?—buying fall apples from a roadside stand, the long curve of the beach at Ogunquit and a hotel where we had tea—and maybe a bootleg cocktail?—on the porch. Finally there were the "pools" like great salt-water puddles, a rundown dock with some sailboats and some lanky, gaunt peeling boys who sailed them, most of whom seemed to be named "Stackpole" (an example of imitative form) and to have gone to Milton Academy. And there was the Schoyer family from Pittsburgh. A tanned dark-eyed mother (no make-up) always dressed in white cotton dresses and white buttoned-up sweaters—it was cold in September; Frani's friend, Polly, who went to Radcliffe, and two brothers, Bill and Preston. Bill, the older one, went to Yale and wanted to be a newspaperman. There was a wonderful moon reflected in the water, which was going to be too icy to swim in, and we ate clams and lobsters, probably, with Parker House rolls.

They had a big white frame cottage with a porch and perhaps a swing; doubtless the paint was peeling and blistering like those tall boys' noses. Upstairs there were white iron beds that could stand paint, too. The person I liked best was Polly's mother, who must have worked very hard to keep it all going. I think her husband had died. When I look back on her, I recall a phrase somewhere in Hawthorne about the dear New England ladies being more *ladies* than any Englishwoman ever could be. I liked that.

In the fall, when Bill, the older brother, came to Vassar to see me, he was driving an old tin can of a car—a real heap. He was a romantic and fell a little bit in love with me, as we discussed literature and some course he was taking at Yale. As a romantic, he decided to rename me "Poppy," which was flattering, but it also sounded foolish. We drove around the Dutchess County roads in his car, talking about books and his plans for his life. I don't think we ever parked. His younger brother, Preston, became a successful war novelist, and Polly's son, his nephew, is a deconstructionist at Yale.

At Vassar Frani and I, even before I moved to Cushing, continued to be friends. But I cannot date events in our friendship. There was an afternoon we spent climbing apple trees together on Sunset Hill over the lake and talking about Shelley, whom neither of us liked very much. Frani's drawling little voice came from a nearby branch saying that Shelley's personality was over-prominent in his poetry, like a too-prominent nose, which made me laugh so that I risked falling out of my tree. That must have been junior year, when we were both in Blake-to-Keats, probably in the spring, when Lockwood was teaching it. Junior year we both read *Sanctuary* and *Death in the Afternoon* and did a lot of deriding of Hemingway. But I am not sure when it was that we used to skate at night on that same lake, below Sunset Hill; it might have been the year before. Freshman year we had both taken Miss Olive Lammert of the Chemistry Department out to dinner at the Vassar Lodge and had artichokes or mushrooms under glass—our two favorite things—and when I mentioned brushing my teeth with some abrasive powder, Miss Lammert said dryly, "Why not Sapolio or Dutch Cleanser?" That humorous thrust has lodged in my mind along with the picture of her, as she was found a bit later in the Chem Lab with an empty bottle of poison near her hand—why? Frani and I discussed it with Kitchel and Sandison, who had been Miss Lammert's good friends, but we never learned any more. Just as we never knew why handsome Miss Tappan of the Classics Department (I had her in Medieval and Renaissance Latin, and she played Phaedra in Greek in Hallie Flanagan's production of the *Hippolytus*) left Vassar our senior year to become an Episcopal nun.

Like me, Frani was taking Classics, which had classes in Avery Hall, the old Riding Academy, behind Main. But Frani was in Greek, and I was in Latin, under stately Miss Haight (*Horace and His Art of Enjoyment*) and others, although I did take a year of beginning Greek with Mrs. Ryberg, which I did not like—too many small untranslatable words like μην and δε. Miss Kitchel declared that my Latinate mind ("Johnsonian," she said, on another day) was too perspicuous for the shadings of Greek; as my faculty adviser, she let me drop Greek after sophomore year—a mistake. But Frani persisted. Having started freshman year, she was able to do both Homer and the dramatists by the time she graduated. Apparently you had to learn a whole new kind of Greek for every author (except that Plato was the same as Xenophon, whom we had in our beginning course). Hearing about those prodigies of language-learning—Dorian, Ionian, Boeotian, Aeolian, Attic—convinced me that I was well out of Greek, after all. It was afterwards that I grew sorry. Old Miss MacCurdy, with her ear trumpet, friend of "dear Gilbert" (Murray), was a saltier personality than gracious Miss Haight, who wore her white hair like my great-aunt Eva's in noble, layered piles on top of her head.

Miss Haight, quaffing the old Falernian (as we pictured her in Williams Hall with Dean C. Mildred Thompson and the rest of her cronies), was slightly a figure of fun. Her absurd opening words to an advanced Latin class remain with me: "When Theseus [pause] came to Athens [pause] as it were [pause] *in medias res.*" And Frani and her friend Clover (who played the fiddle and later won fame as a window-dresser at Elizabeth Arden) had an amusing tilt with her when the new Music building, Skinner, was inaugurated. They were both Music students (Clover was a major), and Music throughout our time had been housed with Classics in Avery but on the top floor. In niches on the stairway were classical statues of Venus and Minerva, which had suffered greatly over the years from the Music girls' practice of running pencils down their marble curves while going by. To honor the new building Frani and Clover and their friends decided to weave garlands and procure wine for a libation from Signor Bruno, a friendly speakeasy-keeper in downtown Poughkeepsie; they took the statues of Venus and Minerva from Avery and set them up on the lawn before Skinner with garlands around their necks. Then they poured wine, played music, and danced. The next day a letter from Elizabeth Hazelton Haight was on the desk of our Chief Justice. "I regret to be obliged to report to you the rape of Venus and Minerva from the Classics Department." If she had not gone on to demand the immediate return of the statues and the punishment of the culprits, Miss Haight might have been felt to be horsing around herself on some old steed of parody. But she did not get the benefit of the doubt, and it was noted that Miss MacCurdy, dear Gilbert's friend, had not added her voice to the denunciation—the rape of *Roman* statues was outside her department.

An amusing story told about Miss MacCurdy had to do with Mrs. Flanagan's production of the *Hippolytus*. Two huge archaic statues of Artemis and Aphrodite made out of papier-mâché by students in Dramatic Production, stood on either side of the bare stage. Phaedra in a classic mask, played by Miss Tappan, spoke her lines in Aphrodite's shadow; across the stage, Hippolytus, played by Phil Davis, a young widower who taught late Latin and eventually turned into Mrs. Flanagan's husband, was under the protection of Artemis. Prexy, once a Greek scholar, played Theseus, entering as it were *in medias res* and taking a position in the middle. I wish I could remember whether they were buskinned. There were also a chorus and a Messenger, played by gaunt Mary Wing, the daughter of Miss Madeira of the Madeira School. Miss MacCurdy with her ear trumpet sat in the front row.

Now, as the story has it, Prexy forgot his lines. But he was a born actor, full of resource: in his head he hastily translated "To be or not to be," which was about the right length, into Greek, spoke the resulting lines, and nobody noticed a thing. Except old Miss MacCurdy, whose ear trumpet could not be fooled by *Hamlet*, in Greek or English. She did not let on till after the performance was over and Prexy was receiving congratulations. Then she added her own.

That must have happened during our junior year, which, I now recognize, was my year of election at college. As I said, Elizabeth Bishop had arrived as a freshman when we were sophomores. But I don't clearly remember her till the next year; we both (I think) lived in Cushing; she took Greek, like her old friend Frani, with Miss MacCurdy, and Verse Writing with Miss Swain. Already that fall, Frani, Bishop, and I began to talk about starting a rebel literary magazine, to be called *The Battleaxe* (my title). I wrote to John about it (he may not have approved of the name), and late in October Frani wrote to her mother: "Some of us are going to start a new magazine, The Battleaxe—Mary, Clover, Bishop, Kay McLean, Nathalie Swan . . . and it is really going to be *good*, a little sock at the Review! Nothing tame, arty, wishy-washy, ordinary or any of the other adjectives applicable to so much college writing." This did not come to pass until senior year, when it was called *Con Spirito* (Bishop's title), a pun joining the musical notation meaning "with zest" to the announcement of a conspiracy.

At Cushing we belonged to the so-called smoking-room set, consisting of Bishop, Frani, Nathalie Swan ("the Sphinx of the smoking-room"), Ev Huntington, Lou McGeehan, Beth Osborne, Louise Crane, then known as "Auntie." There was Rhoda Wheeler, who loved to ride, from Adamsville, Massachusetts; she was another Walnut Hill girl and classmate of Bishop's. Some, like Ev Huntington, who was a senior, did not really live in Cushing, and on some nights the smoking-room would turn into a debating society as girls would drop in from Students or from their own dormitories and we would discuss questions such as "What makes Cézanne's apples beautiful?" I argued that it was purely the arrangement of the shapes and colors, while hoarse-voiced Eunice Clark, editor-to-be of the *Miscellany News*, kept earnestly repeating "But it's the *spirit* of the apples that counts," whereupon I led a round of derisive laughter. In New York we had been impressed by the new Museum of Modern Art, where we saw the famous apples for the first time, and somewhere I had learned about Clive Bell and the expression "significant form," which, to tell the truth, despite my bold assurance, I did not fully understand. Nor do I now. Unless it was only stating that the form is the meaning.

The Cushing smoking-room was a launching-pad for funny stories and songs like the ones composed by Lou McGeehan and Beth Osborne on the French Survey course, which most of us had taken. Snatches from Crouzet—the textbook—were set to a boisterous tune: "Travel'd in India, exotic, *le sud de Madagascar,/* Poems that are *tragiques* and *antiques* and *barbares*" (Leconte de Lisle) or "*Gentilhomme de campagne,/* Died because too stout" (that was Balzac); "Oh, *fille de Necker,* what is it all about?" was Madame de Staël. One great hit was Bishop's composition on living in a room next to the "john":

> Ladies and gents, ladies and gents,
> Flushing away your excrements,
> I sit and hear beyond the wall
> The sad continual waterfall
> That sanitary pipes can give
> To still our actions primitive.

From the first we had called her Bishop; nobody, unless it was old Miss Fiske, who taught her Anglo-Saxon, called her Elizabeth. Miss Sandison tried Bish for a while, but it did not work.

Small, with hunched shoulders, rounded features, and a high hoarse voice like a boy's in the course of changing, at Vassar she anticipated the way she looked in later life. I see her playing a little old man—the heroine's parent—in a dramatization we put on of Dostoievsky's "Uncle's Been Dreaming" (I was Sophia, a neighbor lady). Dressed in a little black suit of clothes, her short frizzy ash-blond hair worn in a pompadour and powdered for the part with cornstarch, she was already her future self.

She had a little cough, a mild clearing of the throat, which sounded apologetic, like an old person's cough. Much of this was due to severe asthma, which had held her back in school and bothered her all her life. She had lived a good deal with an Uncle Jack and Aunt Ruby in Worcester, where the family had a contracting business, and she lived in fear of the aunt, whose long-haired dogs were a torment to an asthmatic. In the summer sometimes she went to Nova Scotia, where there were relatives she loved—her mother's people. To all intents and purposes she was an orphan, like me; her father had died when she was a baby (of drink, I thought, but I now learn it was Bright's disease), and her mother was in an asylum, having tried to kill Bishop with a butcher knife when Bishop was five. The mother did not die till years after the knife episode, which quite possibly (I now think) never happened outside the imagination of some relative or neighbor who claimed to have seen "the crazy woman" eye the child and then eye the big knife. But that was what poor Bishop had been told.

In her background, as in my Minneapolis experience, there had been plenty of old-fashioned cruelty-to-children—orphans in those days seemed to invite it, having no natural protectors. In Bishop's case, as in mine, there had finally been a rescuer; hers was Aunt Maude, her mother's sister. That year we took walks along the Pine Walk and talked of books and socialism (I was the conservative), but we never had a class together. The authors she spoke of were almost all new to me: Dorothy Richardson, Wyndham Lewis, Gerard Manly Hopkins, Sarah Orne Jewett. She was reading *Tender Buttons* by Gertrude Stein, and I was reading Rebecca West. I doubt that she was aware then that Sarah Orne Jewett had "a Boston marriage" (as such relations used to be called) with the wife of a publisher. Or was it already on the grapevine?

Bishop herself was interested—or earnestly trying to be—in a young man on the Cape with whom she went off on a boat that summer, in the company of Ev Huntington. Years later, I learned, she believed that I had put one of her own Boston marriages into *The Group*. I had not, but since she never told me of that unshakable conviction of hers, I could not deny it. When we saw each other, nothing was said of it, and I only learned of it—from Robert Lowell—not long before her death. I did not try to disabuse her mind in a letter and waited till I would see her, which never happened. Probably it was hopeless. Frani, without telling me, had already tried to persuade her that she was wrong; Lowell, too, I think. The day she died I had just mailed a letter to her, but on a purely literary subject—no reference, no hint of the "bone" lying between us.

Nor did I ever guess—what I was told during those years by a young male academic with a grudge against her, in an unsolicited communication—that she had me "on the brain." There was a tin butterfly, he wrote, on the wall of her Boston apartment, in dark allusion to a story of mine, and she used to say of me, "Mary McCarthy? She's an Irish Jew." Well! I am sad about all that, but not very, since it does not affect my love for her work and her, too.

Now that I think of it, I am not sure that Bishop lived in Cushing during my junior year. If she had, what I am about to describe could scarcely have happened. I would have had someone that I belonged with to sit next to in the dining-room. Someone, that is, besides Frani, for I would not let myself depend too much on the beacon of that friendly little freckled face to send out welcome signals as I stood uncertainly in the doorway peering around. Lunches were all right—you were in a hurry between classes and just sat down at any vacant place—but dinner was something else. Luckily I cannot recall my sufferings as night after night I surveyed that noisy dining-room, where most of the tables were already filled. The Vassar system of "grouping" was almost fully operative by sophomore year: at the end of freshman year, you had chosen the girls you would live with and, if necessary, had changed halls accordingly. Thus most nights at the dinner-hour each table in the dining-hall was the preserve of a constituted group. If I did not see Frani from where I stood in the doorway (or there was no empty place beside her), I had nowhere, literally, to go. With Virginia in Waterbury already choosing her bridesmaids, I had no group; my friends in other halls (and by this time there were a few) all had groups of their own whom they ate with. And Frani, I had to remind myself, had other friends in Cushing—Clover Benson, for instance, with her fiddle.

That girls could invite girls from other dormitories and be invited to other dormitories themselves (or go to the Lodge, to the Popover, to Cary's, even downtown to the Nelson House) was the saving element in the system. Not only could a loose end like me go elsewhere; others could, too, so that there would sometimes be vacant places here and there, where a non-insider could sit unchallenged. And that was how, Reader—gradually, very gradually—I came to join the group.

At their table, near the door, there was quite often an empty place. I suspect, thinking back, that it belonged to Kay McLean, a glowing dark girl from Detroit who was the slave of Mrs. Flanagan in DP (Dramatic Production); she was always building scenery and painting flats for "Hallie" and "Lester" (Mrs. Flanagan and Lester Lang, her assistant). Yes, it was Kay, I remember now, who toiled over those statues in the *Hippolytus*. For DP, she would gladly skip dinner night after night and go to Cary's late for a sandwich with paint in her hair. In any case, quite often there would be this empty place.

At first I hardly knew any of these mostly rich and handsome girls to speak to, only the Sphinx of the smoking-room, the untalkative Nathalie Swan, and Julia Denison, who was in my Blake-to-Keats class. Bis Meyer, Eugene Meyer's daughter, who had been one of them the year before, had sat next to me in Miss Snyder's Narrative Writing (looking over my shoulder at the letters to John I was writing), but Bis had left to do a junior year in Munich. Another one I knew slightly was Maddie Aldrich, she of "a pissing-while" in Miss Sandison's Shakespeare, but we had never talked, and I understood that she cared only about horses and hunting. Rosilla Hornblower I remembered by name unhappily from Davison in our freshman year. Of them all, the one I liked best was Julia Denison, who looked like Kay Francis in the movies and came from Cape Elizabeth, Maine. Her best friend was Dottie Newton, from West Newton, a suburb of Boston.

On nights when there was an empty place Julia would smile at me encouragingly as I surveyed the diners from the doorway. "Come on, sit with us," she pantomimed, and the full-breasted, inscrutable Nathalie Swan, who looked like an Edwardian beauty in a corset, would nod a greeting. As it turned out, Nathalie and I, rather than Julia and I, were the ones to become close friends—Julia was inseparable from Dottie, while Nathalie was a loner; she planned to be a landscape architect and took Botany, Art, and Math. Since she liked to read and was Modernist in her tastes, from her corner in the smoking-room she eventually became friends with Frani and Bishop, too. She had a bored voice and a tremendously posh accent, the most so of all those débutantes who had gone to Chapin. Her mother and another young woman had founded the Junior League, which at the start was a social-service endeavor on the part of rich young women not wishing to be idle. Her mother, who had gone to Barnard, "kept up" with Einstein's second field theory, Nathalie said dryly, on a note of deprecation. This odd, inarticulate girl, so much like a fashionable matron of his youth, greatly discombobulated Edmund Wilson when he met her. "She said she admired Gertrude Stein's use of metaphor," he reported with alarm, since the most notable feature of Miss Stein's writing was precisely the lack of metaphors. I reflected. "She means paradox," I decided, to his vast relief. At Vassar I was surprised to discover that Nathalie liked me.

Nonetheless the suspense of the dining-room went on for what seemed like months. Not every night, of course, for some nights I ate with Frani and Clover and sometimes I went to another dormitory or off campus. I did not want to abuse the privilege that group was according me. So sometimes I avoided the invitation in Julia's eye (large and green like my flattering notion of my own) and went to find a seat at some inferior table far down the room. But bit by bit it came to be accepted that my place was *there*, with those select girls; nearly always there was a vacant seat—if it was not Kay painting flats, it was Maddie gone off hunting with a cousin, or Kelly, having supper with her little protégée, Tassie Gesell. I suppose there must have been a dispute among them about allowing me to become a fixture at their table, but they were too well bred to let me sense it.

Upstairs, as it happened, my room was on "their" corridor, almost opposite Nathalie's—Frani was on the other side of the building. When we were not in the smoking-room playing bridge or pounce, I spent a lot of time in Nathalie's untidy room (she wore a handsome mandarin coat that her aunt had brought her from Peking), talking till very late at night. I went to Julia's room, too, but Julia tired easily—she was having some nervous disturbance that caused her pure olive skin to break out. It may have had something to do with her family's losing their money; when I went to stay with her at Cape Elizabeth over Thanksgiving the following year, I found that they had no servants, so that family and guests all pitched in to make beds and wash dishes while Mrs. Denison, who was an intellectual, cooked and discoursed. Or did Mr. Denison cook and Mrs. Denison discourse? He was a Beaux Arts architect who no longer had clients. They treated the housework as "great fun"—New York society parlance to this day—which was not my attitude, though I threw myself into setting the table for breakfast with Chelsea ware. Like Frani's mother, the Denisons had wonderful china, but Mrs. Denison at the head of the table did not go through the charade of washing the breakfast dishes at the table since there were no maids to bring her bowls of hot water and snowy linen towels.

But I am anticipating. Back in the Cushing smoking-room, it is still junior year, and it is then in the late spring without my knowledge that my life's course is being decided. Room-drawing. Juniors drew numbers to determine what rooms they would get the next fall as seniors in Main. A low number was good. Frani and Clover and I had made up our minds to be a group of three and, to our amusement, our group drew quite a low number, which was wasted on us since we were only three and did not care where we lived. The nicest rooms were the suites in the two towers, but for those you had to be six or eight.

Meanwhile the group consisting of Julia, Dottie, Maddie, and so on had got a high number. This was sad for them because, being six, they had hoped to get one of the towers. In Cushing they had been seven, but Nathalie had decided to do her senior year at the Bauhaus in Germany, studying architecture. Six with a high number risked being strung out over the top floor of Main or even being separated. Hearing about our low number, the group woke up to the interest of making a deal with us. If they were to take two of us to "group" with them, using our low number, they could get the South Tower. The two towers were considered the most desirable because each tower was completely by itself, with the bedrooms opening off a common sitting-room and its own baths and toilets; of the two, the South was the nicest. Calculations were swiftly made. Two of us could join the group from Cushing, with whom I was friends anyway, and the third would live in the North Tower with a group of "achievers" that had a fairly low number but was lacking one member. In the event, that proved to be Frani, who had an "achiever" side herself, thanks to her mother, and so got along well with them. In our last year, then, Clover and I lived in single rooms opposite each other in the South Tower, while Frani, on the other side of Main, across the roofs, roomed with Alice Dodge in the North Tower.

The arrangement worried Miss Sandison. She was fond of Frani, and the association with the "achievers" seemed to bode ill. What could I do, she asked me, to counter the influence? It was pleasing to be consulted, begged even to help, as though the two of us would be saving Frani from the clutches of Satan, when it was the president of Students, the vice-president of Students, the president of the senior class, a hockey-playing stalwart of the Community Church, the editor of the *Vassar Review*, we were speaking of. No better example could be found of non-conformity as an intellectual principle than Miss Sandison's lively fear of the corrupting potential of those squares. She dreaded what they might do to Frani's integrity—I can hear the word pronounced in her pretty, fastidious voice—just as she was concerned over what Dr. Bowdler's shade could do to the integrity of a Shakespearean text: Launce and his dog.

But what of me, Reader? Did nobody ever worry about the effect on a girl from the Northwest of exposure to the contagious disease of snobbery and the New York Social Register? Perhaps my teachers counted on the counter-influence of Johnsrud. Or else they considered that in my case the damage had already been done, the fat was in the fire, *alea jacta est*. But it may be, too, that, in their view, social ambition occurred too classically in literature to be regarded as greatly harmful, lying so very close, as it did, to the passion for excellence, beauty, fine ornament, and to the gift of worship. What English major was—or ought to be—free from the vice?

9

That summer I did not go home to Seattle. The summer
before—after sophomore year—had been the last time,
had I only known it. When I came back to Seattle after that,
it was for visits, even if my grandmother continued to speak
of "Mary's room." And the trains were different.

The trains were part of being a girl from the Northwest.
It took nearly four days to cross the continent. Coming home
from Vassar on the Lake Shore Limited or the Wolverine,
you changed at Chicago for one of "our" trains—the Chicago, Milwaukee, and St. Paul, the Great Northern, the
Northern Pacific. They took different routes, and I think
they had different depots in Seattle. The one I liked best
was the Chicago, Milwaukee, and St. Paul, which was
a bit like preferring Diderot, given the choice Voltaire-

Diderot-Rousseau, or Turgenev, given the choice Turgenev-Dostoievsky-Tolstoy. I loved its route, midway between the other two; for nearly a day it followed the course of the Missouri, so that out the window you could watch the great river's story unroll from its source as a "forks" or confluence of three Rocky Mountain streams, to its union with other streams—the Milk? the Platte?—even if you had to miss its final glorious meeting with the Mississippi above St. Louis.

Unless I am mixed up, and it was not the Chicago, Milwaukee but one of the others that followed the Missouri? No current map is useful, for current maps do not show railroad lines—still less, *defunct* railroad lines—but highways. With a magnifying glass, I can trace the Missouri from its headwaters (found by Lewis and Clark) on the border between southwest Montana and Idaho, then north to the Dakotas, then south again to the Nebraska line, but where the railroad tracks lay (or still lie?) remains dark to me.

Anyway, as I remember, the Chicago, Milwaukee went through more varied and interesting country than the other two. It was not a prairie train nor an iron horse of the wilderness; it stopped at Butte in Montana rather than at an entrance to Glacier or Yellowstone Park, with grizzly bears or geysers. I forget which of the railroads went through the Bad Lands of South Dakota—a fearsome spectacle, only equaled by the so-called *terre squallide* of central Sicily.

The Chicago, Milwaukee, and St. Paul was anchored on St. Paul, while the other two were anchored on Chicago, so I suppose it was the train my parents took to go to Minneapolis in 1918, when we all sickened with the flu. It would have been the natural choice, and I wonder whether the reason I preferred it, without even guessing at this history, was that the scenery it traversed was for me quintessential train scenery, its route, half-recognizable, was *the* fateful route.

Yet for some reason—perhaps because the Chicago, Milwaukee was on the verge of receivership during the time I was at Vassar—I usually went east on the Great Northern, Jim Hill's line ("I like Jim Hill,/ He's a good friend of mine,/ That's why I am riding down Jim Hill's main line"), the most northerly one, which was to northwestern railroading what the Yankees were to baseball. And just for that reason, because it was the most powerful, I did not care for it.

I never liked the Yankees or Babe Ruth or Lou Gehrig or any of those Sultans of Swat. I was a Giant fan, a passionate Polo Grounds–goer; my loves were Bill Terry, Blondy Ryan, Dick Bartell, Travis Jackson (the captain and third baseman), and of course Carl Hubbell and Hal Schumacher ("Prince Hal"); I did not even reject "Fat Freddie" Fitzsimmons, a pitcher who was getting old. It will be seen that, apart from pitchers, my favorite players were all infielders—the brains of a baseball nine. In those days, most intellectuals, I think, were Giant fans, except for an element, still in school then, that was for the Dodgers, and another, smaller, for the Cardinals. All National League teams.

Well! It must have been my grandfather who chose the Great Northern. To me, it was epitomized in the "Great Big Baked Potato" featured in its promotional literature. On the Empire Builder, the star train, they made a point of the hefty meals served in the diner—big manly steaks and chops to accompany that Idaho potato, lathered in butter (this was before sour cream and chives), when at the time my taste ran to refinements on the order of mushrooms under glass.

All our railroads were proud of their linen napery and the hotcakes they served for breakfast with sausages and lots of maple syrup. Real? I now ask myself. No; most likely, imitation. Probably the catering services reckoned that Far Westerners could not tell the difference. Certainly I myself did not know the difference then between Log Cabin and the real thing. Indeed I thought that Log Cabin *was* the real thing and would faithfully ask for it by name in a grocery store, the way I asked for Del Monte peaches, testifying to my consumer education. (As you can see, Reader, I do not care for that side of myself, which I have not completely

237

shed, however; how can I as long as *knowing* concerns me?) And while we are on that subject, I can quote Proust, speaking of Swann as one who had inherited from a rich and respectable middle-class family "the knowledge of the 'right places' and the art of ordering things from shops."

In their accommodations, the trains of the Northwest were pretty much alike. It was before the days of roomettes; I traveled in a lower, behind dark-green curtains, which the porter would twitch to wake me in the morning. Night and morning, to avoid acrobatics in the berth, I changed from day to night wear and back in the ladies' room, which had a toilet, hot and cold water for washing and drinking, plentiful towels, and, in front of a long mirror, a row of receptacles for hair combings. All the trains had observation cars— sometimes an open one (more adventurous) coupled onto a glassed-in one. In the open one there was giggling about kissing in the tunnels (it was pitch-dark), and until electrification came you could get a cinder in your eye. Off the closed-in observation car, also known as a lounge, with swivel chairs and a beverage service, there was a bathroom, in which you could arrange with the porter to have a bath or a shower. The eastern trains, between New York and Chicago, had a telephone in the observation car, but I don't think our trains had that—only telegram blanks. The porters shined your shoes and brushed your clothes. There was a booth for playing cards, and warnings posted against card sharps. Even if nothing much happened, the trip was a continual excitement, and I was almost sad each time when it ended.

As for Seattle, in the last two summers I spent there, it had showed itself in quite a new light. Having reached the age of eighteen, I was allowed finally to go out with boys, and soon a number of young men were calling for me in their cars. The one I liked best was homely, with yellow hair and big teeth and a stooping walk. John Powell had graduated from M.I.T. and so was slightly older, about twenty-three; he drove an old touring-car. My grandfather, who knew his parents, took a shine to him. "He certainly is a handsome man," he would say without fail, to the amusement of the ungainly subject himself when I repeated it. The thing that attracted me most in John Powell was that he did not try to "make" me or not very hard. He just liked to talk and drink. He had a brother, George Powell, who was at Princeton and fought to get his hand up my skirt night after night tirelessly in his two-seater car. When he gave up hope, he ceased to ask me out. There were a number of other boys, the Badgeleys, for instance, Chick and Ed, who went to the University (Ed was my friend), and Hal Gates, a small flashy Californian with a new red Ford touring-car. With the exception of John Powell, all of them "wanted only one thing." The sole difference was the degree of persistence. When they saw they could not get beyond necking, they were irritated, though some showed it more than others. The younger they were, the worse.

On the other hand, there was the Navy. Every summer, the fleet was in, eager to meet girls and go dancing. My friend Francesca Street and her sister Mary McQueen had many beaux among the young officers, and now I, too, during "Fleet Week," was able to go aboard the ships with them and to the hotels in town where you could dance. The ship I came to know best was the *Maryland*, where there was a popular officer, a lieutenant j.g. known as "Steamie" Stone, who was a great organizer of fun and parties. To my relief, the Navy was much less aggressive with girls than the Seattle boys. Perhaps it was just more sophisticated. The only problem with the young officers was that they expected you to take an interest in the ship and its fittings, an interest I found it hard to simulate. The cannon they showed me, the nests of guns on the deck, all in a high state of polish, the winches, pulleys, compasses, cleats, barometers, wheels, all that nautical ordnance was the same from ship to ship, that is, boring: when you had seen the *Maryland*, you had seen them all. Nonetheless I enjoyed the slightly racy stories these Annapolis men told and the funny songs they knew.

Besides the randy boys and the young officers in summer whites, there were also the men. The Street girls' father, Mr. Street, a widower, and Broussais ("Bruce") Beck, whose wife owned the Bon Marché department store and who pretended to an interest in the fine arts. Twice he got me to meet him at the Washington Hotel and tried to persuade me to go up to a room he had taken. It must have seemed strange to him that I agreed to meet him at the hotel, on the mezzanine floor, and then jibbed at what should have been the logical sequel. To me, what seems strange is the opposite: my inability to refuse in the first place—was it curiosity? The most embarrassing part of being pursued by Bruce Beck came when he started calling me at home. "Who was that man?" my grandmother would say sharply, as if his mature years were imprinted on his dulcet voice. I would have to make up some lie to shield him, for his wife, Mrs. Beck, was a devoted client of my grandfather's and later of my uncle's, and it would be shameful if my grandfather or Frank discovered what Bruce was up to. In fact, as I eventually learned, his habits were no secret in the town; my only distinction was to be a bit young for him.

Thinking back, I see that those two summers home from college were an illustration of what, except for Johnsrud, I might have become, now that I was starting to fit into Seattle. My grandmother had concurred in my joining the Tennis Club, the place to belong for the younger set; it was on Lake Washington, not far from our house. I swam and watched tennis matches and gave an occasional small luncheon. On the raft there was a good deal of repartee, denoting social acceptance, though my feelings were hurt one day when I overheard two boys assess me as I stood poised for a dive: "Kind of broad in the beam?" said one, and the other agreed. I was and always would be a flat-chested, wide-hipped girl; it was a matter of bone structure, everyone said. I was also bow-legged—had I been allowed to walk too early?—and this greatly bothered me. I read of operations in which they broke your legs and reset them again straight, but my grandmother, of course, would not hear of that. I was not a movie star, she tartly pointed out. Having experienced the dire effects of an unsuccessful face-lift, she was unlikely to sympathize with my dream of cosmetic surgery on my legs. And perhaps she was right that the malformation was not very noticeable. As I grew older, I forgot about being bow-legged and only remembered, briefly, when I looked at full-length photographs, especially those taken from the rear. Yet even now, out of the blue, I wonder whether that operation would have made me taller, not that I am short. And anyway why should I care now, when nobody but a doctor is studying me from the neck down? In a bathing suit on the Seattle Tennis Club raft every one of my bodily shortcomings was conspicuous.

The queer thing is that I enjoyed those summers. Though I considered myself "engaged" to Johnsrud, that did not inhibit me with other males. Once I even made love with a man I met at the Becks' summer place, on Three Tree Point: George Guttormsen, a University quarterback, who, I think, was All-America and who was now in the Law School—later he joined my grandfather's firm. He was an intelligent young man, a sort of intellectual even, a freak case of a football star who was Phi Beta Kappa and good-looking as well. But it was the end of my last summer (1931) when we met and excitedly made love. So that I never saw him again. When finally I came back to Seattle—from Reno, by Union Pacific, after getting a divorce—either he was married or I did not know that he was with Preston, Thorgrimson, and Turner. In an alternative life, I hope, he could have been mine. On a loose page of one of my Vassar letters to Ted Rosenberg (undatable, as the first page and envelope are missing), I have come upon this: "You say you suppose I have forgotten about George. No, I haven't, completely. I shall be very much interested in any bit of news you can send me. . . ." So I told her about him. I wonder how much.

Except for that and evenings with Evelyn Younggren at our "Symphonies under the Stars," I have no recollection of anything intellectual or cultural in those two entire summers. Not of books I read, pictures I looked at, plays I saw. I don't even remember a movie from that time. I did go to typing school the first summer, but that was my grandfather's idea. It was as though the whole mental side of me had been switched off and the current diverted to swimming, the Tennis Club, the Navy, clothes from I. Magnin, from shops named Helen Igoe and Henry Harris—I had a semi-real French designer suit ("Patou first copy") to wear back to college which I did not tell my grandmother the true price of. The sole revelation that burst on me in those vacations was tequila served in a glass whose rim was rubbed with lime and sprinkled with salt. And—oh, yes—a discovery John Powell and I had accidentally made: hard cider, if you freeze it, will turn to applejack.

My reason for not going home the summer after junior year was of course Johnsrud. After two up-and-down winters on the fringes of Broadway employment, he had got a job with a rich young man named Shepard directing a summer theatre at Scarborough, New York. It was up the Hudson, near Tarrytown, on the edge of the Vanderlip property; a young lawyer who represented the company lived with his actress wife in the gatehouse of the estate.

It was a very ambitious program John was going to do: eight new plays in an eight-week season. Only an amateur producer would have dreamed of it. In the normal summer-stock program there may be a couple of new plays; the rest are stand-bys—*Auntie Mame*, *A Lion in Winter*, *Amadeus*. When the producer acquires the rights, he can buy, from Samuel French, what they call in the profession the stage-manager's working script: every cross, every entry, every exit, every piece of stage business of the original production is noted—in those days a copy of that used to cost around

$1.95. But with eight new plays, Johnsrud had to map out the stage business himself every week for eight weeks. I don't know whether the idea of doing all those new plays was his own or Shepard's. And if the producer was a débutant, John, who was twenty-nine, had never directed a play in his life—the closest he had come was being assistant stage manager for Jed Harris' *Uncle Vanya* and *The Inspector General*. Knowing nothing about the theatre professionally, I did not guess what a crazy enterprise this was.

Only one of the eight plays had ever been done anywhere—a Victorian melodrama called *The Ticket-of-Leave Man*, which had not been played for fifty or sixty years. So naturally no working script existed. John's thought was to stage it straight, counting on the laughs to come from the material itself. This was before *The Drunkard*, and a fairly original idea—John and his actors had fun with it. But *The Ticket-of-Leave Man* was far and away the *easiest* play they put on. In my memory, the best was probably *The Heavenly Express*, by Al Bein, a proletarian play about hoboes, set in a box car and on a siding. Bein was a rhapsodist, and it had a wild, poetic quality, as if written for strings, but when it finally reached Broadway—not till 1940—it failed.

Then there was *Blow, Whistles*, by Sarah Atherton, a Bryn Mawr woman in her early forties who was the daughter of a Pennsylvania mine operator. John had helped her adapt it from a factory novel she had published called *Blow Whistles, Blow*. She was a hospitable person who lived in South Norwalk with her husband, Luther Bridgeman, a telephone-company executive. Both these well-meaning, high-minded people thought the world of John and often had him out to stay. Mrs. Bridgeman was trying to escape from her class and did her own cooking; it was from her that I learned how to be sure your egg whites are stiff enough for a puffy omelet or a soufflé: invert the bowl, and if they don't slide, they are ready. I still use that test (better than the one where you drop a whole egg on the surface; if it doesn't sink, they are OK), and think of her while I do it—

243

that is immortality. And I have passed the torch on to younger people who don't use a mixer.

Among the actors that summer I remember Richard Whorf, who in the theatre was like a utility infielder in baseball— he could do anything from painting scenery to writing scripts. And it was that summer, I think, that John first worked with Lloyd Nolan, a wonderful actor. And there was Joanna Roos, who had been with John in *Uncle Vanya*, playing Sonia; Joanna's much older husband, Edward Rickett, a church organist, was the collaborator of W. S. Gilbert after Sullivan's death.

Most of the company lived in dormitories—a converted barn and stables on the Vanderlip property. Rehearsing next week's play while this week's was playing got everybody on edge. And because of rehearsing late, John usually stayed over; he had a bed with the Sherwoods in the gatehouse. But then he would stay up drinking with his younger brother, Byron, whom he had brought on to help out. Though Byron planned to be a newspaperman, he could drive a car to meet trains, move furniture, hold the prompt book, and hear actors who needed it in their lines. He was a smallish, sandy person with a sharp nose and reddish-brown eyes; the mother's Irish blood had come out in him, and his favorite word was "cock-eyed." He and John drank a lot and sometimes Byron fought with him. I knew about it because Kay McLean, my classmate, had landed a job as a stagehand with the company, moving and painting flats; she and Byron were having some kind of love affair—what it amounted to in those dormitory conditions John and I could not tell. After the first weekend, when John and I had quarreled coming up the Hudson in a friend's erratic motorboat, I tried to keep out of his way and not make any demands, even though I had stayed in the East for the sole purpose of being with him. I spent Saturdays with him, coming up by train, seeing the play, discussing it, and going back to New York the next morning.

I had a job. I had guessed that my grandparents would

let me spend the summer in the East if I found some work that paid a little and was connected with the arts; hence I jumped at the chance offered me by the theatre's publicity agent, a friendly girl from Cleveland named Terry. She introduced me to E. J. Rousuck, an art dealer, also from Cleveland, who agreed to hire me as a secretary for eleven dollars a week. What Terry did not say—did she know?—was that the Carleton Gallery, where I would be working, specialized in dog paintings. I found a cheap room in a brownstone house in the East 60's belonging to the parents of a classmate; several other Vassar girls were camping out there, too.

Thanks to my grandfather's foresight, I knew how to type, and my lack of shorthand made no difference to Mr. Rousuck. Instead of taking dictation from him, I wrote our letters myself directly onto the typewriter. Mainly these were letters inviting people to have their dogs painted by an English sporting artist, Maud Earl, who also did Chinese silk screens of birds and flowers which we were empowered to offer, too. Miss Earl, who was close to eighty and a celebrity in her field, got a good likeness of the poor animals we sent up to her apartment from our gallery whenever one arrived by Railway Express, in a cage, barking furiously and usually—we could tell—unfed.

We also sent out letters describing already painted paintings of dogs—nineteenth-century oils, usually pointers and setters posed in profile—and once in a while a horse painting of some famous steed or of mares and foals. For a few days (on consignment) we had a Remington bronze for sale. We did not handle cats.

Mr. Rousuck was a dog fancier and had once had a kennels, where he raised Boston bull terriers; he was the author of a book, the classic, on the Boston bull terrier, which, as became clear to me, he could not have written himself. An old lame sporting Englishman by the name of Freeman Lloyd who wrote for *Field and Stream* had been Mr. Rousuck's "ghost" before I entered the picture. He could de-

245

scribe the fine points of an animal in technical language; he knew pedigrees and blood lines and the folk lore of turf and field, while I was barely learning to say "dog fanciers" rather than "dog lovers" in my letters. But Mr. Rousuck, while appreciating all this, preferred to have me as his scribe. He had concluded that Freeman Lloyd knew about dogs and horseflesh, but that I wrote a better letter. Perhaps there came days when he would have liked to "cross" us.

A third kind of "missive" to prospective clients (not "customers") went out under the Carleton Gallery letterhead over E. J. Rousuck's signature. That was our art-as-investment letter, combined with a general invitation to visit our gallery: "In these times art is a peerless investment, and above all sporting art, which is only now coming to be regarded with due seriousness by connoisseurs of the brush and can still be bought advantageously by those in the know. Do drop in and let me show you, among other treasures, a delightful sporting primitive by the eighteenth-century master, Seymour." These letters went out to Paul Mellon, John Schiff, Mrs. Hartley Dodge, Ambrose Clark, William Woodward, Walter Jeffords, et al. Apparently some of the recipients actually read them, for now and then a client would "drop in."

"Gallery" was a funny name for our place of business, which consisted of three rooms on a high floor of an office building—the French Building on 46th Street and Fifth Avenue (I never knew where "Carleton" came from, perhaps from a misspelling of "Ritz Carlton"). The first room, hung with red velvet, was the gallery proper, where our few paintings were displayed. Behind that was a back room, also velvet hung, where Mr. Rousuck received customers and allies. To one side was my little office, in which, if we were lucky, a dog was confined, waiting to be taken up to Maud Earl's apartment to "sit." Elliott, a young black man whose job was to move pictures around, mostly stayed in the office with me. It was too bad that I had a phobia about dogs, having been rolled down a snowbank in Minneapolis by a

246

big one when I was small: if Elliott or Mr. Rousuck let the dog we were boarding out of its cage, I could not keep myself from jumping onto the desk until someone caught it and put it back in. In addition to Mr. Rousuck, Elliott, the transient dog, long-staying visitors such as Freeman Lloyd, a dealer called Nick Aquavella and another called Du Vannes, there was Mr. Rousuck's red-haired mistress, "Cissy" Bozack, from Scranton, Pennsylvania, whom we often had with us, too. Cissy was well fixed but she drank—her husband had met his end by diving drunk one morning into an empty swimming pool.

Mr. Rousuck, I discovered, sometimes slept in the gallery, on the velvet-covered couch where he showed paintings to clients. This was probably when he had been locked out of a hotel room for non-payment of rent. Now and then, I gathered, he would sleep at Cissy's but did not like to because of her drinking. I suppose that she lent him money to make sure that he ate when he was by himself. It was not a situation in which I could hope to collect my salary; I forget how many weeks he was behind with it, and now and then he borrowed a little money from me. In my opinion, the most imperative thing was that he pay Elliott, which he sometimes did, probably as often as he could. We all, including Elliott, lived in terror of a visit from the city marshal, who might try to hold a sale of the property to collect some unpaid bill. But he appeared only once that August, while Mr. Rousuck was out, and I managed by my tears (unfeigned) to send him away, thus rendering myself invaluable.

The friendship with Mannie (Emmanuel) Rousuck ("Jay" later on, to his social friends; the surname was pronounced like Russeks department store) lasted till he died, in 1970. It even weathered my putting him in a book and his making motions to sue me unless I changed the text. I did, with his assistance, but of course not enough to disguise him from other dealers, who were not deceived by seeing our Maud Earls changed into crystal cuff-links with miniature likenesses of dogs in them. By that time, his gift for salesmanship had inspired a series of important firms to take him on. In the end (I hope) he forgave me, which was large of him. He told me long after how he did it: "I said to myself, 'If I am not man enough. . .' "

I kept on writing letters for him long after I was a professional author: he would send paintings up for me to look at in Wellfleet or wherever I was living, and the delivery boy (a Jewish Elliott, better paid) would wait for me to write my description before taking them back to the gallery—which, after being Ehrich Newhouse, Newhouse, Scott & Fowles ("E. J. Rousuck, Proprietor"), eventually became Wildenstein's. Over the years the works of art I wrote about increased in value, although he never sent me a Rembrandt, even a debatable one. Apart from the letters, I did brochures and catalogues signed with his name for shows of Fantin Latour, Ben Marshall, Stubbs, Munnings, perhaps Augustus John, and others I forget.

Edmund Wilson always said that it was my "outlaw side" that was appealed to by Mannie. Perhaps so. Was it my outlaw side that liked being taken to lunch at good restaurants (such as Wilson did not go to), from Voisin to Luchow's to the Colony? And I liked hearing Mannie's troubles—it was impossible for him to go straight altogether—and giving him advice. He trusted me (which was not the same as being willing to do what I told him) and depended on me. If he represented an outlaw stripe in my nature, I may have represented for him a "moral" streak in himself. His mother had been maid of honor at the wedding of Rose Pastor Stokes, a once-famous Russian-born Jewish radical and heroine of a "Cinderella story" of the turn of the century. Having first got work in a Cleveland cigar factory (1892), she married a Wasp railway president, who moved out of his Fifth Avenue mansion and into a settlement house—an early illustration of downward mobility. Mannie was fond of telling Socialists, whenever he happened to meet one, that his mother had been Rose Pastor Stokes' maid of honor, but in later years he did not often

248

meet anyone old enough and radical enough to appreciate what that meant. Once in a presidential election I persuaded him to vote for Norman Thomas; it was easier for him than it might have been to explain it to his new, "Jay," friends because Norman Thomas raised dogs—Sealyhams, I think.

I ought to add that the later Mannie paid me extraordinarily well, which was certainly part of my motive for continuing with the letters and brochures. And his own motives were a little mixed, too; toward the end of a lunch at, say, the Lutèce, he would pass me his gold pencil and gold-framed memo pad—"Just give me a few lines on Cooper-Henderson." We never had a love affair, not even what he called "an affair," and thanks to my intellectual pursuits could not be intimate friends, sharing only a taste for the theatre. Yet his death in 1970 was the first in a series that brought down the pillars of my life. Dear Mannie, who died, charmingly, while being shaved in his Park Avenue apartment, was followed in a few months by Heinrich Blücher (Hannah Arendt's husband), Rahv, Chiaromonte. . . .

Like Wilson, Johnsrud did not like Rousuck. John knew that he was failing to pay me most of the time and probably knew, too, that he occasionally borrowed bits of money from me. When the Scarborough season ended, I stopped work at the Carleton Gallery and left Barbara Mosenthal's family brownstone to move into a furnished apartment with John. We had a month before college reopened, the worst month, I believe, of my life. I had not thought that anyone could suffer so much. I cried every day, usually more than once; it would not be false to say that he *made* me cry every day, for there was a kind of deliberateness in it, or so it appeared. And almost the worst was my total mystification. What made him so hateful I never found out, and this left me with a sense of being hopelessly stupid, which I fear John liked.

The place we had rented was only a furnished room, across

from Cherio's restaurant in the East 50's. Our landlord was a horrible Mr. Schatz with a heavy accent who, obviously guessing that we were not married, pestered us with threatening visits to make sure we were not damaging his property. Its main feature was an outsize "studio couch" covered with a smelly black velveteen drape. It was hot, not a breath of air, not a fan; this was long before air-conditioning. John blamed me for Mr. Schatz (whose name he derided as a variant past of "shits"), and maybe I *was* the one who had found him in an ad in the paper. But our landlord, I think, was only part of a more general grievance he had against me, for wanting to live with him, I suppose, when he wanted to be alone. After those tense weeks with the theatre, his nerves were bound to be irritable. But I was too young to make allowances for that and could only sob at the streams of abuse he subjected me to—sarcasm, irony, denunciation. We must have made love in the midst of all that, but I have no memory of any love-making on or in the studio couch, only of my tears and shaking shoulders, which of course exasperated him all the more.

My being there, clearly, was what he resented. Perhaps he had someone else—one of the actresses from the Scarborough company or more than one. But in that case why had he moved into this room with me? Whosoever suggestion it was, he had not had to accept. Or maybe, since he was not working, he just felt the rent was too high. I was surely the one who had wanted to live in the East 50's. Whatever it was, he was drinking more than usual, spurred on by his brother, Byron.

Byron and Kay were an aggravation, in every sense of the word. Something in the relation between them made them feel and act superior, above all to me. She in particular behaved with an incredible tactlessness; Byron was just rather boorish in a young man's way. They kept dropping in, on me alone or on the two of us together, frankly to size up how things were going between us on that day or night. Kay was positive that I was losing him, in fact had already lost him. It was all over, she told me repeatedly in her loud, authoritative voice. "Yeah," confirmed Byron, from better knowledge of his brother. They both found food for derision in my claim that we were engaged. "You're just another feather in the Johnsrud cap," Kay assured me; that phrase, dinned into my ears throughout a month, is "memorable" to me still.

I do not know whether or not John was aware of their prophecies. As long as either of them was around, I did not let my misery be visible. My pride was at stake. Even to myself, I was not going to admit that John was on the verge of "throwing me over," as we said then. Yet when I went back to Vassar in September to take my place in the South Tower, I really did think, numbly, that it was over with John. And with Kay living in the room next to mine, it seemed likely that the other group members had heard that he was "ditching" me, that I was just another feather, and so on. My senior year, with the prospect at the end of it of returning to Seattle with my tail between my legs, ought to have been grim. Yet it was not, even at the beginning, when John went off to Hollywood. Senior year was a peculiar mixture; several streams of experience ran through it, independently and as though oblivious of each other, like in one of those "histo-maps," colored pink, yellow, pale blue, green, showing the rise and fall of cultures. There was John, there was the group in the Tower, there was Miss Sandison's Renaissance seminar—we did *The Faerie Queene* that year. There was the *Con Spirito* stream, with Frani and Elizabeth Bishop, Muriel Rukeyser and the Clark sisters; there was the placid stream of Miss Peebles' Contemporary Prose Fiction, which led to Sacco and Vanzetti and thence to *The New Republic*.

There were other streams that felt like torrents but that eventually dried up: Waterbury and Dick Goss's cousin, Harry Wayne; my paper for Miss Beckwith on Ge, the Earth Mother; dictatorial Mlle. Monnier, whom I foiled. It is hard to describe these individual trains of experience while keeping to a linear narrative, and it must have been hard, also, to live them side by side, all at the same time. A few chapters back, of my senior year at the Seminary, I said that it was a jungle of incompatibles. That was even more applicable to my senior year at Vassar. Perhaps senior year is when everything comes together before, once again, separating.

In the fall, John was hired as a writer by MGM at a salary of $200 a week. Out there he lived in a house in Laurel Canyon and did not come back till May of the following year. In time to see me play Leontes in *The Winter's Tale* in the Outdoor Theatre and tell me I could never be an actress. I have told how the year before he had seen me play Arcite, also in the Outdoor Theatre, in a modern-language version of Chaucer's *The Knight's Tale* and how the audience had roared when I, a supposed corpse struck down by a dragon, reached out a hand as I lay on the floodlit grass, and pulled the skirt of my costume down. Yet it was not that girlish performance that decided John on my unfitness for the stage. No, it was my Leontes the next spring: "Inchthick, knee-deep, o'er head and ears a fork'd one!/ Go play, boy, play; thy mother plays/ And I play too, but so disgraced a part whose issue/ Will hiss me to my grave: contempt and clamour/ Will be my knell. Go play, boy, play." In the tryout I had read brilliantly (often true of bad actors, I hear) but all through rehearsals I had been getting worse and worse and did not know what to do about it.

John told me that I would never make an actress. Miss Kitchel had told me not long before that my gift was for criticism, not for imaginative writing. Perhaps they were both right. At any rate I accepted their judgment. Nor did my prospects for marriage look good. That awful month in New York, with Kay and Byron Johnsrud acting as chorus, had somehow put an end to whatever there had been between John and me. From Hollywood he wrote to me often and with a peculiar energy—very strange repellent letters that were about screen writers and sex, studio executives and sex, stars and sex, nothing but that. I knew some of the names or came to know them—Thalberg, Harry Cohn, Paul Bern—but all those men sounded like characters in Krafft-Ebing ("He was first immoral with a hen at the age of eight"), whose *Psychopathia Sexualis*, at John's recommendation, I had just bought. John did not say that he took part in the incessant saturnalia he described, but he did not say that he didn't. I was left to draw my own conclusions. There was no word of love in those letters, not even the S.L.O.C.Y.K., which had become his mechanical sign-off. And they were too shocking to show to anybody—certainly not the group—so that the pain of reading them could be lightened by submitting them to someone else's judgment.

Yet in the end it let up. I had passed the limit of suffering, I concluded: whatever he did, I could not feel it any more. In fact, as I decided afterwards, he had killed my love for him. And it struck me that I had made a discovery: it really could happen that a person you had loved could exhaust your capacity for suffering. That cannot be true for everybody, I now see—not for masochists, surely. But I think it is still true for me. In any case, that spring, when he wrote me that he was coming back east (Metro was letting him go), I did not know what to feel.

Neither then nor later did he ever let me know what his own feelings had been during that winter. Presumably he was still attached to me despite those letters. Because, on his way back from California, he stopped in Seattle and stayed with my grandparents. According to his account, he made a conquest of them. My grandfather came to his room in the mornings with a little shot glass of bourbon—surely a friendly indicator—and he must have taken him to the Rainier Club for drinks and a rubber or two of bridge. I do not know what my grandmother served him at home—no doubt Olympia oysters, for one thing—but it sounded to me as if they were treating him as a future son-in-law, or, rather, grandson-in-law. For my critical grandmother, his bald dome and broken nose could not have been a great shock, since after all she had seen him more than once on the stage. On his side, certainly, his *going* to Seattle represented a decision about me.

What a pity, then, that just at that juncture, I had started on a little love affair of my own, with a young man a year or so out of Yale who lived with his mother, Flora, in the Westbury Hotel and was trying to write the novel that so many just out of Yale, Williams, Harvard were trying to write—it was a purely male drive. A friend of John's, Lois Brown, took me to a Sunday-afternoon cocktail at Alan's. Everyone was getting fried, as he called it. He shook Bacardis in a silver shaker; there were little things to eat on trays; he had friends there like Winsor French and George Antheil and Jerome Zerbe, the fashion photographer, who while at Yale had received in his rooms in an evening gown; Alan himself was very charming, with dark-brown witty eyes and a slight lisp; when the others started leaving, he asked me to stay.

That was during Easter vacation, while John was still in California, and it was over almost before it began. But if Alan had wished to continue it, I would have been responsive. Instead, we became friends, and the friendship, with some hiatuses, lasted a lifetime. He did not write "the" novel and eventually turned into a newspaperman, getting his start on a paper in Beaumont, Texas. Then, as Alan Barth (his mother's name; his own, Lauchheimer was too hard to spell), he went to work for the Washington *Post*, where for years he was chief editorial writer, specializing in constitutional questions. Despite the rather fast and worldly friends he had made at Yale, there had always been a civic streak in Alan; in his first years in New York, living with Flora at the Westbury and writing unsalable fiction, he got himself taken on as a poll-watcher for the Democratic Party in the silk-stocking district.

After our affair—of a very few days, I think—I had gone back to Vassar beglamoured by Alan's familiarity with night clubs and with entertainers like the black pianist Jimmy

Daniels, and John had come back East from California. Maybe this was when he lived at the Wellington Hotel, on Seventh Avenue; he had moved out of the Bank Street place that he shared with his friend Phil Huget. He got onto some new friends, very quickly, as always happened with him: two artists, Harry Sternberg, a Communist, who painted his portrait, making him look like Lenin, and Dick Kingsbury, a commercial artist, very good-looking, very unhappy, and a drinker, whose social wife from Rahway, New Jersey, had left him because of that last. Dick had a studio on 8th Street, where he drew men's clothing ads, but he also spent time in Sullivan County, on the Delaware, in a place called Callicoon, where he invited John to come and stay. The house was what in Maine they call a "camp." There were other people living there, too, an old man called George and a young man called Ralph, possibly his grandson; the two of them drank and quarreled, arguing about who had more true Scottish blood in his veins ("Yer nae a MacGregor," the boy would yell, sobbing, at the ossified old man). In Callicoon it was easy to get applejack—I did not like the taste—and when John came up to college, he brought a bottle to Miss Sandison and Miss Kitchel, from which we had drinks on their porch in the late spring night. This may have been the time when he saw me play Leontes and pronounced his verdict (he was right, by the way).

It was not clear to anyone whether John and I were going to be married or not. This was partly because John in his histrionic style could not accept the thought of being predictable. But, as I said, my own feelings had changed, mainly because of what John had put me through, overestimating my capacity for suffering. Yet I was slow to recognize what had happened; at first, I think, I was barely aware of my lack of joy in having him back—smiling ironically, quirking his eyebrows, bowing, being courtly. What must have made it harder to "sort my feelings out" was that his return was a great triumph for me, to put in the eye of the egregious Kay McLean (whom I had come to positively hate) and all other doubters and skeptics. Just to have him on campus was to show them.

Around that time I "made" Phi Beta Kappa. One morning, in the tower, I heard my name called from below, and, looking down from my window, I saw the whole group making signs to me and clapping; they had my cap and gown, which they had brought down when they found the announcement in my mailbox, so that I could don them and go to the chapel for the ceremony. John had been Phi Bete at Carleton and as soon as he heard, he offered to give me his key, so that by not sending for mine I could save the six dollars. This struck us as clever, I am afraid, like a high-brow equivalent of being "pinned" by your man's fraternity pin—the little gold key in my eyes was a convention-defying kind of engagement ring. An alternative we considered was that I should order mine and wear the pair as earrings. Having rejected that piece of silliness, I have never had a Phi Beta Kappa key of my own.

Clearly I still considered myself engaged to him. I am not sure whether he had noticed a cooling in me—at Vassar, when he came up, or when I went to Callicoon one week-end to see him. As a performer, he was bound to be sensitive to audience-reaction, and it is conceivable that he noticed a change in me before I noticed it myself. That would explain his attempted suicide, if it *was* an attempted suicide rather than a case of O.U.I.

What happened was this: late one night he drove his car off the road and over a bank heading toward the Delaware River. Instead of going into the stream, the car hit a tree and turned over. All the way: Johnsrud was able to let himself out, climb up to the road, and walk jauntily home. The car—a second-hand Hupmobile that he had driven back from California—was undamaged except for some holes in the ceiling upholstery where acid from the battery had dripped. There were also some small holes in John's hat.

He told me that he had been trying to kill himself, but he told Dick Kingsbury that he had been operating under the influence and missed a turn. I don't know what he told the police—the tow truck that pulled the car out must have reported the accident. On the whole, I believed the suicide version and was much impressed. If there was a single factor that decided me to go on and marry him, it was probably that. Obviously I would have wanted to keep him from trying it again, but that was not the whole reason. No, it was that I admired him for what he had done, and the picture of those little acid-holes in the ceiling upholstery and in his snap-brim hat kept that admiration vivid.

I did not imagine that he had sought to kill himself on my account—I had too much sense. I felt that he had done it from an immense and wild misery, which I honored, and if drinking had played a part in it, that fitted, for he drank to drown his sorrows, being a Norwegian and Irish, too. Though I might be tired of John, it did not affect the awe in which I stood of him. I firmly believed that he was a genius, that he was going to win, first the Pulitzer and then the Nobel prize, that he had a more than Shavian wit, and finally, to cap it all, I now discovered that he was *colossally* unhappy. Byronism, Miss Kitchel could have told me, but Byron was always my favorite among the Romantics. As our class prepared for graduation, I was wearing his key on a chain.

In the meantime, there was *Con Spirito*. This was the rebel magazine that Frani, Bishop, and I, working now with some others, finally started in December of senior year. The title was a joke on the idea of a conspiracy, for our magazine was anonymous. All our contributions were unsigned; we did not know ourselves, except by guessing, who had written what. The point was to protest against the tame *Vassar Review*, which we thought was run by a clique too well acquainted with each other and too fearful of disturbance from the "outside."

We of *Con Spirito* would meet in a room in Students (later

in the Poughkeepsie red-wine-and-white-coffee-cups speak-easy owned by Signor Bruno); manuscripts for submission were put, unsigned, on a wooden chair, to be read and argued over. Though the make-up of our board was supposed to be a secret from the campus at large, naturally we knew each other, in most cases well: Frani, Bishop, Eunice Clark, her sister, Eleanor, Muriel Rukeyser, Margaret Miller, me. Margaret was an Art major, in Bishop's class, who wrote a remarkable piece on Surrealism for us, afterwards studied with Meyer Schapiro, and worked for years at the Museum of Modern Art. The others are self-explanatory. Occasionally we published something not written by one of our number (though there was no way we could know for sure), and once, according to rumor, a hoax was perpetrated on us by somebody who sent us a poem, which we accepted, by a patient in the state insane asylum. "So what?" was our reaction, but on campus there was a lot of crowing at the sight of that poem in print.

Con Spirito was my first encounter with "motiveless malignity" touched off by a good or morally neutral deed. The phrase is used of Iago; "He hath a daily beauty in his life that makes me ugly," which he says of Cassio, being the best explanation of his conduct he ever vouchsafes. Our magazine, which we advertised by posters we nailed up on trees in the dark of night, contained nothing libelous or obscene, attacked no person by name or insinuation, was well printed, inexpensive (15 cents), in other words incapable of harming anyone, yet it was met, dear frail gay little bark, by a tide of hatred. Because it was unsigned. That was the outrage, the shameful crime, treated as such even by some of the faculty, who breathed the word "anonymous" as though it were married to the word "letter," denoting something so scurrilous that it dared not sign its name. We were reviled as cowards since we did not come forward to claim our publication; in all the furor, nobody stopped to think of the *Times Literary Supplement*, which had been publishing unsigned articles and reviews for years.

Miss Sandison was torn between amusement and anger on our behalf. She at once picked out Frani, Bishop, and me as the arch-Conspirators and wanted to hear who the others were. I don't remember Miss Kitchel's part in this; evidently she was still working in the British Museum when our first number appeared. But Miss Sandison, as she put it, "went to the mat" for us, and Miss Kitchel must have taken our side on her return. It would not surprise me if Miss Sandison had even used her position as head of the English Department to overpower our enemies. This delicate small person was a fighter.

Looking over old copies of the magazine, I see that her sharp literary eye must have had no trouble identifying the authors of quite a number of the pieces. I can find myself— a prose poem against Hitler and Mussolini and two long book reviews; I find Frani doing an extended metaphor on the structure of an onion; I find Margaret on Surrealism and Eunice Clark in a story called "The Bite," about (so we thought) her sister, Eleanor ("the Baby"), herself ("Sister"), and their mother, who bit the Baby to teach her a lesson for biting Sister. Finally and far beyond the rest of us, I find Bishop with "Then Came the Poor," a marvelously amusing story, laid in the near future, of a revolutionary takeover. In November, 1933, after our graduation, there is Eunice again, surely, reviewing John Strachey's *The Coming Struggle for Power* and *The Menace of Fascism*. But I do not find any "crazy" poem nor any Muriel Rukeyser, unless she was the author of "Lecture by Mr. Eliot" in the third number:

> The audience crumbles in cerebral whoredom
> devoted lustfully to a conceit's expansion
> to an obscure line's scansion.
> These Fantastics bow and nod
> homage to prosody as a god.
> Somewhere beyond these windows,
> China moans. . .
> In Alabama are beated nine dark boys,

and quenched—while poets practice smiling
contemptuously at the seventh row.

The Scottsboro Boys. Yes, that sounds like Muriel, and the
reference would be to a reading by Eliot in Avery during
our senior year, when he gave us one of the early Possum
poems. Too bad about the typos: "crumbles" was probably
"crumples," and "beated" certainly "beaten."

Another appearance in Avery, that fall or winter, escaped
the notice of *Con Spirito*. That was when Edmund Wilson,
known to us as the author of *Axel's Castle* (1931), which none
of us can have read, lectured to us on Flaubert—manifestly
a try-out of one of the essays in *The Triple Thinkers*. He was
heavy, puffy, nervous, and a terrible speaker, the worst I
ever heard, including a stutterer, years later at a New York
meeting I chaired, who pronounced "totalitarianism" in
twenty-one syllables—someone counted. Wilson's delivery
was characterized by harrowing pauses when we did not
know whether he was going to continue or had stopped
altogether. Watching this happen, Miss Sandison, who had
introduced him, hurried down to the basement to try to
find a glass of water—none had been provided at the lectern. *"Vox exhaurit in faucibus,"* she said to me afterwards:
his voice was expiring in his jaws. I have never identified
the Latin quotation. Her shock—and Miss Kitchel's—at my
marriage to Wilson, and relief at the end of it, went back to
that evening in Avery. "Tell us," said Miss Kitchel, over
her Old-Fashioned in the Poughkeepsie restaurant when I
was back in the Hudson River Valley, teaching at Bard, and
a divorce was impending. "Tell us," her fading blue eyes
supplicated, "you didn't marry him for love." It was in love's
name that the two spinsters begged for reassurance, and
we all three laughed when I said no.

Frani and I were both taking Miss Sandison's Renaissance
seminar. My senior thesis I divided into two parts, one on
Sir John Harington, Elizabeth's witty godson and translator
of Ariosto; the other on Robert Greene ("For he left his pretty

boy,/ Father's sorrow, father's joy"), Shakespeare's immortal detractor ("His tygres heart wrapt in a player's hide . . . the onely shake-scene in a countrey") and friend of Nashe, author of a manual on the art of cony-catching and of a very curious work of deathbed repentance (*Greene's Groatsworth of Wit Bought with a Million of Repentance*) whose sincerity is impossible to determine. Both halves of my thesis were portraits of a kind, and you could say that the sitter for each was a distant cousin to Sir Gawain. The one on Harington (also the inventor of the toilet, described in his *Metamorphosis of Ajax*—a jakes) was published in the *Vassar Journal of Undergraduate Studies* and won half the Furness Prize, given for a work on an Elizabethan subject. I was happy with these honors and even more so in Miss Sandison's approbation. If I have ever had an academic field, it is English Renaissance, and there I feel my home is, in the music of the period, too. I did not greatly care for Spenser—the only parts of *The Faerie Queene* I really responded to were the mutability cantos—there were quite a number of Elizabethans, poets and wits, major and minor, that I preferred. My real and lasting love, not counting Shakespeare, was Thomas Nashe ("Brightness falls from the air"), to my mind the embodiment of the genius of English prose. I am thinking not so much of *The Unfortunate Traveler*, often called the first English novel, as of the high spirited pamphlets, for instance, *Have With You to Saffron Walden*, an attack on Spenser's crony, the ineffable pedant Gabriel Harvey.

Frani was smitten with the Elizabethans, too; in the apple country, not far from the college there was an inn, the Silver Swan, that we used to frequent with our friends, partly on account of its very Elizabethan name. On occasion, Elizabethan airs were sung at table. In classes, as I said, I had been taking Renaissance French with Miss De Schweinetz and Renaissance Latin with Miss Tappan.

Yet despite my love of Elizabethan language and sense of being at home in the period (still powerfully operative the instant I hear the lascivious pleasings of a lute, and/or Wil-

261

liam Byrd, Dowland, Campion), the course senior year that had the greatest visible influence on my future life was Miss Peebles' Contemporary Prose Fiction, in which we studied the "river-novel" and something she called "multiplicity." As I have related elsewhere (*Occasional Prose*), we read Dos Passos' *The 42nd Parallel* (perhaps merely as an example of multiplicity), and, one thing leading to another, I was prompted to go to the library basement and find Dos Passos' pamphlet on Sacco and Vanzetti, which turned me around politically from one day to the next (or so it seemed). There was no more talk from me about royalism; instead, I was pursuing the Tom Mooney case through the back numbers of *The New Republic*.

That was how it happened that one day in the spring I went to *The New Republic* offices on West 21st Street and asked to see the book editor, who (though I did not know it) had once been Wilson and was now Malcolm Cowley, smoking a pipe. I had brought along a copy of *Con Spirito*, which had in it "Two Crystal-Gazing Novelists," my review of Huxley's *Brave New World* and of *Public Faces*, a future-laid satire by Harold Nicolson. With characteristic perversity (you may think), I had preferred the second and said so, roundly. Cowley looked over the magazine, pursing judicious lips and making no comment. If I had brought the second number—April—also, he might have found "In Pace Requiescamus," in which my doggerel verselets (*"The Jews gave Heinrich Heine,/ Felix Mendelssohn, too;/ But the Prussians taught the goose-step./ Take your choice of the two"*) alternated with syncopated prose ("The Vatican doors open and the Pope steps out. But the Pope is an ex-mountain climber of seventy-odd, who composes new encyclicals on birth control, and sets new red hats on his prelates' bald heads, while the Italians increase and multiply as the Lord commanded them, and the Nazis, Poland looking, test their clubs on Communist pates"). Clearly, I had been "radicalized." Cowley, who was one of *theirs*, pulled at his pipe and nodded. Finally he told me that to get a review assignment from him, I would have to be either a genius or starving. "I'm not starving," I said gayly. In the end, he allowed me to do a tiny review for him, of Glenway Wescott's *A Calendar of Saints for Unbelievers*, a sort of deadpan *Lives of the Saints*, for which the magazine paid me three dollars. When the check came, after we were married, John wanted to frame it.

None of this, as they say, was happening in a vacuum. During the summer, while I was working for Mannie and living at Barbara Mosenthal's parents' house, newspaper headlines proclaimed an important election in Germany: "Hindenburg Wins" sounded good, but in reality it was a Nazi victory, as old Hindenburg rapidly stepped down and was replaced by Hitler. In the fall came Roosevelt's election and, after that, in the spring, the bank holiday, when we at Vassar, like everyone else, lived for a surprising week without money. I also remember the milk strike—farmers were dumping huge cans of milk on the roads; I wrote a story about it for Miss Swenarton in Advanced Composition. Miss Newcomer of the Economics Department kept going to Albany, and Prexy had lunch with Roosevelt on a tray in the White House. 3.2 beer became legal, and a repeal of the Volstead Act was promised.

But while the nation was enduring the Bonus March and experiencing the first labor pains of the New Deal, I myself was getting to know the rich. The South Tower group, being well brought up, was always good about inviting me to stay with one or another of them during holidays, which were too short to permit my taking the long train trip back and forth to Seattle. Thanksgiving, Christmas, mid-years, Easter—this year I might have spent them at college since John was not around. Instead, I stayed at town and country houses, with Kelly or Maddie; at Thanksgiving I had visited Julia on Cape Elizabeth and would go to Frani (though not a group member) in Pittsburgh for part of Easter. I had become familiar with butlers. Already, junior year, Nathalie Swan had

had me to stay with her in the country and, in town, in the East 80's. I learned the uses of parlormaids: having my suitcase unpacked and my clothes laid out or taken away to press. I grew accustomed to morning trays and hot milk with coffee.

The Swans' butler (French) was named Charles. Mr. Swan, who was something of a sybarite, was interested in old furniture and in his rock garden; in the country, he drank wine with his meals and in New York, in his Georgian town house, he drank a whiskey-and-soda. It must have been a New York custom—Mr. Kellogg, I think, did the same. Mr. Swan was an investment banker, and Mr. Kellogg was in the contracting business, which sounded less elegant, but his wife was a Winthrop.

At Maddie's country house, Rokeby, where I spent Christmas, austerity was the rule. The Aldriches were elderly and fairly poor (he had been the music critic of the *New York Times*), and Mrs. Aldrich, the Angel of Porto Rico, was a fanatic teetotaler. The nicest part of staying there—in Hudson River estate country, near Barrytown—was listening to the two-piano duets played by Mr. Aldrich and his brother Chester, of Delano and Aldrich, architects. Tall, white-haired, dark-eyed Mrs. Aldrich, a strong Democrat, often spoke about the Webbs ("dear Sidney and Beatrice"), and one night at dinner (estate-bottled grape juice) she interrupted one of her historical reminiscences to ask graciously, "And what part did your ancestors play in the Civil War?" I was able to answer that my great-grandfather had been a colonel, retired as general, on the Union side. I did not say that he had commanded a Negro regiment, because I did not know it then. On another evening I was surprised to hear Mr. Aldrich, who had a speech impediment, stammer out an objection to the conservative politics of young Dickie, just out of Harvard and working at Proctor & Gamble. "It is qu-qu-quite all right for me," he said, "at my age to be a Republican but not right for Dickie." Chester agreed. It was interesting that the most civilized of the families I stayed with—the Aldriches and the Denisons—were also the only poor ones.

I was conscious, naturally, of seeing my girlhood wishes—all those mornings spent immersed in *Vogue*—come improbably true, and it delighted me to be staying not merely with rich society people but with old-family patricians unable to afford central heating. And it was a strange coincidence—the return of the repressed?—that my old Seminary friend the very fast Helen Ford, from Montana, should turn up close to Rokeby, in the very same neighborhood, indeed just down the road, near the old country town of Red Hook, as a widow and running a chocolate factory painted the color of a Hershey bar, with a house to match next door. She had married the son of the popular author James Oliver Curwood, whom she met on a world cruise of "the Floating University"; he died, leaving her a chocolate business, originally located in Barrytown and named Baker's, but which was not the same as *the* Baker's. After going over from college, once, for dinner, I did not pursue the relationship and was startled years later to find that Maddie knew about her and had been curious to meet her.

In the sitting-room of the Tower, Clover had painted a mural of us all in the nude, which produced the inevitable scandal even though the likenesses were no closer to photographic realism than "Les demoiselles d'Avignon" by Picasso. It was felt to be very shocking that we invited men to tea in the presence, so to speak, of ourselves in the altogether. That was the only scandal. Among us, there was occasional dissension as to who should wash the bathtub—we had one for eight people. Otherwise there were no special incidents unless we made the mistake of playing Truth or Consequences.

Yet my relation with the group underwent a change. Extraordinary to relate, they became possessive about me. Besides Bishop and Frani, I had a lot of other friends—Betsy Strong, Fran Rotter, Martha McGahan, Rosemary Paris (who had played Perdita to my Leontes and later married Arthur

Mizener)—and the group did not like it if I ate dinner at their tables or went off campus with them to the Popover Shop or the Lodge. Or down to Signor Bruno's to drink wine out of coffee cups with the *Con Spirito* board, though this was usually not at meal-times and it was the dining-room—an empty place at table—that bothered them most. I was unaware of this and perhaps should have been flattered when a delegation came to me to suggest that I eat a bit more often with my own group. But actually, I was depressed by the clannishness of their behavior, typical, I now know, of society people, who are great stickers-together.

It was mid-June the morning we graduated, and I fainted in the chapel from the heat. Afterwards Frani's parents took several of us to lunch at the Silver Swan. My grandparents had not come on for the occasion, to hear me get my *cum laude* (no *magna*); they sent me the money the trip would have cost them. That was my graduation present, and perhaps it was just as well that they were spared Clover's mural. Besides that, my grandfather sent me a check for what they might have given me for a trip to Europe, such as Frani was getting from her parents—*that* was a wedding present, he wrote. Yes, the decision had eventually been made. We had even sublet an apartment, furnished, on East 52nd Street, from Miss Sandison's sister, Lois Howland, who taught Latin at Chapin. Feeling the depression, she and her husband were moving down to the National Arts Club and leaving us their very nice things. It was over a "cordial shop" (liquor store) and next to a dry-cleaner's; at the end of the summer, when the Howlands' lease ran out, we would have to find a place of our own.

We spent the night in the apartment, then took a taxi down to St. George's Church, on Stuyvesant Square. We had already had an interview with the curate, and it was exactly one week after Commencement and my twenty-first birthday when we "stood up" together in the chapel. I had a beige dress and a large black silk hat with a wreath of daisies. Most of the group were present; Frani had already sailed for Fontainebleau to study music, and Bishop, I think, was not there either. We had a one-night honeymoon at an inn in Briarcliff, and there all of a sudden I had an attack of panic. This may have had something to do with an apple-jack punch we served at the reception or with the disturbing proximity of Scarborough, suffused with bad memories of the summer before. As we climbed into the big bed, I knew, too late, that I had *done the wrong thing*. To marry a man without loving him, which was what I had just done, not really perceiving it, was a wicked action, I saw. Stiff with remorse and terror, I lay under the thin blanket through a good part of the night; as far as I could tell from what seemed a measureless distance, my untroubled mate was sleeping.

BRIEF BIOGRAPHICAL GLOSSARY
OF LESSER-KNOWN FIGURES

by Carol Brightman

George Antheil (1900–1959): American pianist and composer. His *Zingareska* for orchestra, one of the first symphonic works to incorporate jazz, was performed in Berlin in 1921. When he moved to Paris in 1923, he was taken up by Joyce, Yeats, Satie, Picasso, and Pound (who wrote a book about him). In November 1923, two violin sonatas commissioned by Pound—who performed the part for tenor and bass drums at the end of the second—had their premiere. In 1924 Antheil began working with Léger and the film maker Dudley Murphy on *Ballet Mécanique,* which was scored for sixteen player pianos controlled from a switchboard, but the synchronization with the abstract film proved impossible, and they became autonomous works. *Ballet Méchanique* was performed in Paris in 1925 with eight pianos, one player piano, four bass drums, and a siren; in 1927 it was done at Carnegie Hall.

He became musical director for the Berlin Stadttheater in 1928.

In May 1930 his first opera, *Transatlantic*, was performed at Frankfurt am Main. The libretto centered on an American presidential campaign and presented a wild caricature of life in the United States. During these years he also wrote ballet scores for George Balanchine and Martha Graham. He returned to the United States in 1933 and became music director for Eastern Paramount Studios. In Hollywood, starting in 1936, he composed incidental music for major films. He also did a syndicated lonely-hearts column, acted as a war-analyst for press and radio, and under a pseudonym published several detective stories inspired by a fascination with "glandular criminology."

Sarah Henry Atherton (1889–1975): child-welfare activist and novelist—*Blow Whistles, Blow!* (1930; as a play, 1938), *Brass Eagles* (1935), *Mark's Own* (1941). A Bryn Mawr graduate, 1913, she made a study of female adolescence for the National Consumers League, investigated child-labor conditions for the Department of Labor, and in 1934 supervised the WPA's Federal Art Project in Fairfield County, Connecticut.

Alan Barth (1906–1979): editorial writer for the Washington *Post* and author. As Eric Pace wrote in an obituary in the *New York Times:* "Mr. Barth advanced his liberal political views tirelessly over four decades in books and speeches. . . . In the strongly partisan atmosphere of the McCarthy era, his book, 'The Loyalty of Free Men,' an indictment of what he called 'the cult of loyalty,' was removed from the public shelves of United States Government-run libraries abroad on orders from Washington. But Mr. Barth went on to write other outspoken books, including 'Government by Investigation,' which decried abuse of the power of legislative bodies to investigate. . . . In his 1961 book, 'The Price of Liberty,' Mr. Barth contended that neurotic anxiety about crime was helping breed a police-state frame of mind in the United States; an exaggerated concern for order, he said, was endangering liberty." A graduate of Yale, Barth worked in Washington for the McClure Newspaper Syndicate from 1938 to 1941; then at the Treasury and the Office of War Information. In 1943 he began thirty years as a Washington *Post* editorial writer. He was a Nieman Fellow at Harvard in 1948–49 and won awards for distinguished writing and for his service to journalism.

Al Bein (1902–   ): American playwright and novelist born in Rumania. One of his earliest works, *Little Ol' Boy* (1933, adapted from his novel, *Road Out of Hell*), dealt with a juvenile delinquent, played by Burgess Meredith; it marked Joseph Losey's debut as a director. *Let Freedom Ring* (1935) was based on Grace Lumpkin's novel *To Make My Bread*. *Heavenly Express* (1940) starred John Garfield as the Overland Kid who leads an army of hoboes (one played by Burl Ives) to whiskey heaven. In 1943 Bein wrote, directed, and produced *Land of Fame*, in which Greek guerrillas battle Nazis.

Maurice Browne (1881–1955): founder of the Little Theatre movement in the United States, and producer of the great theatrical success *Journey's End*. Before the First World War he married the young actress Ellen Van Volkenburgh and migrated to the United States. In 1912 they started the Chicago Little Theatre, parent to all the others. In 1918 Browne organized a repertory company that presented *Medea*, *The Trial of Joan of Arc*, *Candide*, and *Dr. Faust*.

Then in 1928 Browne found himself penniless in San Francisco and worked his way back to England, where he became a success as an actor in the West End; he played Adolf in Strindberg's *The Creditors*. He produced *Othello*, with Paul Robeson, Peggy Ashcroft, and himself as Iago. Then he met the young insurance agent R. C. Sheriff, whose first play, *Journey's End*, earned its producer a fortune. In the 1940's Browne lost his fortune on less-favored productions, including a John Gielgud *Hamlet* and the blockbuster *Wings Over Europe* (1942), which starred Van Volkenburgh, and nearly bankrupted him. In 1949 he returned to California to become artist-in-residence at the University of California; there he wrote a peculiar autobiography, *Too Late to Lament*, and married another woman. The marriage failed, and he went back once more to England. He and Van Volkenburgh were associated with the Elmhirsts and Dartington Hall.

Kenneth Callahan (1905–1986): painter born in Spokane. He had his first one-man show at a stationery store in San Francisco. In 1927 he went to sea as a steward, crossing to Asia and Europe. In 1930 he made his first trip to Mexico and Central America. In Mexico he knew Orozco and Tamayo, and their influence was visible in his work, which appeared in regional exhibitions with increasing frequency. In 1933 he took a job as program director for the Seattle Art Museum, a position he held for many years, and became a regular contributor to local and national periodicals. Like many painters of his time, he worked for the mural division of the WPA during the 1930's. Murals by him were commissioned for post offices in Centralia and Anacortes, Washington, and Rugby, North Dakota and in 1939 he completed one for the Weyerhaeuser Timber Company in Everett, Washington. In 1942 he got a regular summer job as a ranger in a one-man lookout post in the Cascades, which seems to have encouraged the sweeping vision of nature characteristic of his middle years. By the 1940's his style was largely non-representational. He taught painting and lithography at Washington State University, the University of Southern California, the Skowhegan School in Maine, and Syracuse University. In 1959 he was one of eight American artists whose work was selected for a State Department–sponsored tour of Europe, South America, and Southeast Asia. He was personally invited to accompany the ten-month tour "to explain the position and life of an American artist."

In 1963 Callahan lost his entire collection in a fire that burned his Granite Falls, Washington, studio to the ground. He established a new studio in Long Beach, Washington, and began to work on several large murals and a series of terra-cotta sculptures. In 1968 he won an American Academy of Arts and Letters Award. His work can be seen in dozens of major collections.

Eduardo Ciannelli (1887–1969): Italian character actor highly esteemed in Hollywood. Once known as the "thinking man's gangster," he played Trock Estrella in the film version of *Winterset* (1936) and Lucky Luciano in *Marked Woman* (1937). His last appearance was in the 1959 television series *Johnny Staccato*.

Warwick Deeping (1877–1950): British physician and novelist. When *Love Among the Ruins* became a best seller in 1904, he left medicine for fiction writing, publishing sixty-nine books. Praised for his "gentlemanly goodness and fun, and well-woven plots," he was incapable of penning an unhappy ending; even his World War I novel *Sorrell and Son* (1925) ended happily.

Maud Earl (1848–1943): daughter and student of the nineteenth-century British sporting painter George Earl. She specialized in dramatized portraits of pedigreed and prize-winning dogs. Among her more famous subjects were the dogs of Queen Victoria and of King Edward VII. Her work appeared in several Royal Academy exhibitions between 1884 and 1901; "The Dog of War" and "Dogs of Death" remained two of her best-known pictures. Her work was popularized in England and the United States through engravings, which included twelve dogs engraved for *The Sportsman's Year* in 1908. In 1917 she went to the United States, and in 1933, at the age of eighty-five, began to execute decorative screens and murals for the American market.

Albert Parker Fitch (1877–1944): celebrated Protestant clergyman and public speaker in the 1920's and 1930's. A graduate of Boston Latin School, Harvard University, and Union Theological Seminary, he became president of Andover Theological Seminary in 1909. In 1917 he was named Professor of the History of Religion at Amherst College and later gave similar courses at Carleton College in Minnesota. In 1927 he was made pastor of the Park Avenue Presbyterian Church in New York City, a post he held until 1932, when poor health forced his retirement. A popular commencement speaker and university preacher, he was well known for his unconventional social views. He was the author of three books about religion and society, including *Can the Church Survive in the Changing Order?* (1920), and a novel, *None So Blind* (1924).

Ferdinand Foch (1851–1929): French marshal. He planned the strategy that stopped the Germans at the Marne in 1914, directed the battle of the Somme in 1916, was chief of the French general staff in 1917, and became supreme commander of all Allied armies in 1918.

Kay Francis (1899–1968): From *The Film Encyclopedia:* "Despite a slight lisp she was one of Hollywood's most glamorous and most highly paid stars during the 1930's . . . portraying stylish, worldly brunettes in romantic melodramas. . . ." She was convent educated. Among her films were *Gentlemen of the Press, Cynara,* and *The White Angel.*

Winsor Brown French II (1905–1973): society figure and travel writer who was a movie critic and travel columnist for the Cleveland *Press* from 1933 until his retirement in 1968. He was briefly married in the 1930's to the stage actress and director Margaret Perry.

Harold Cooper Johnsrud (1903–1939): stage actor, playwright, and occasional director. Son of Iver and Molly (Cooper), he was born in St. Cloud, Minnesota. As an actor, sometimes doubling as assistant stage-manager, he worked for Arthur Hopkins, Jed Harris, Guthrie McClintic, and during several seasons for the radical Theatre Union. He played a blind man in two plays simultaneously, commuting by cab between theatres—in Maxwell Anderson's *Winterset* and Archibald MacLeish's *Panic*. He had a part in Max Reinhardt's *The Eternal Road* (1937), a pageant of Jewish history designed by Norman Bel Geddes, written by Ludwig Lewisohn, scored by Kurt Weill, starring Lotte Lenya and Sidney Lumet (then a child actor), which was described at the time as "one of the costliest failures in Broadway history." Though an option was held on his comedy *Anticlimax*, no play of his had been produced at the time of his death. Only his adaptation of the Viennese comedy *Jewel Robbery*, with Basil Sydney and Mary Ellis, was done, in 1935. *New York Times* news stories of December 23 and December 24, 1939, relate the circumstances of his death:

ACTOR BADLY BURNED IN FIRE IN HOTEL SUITE;
Harold Johnsrud Hurt Trying to Save Belongings
"In an effort to retrieve personal belongings from a fire in his rooms at the Hotel Brevoort, Fifth Avenue and Eighth Street, Harold Johnsrud, actor, director, and playwright was critically burned early yesterday.

"Although the blaze was confined to Mr. Johnsrud's two-room suite on the second floor, forty of the 150 guests of the hotel went to the lobby after a telephone warning. There was little excitement but a crowd gathered on Fifth Avenue as smoke and flames poured from the room.

"Mr. Johnsrud, who is 35 years old, discovered the fire at 5:29 A. M. and after notifying the night manager, Lawrence C. Finn, he went to the apartment adjoining, where Mr. and Mrs. Charles Ellis were asleep. The couple are fellow actors of Mr. Johnsrud in the play 'Key Largo.'

"Instead of following the Ellises to the lobby Mr. Johnsrud returned to his room, where he collapsed. Fire Lieutenant Clarence

273

Cullen of Hook and Ladder 3 found him slumped on the floor of the bedroom and carried him to the hallway. He was taken to Bellevue Hospital suffering from first, second and third degree burns of the face, hands and body.

"The cause of the fire was undetermined.

"Mr. Johnsrud has been active in the theatre since 1927, when he appeared with the Provincetown Players. He has staged plays and recently wrote one, as yet unproduced. His part of 'd'Alcala' in the Maxwell Anderson play at the Ethel Barrymore Theatre was played last night by Mr. Ellis."

BURNS FATAL TO JOHNSRUD, ACTOR

"Harold C. Johnsrud, 35 years old, an actor and member of the cast of 'Key Largo,' who was burned Friday morning during a fire in his hotel room at the Hotel Brevoort, died yesterday afternoon in Misericordia Hospital. Mr. Johnsrud had suffered severe burns of the face, hands and body."

The "belongings" were said to be the manuscript of a play.

Anna Theresa Kitchel (1882–1959): English professor. A graduate of Smith College, she began teaching at West Davison High School in Milwaukee. She received an M.A. and a Ph.D. from the University of Wisconsin and joined Vassar as an English instructor in 1918. She rose to be full professor. During 1923–24 she held a Markham Fellowship for study at the British Museum. Her *George Lewes and George Eliot* (1933) was the first biography to approach the relationship between the famous novelist and G. H. Lewes from the side of the latter. She also wrote *Quarry for Middlemarch* (1950).

Eugene Meyer (1885–1959): publisher of the Washington *Post* and first president of the International Bank for Reconstruction and Development.

Lloyd Nolan (1902–1985): stage and screen actor. In 1931–32 he played in Robert E. Sherwood's *Reunion in Vienna* with the Lunts. The following year he was Biff Grimes in *One Sunday Afternoon*, which closed after an assassination attempt on Franklin Roosevelt and reopened to run for 338 performances. In 1953–54 he gave the first of his highly praised performances as Captain Queeg in *The Caine Mutiny Court Martial*, on Broadway. He received a New

York Drama Critics award for Queeg. He appeared in *Hannah and Her Sisters,* released in 1986.

Adelaide B. Preston (1871–1965): educator born in Torrington, Connecticut, in 1871. She was graduated from Smith College in 1895 and began teaching at the Morgan School, in Portsmouth, New Hampshire, in 1895. She taught mathematics and Latin in various private schools and was principal of Annie Wright Seminary in Tacoma, Washington, from 1913 to 1929. She then founded Miss Preston's Outdoor School in Phoenix, Arizona.

Harold Preston (1858–1938): lawyer and state senator. Born in Rockford, Illinois, he was educated at Iowa College and Cornell University. He studied law in Newton, Iowa, and was admitted to the Iowa bar in 1883. After moving to Seattle that year, he got a job writing abstracts; two years later he opened his own law office. The firm prospered under various partnerships, and Preston's reputation for intelligence, integrity, fairness, consideration, and a passion for thoroughness and hard work grew. In 1888 he married Augusta Morgenstern; they had two sons and a daughter.

Preston was chairman of a commission that, in 1895, formulated Seattle's second charter, which is the framework for its government today. From 1897 to 1901 he was a member of the state Senate and then and later played a prominent part in the enactment of progressive laws. Among these was a statute he wrote that established employers' liability for injured workers, passed in 1911. This first workers' compensation law was upheld by both state and federal Supreme Courts. In 1903 Preston was a candidate for the U.S. Senate, but was narrowly defeated by a vote in the legislature. He served as president of the Washington State Bar Association in 1898 and of the Seattle Bar Association in 1909–10.

Joanna Roos (1901–   ): actress and minor playwright. She was married to the composer Edward Rickett (Gilbert's collaborator after Sullivan's death). In 1928–29 she appeared in *Grand Street Follies,* and in 1930 played Sonia in Jed Harris's *Uncle Vanya* with Lillian Gish and Osgood Perkins. In 1934 she was seen in the comedy *Tight Britches* and, with Orson Welles, in Archibald MacLeish's short-lived *Panic*. Leading roles followed in *Abe Lincoln in Illinois* (1938) and *Orpheus Descending* (1941). With Alexander King and Lehman Engle, she wrote a musical, *Mooncalf*, in 1953. She was a founding member of the Association of Producing Artists in 1960 and appeared with this company. Throughout the 1960's she played Shakespeare, Ibsen, and Chekhov in summer-theatre festivals around the country.

Siegfried Rumann (Sig Ruman) (1885–1967): German character actor. He appeared in 130 films, including the Marx Brothers' *A Night at the Opera, Ninotchka*, with Greta Garbo, *The Hitler Gang*, and *Stalag 17*. He played on the American stage with Tallulah Bankhead, Ethel Barrymore, and Katharine Cornell.

Helen Estabrook Sandison (1884–1978): Elizabethan scholar and member of the English faculty at Vassar College from 1919 to 1950. She graduated from Bryn Mawr in 1906 and got her Ph.D. in 1911. She taught English and Latin at Brookville (Indiana) High School from 1907 to 1908. In 1913 she became a Reader in English at Bryn Mawr; in 1919 she was appointed Assistant Professor of English at Vassar. She became full professor in 1929, chairman of the English Department in 1931, and was chairman of the Committee on Admissions from 1923 to 1930. From 1931 to 1936 she was a member of the Modern Language Association's Executive Council. She was also the author of *Chanson d'Aventure in Middle English* (1913) and, with Henry Noble MacCracken (Vassar's president), *Manual of Good English* (1917). Her lifetime work was her edition of the English poems of Sir Arthur Gorges, Ralegh's friend and translator of Lucan (1953).

Preston B. Schoyer (1912[?]–1978): author of four novels—*The Foreigners, The Indefinite River, The Ringing of the Glass*, and *The Typhoon's Eye*—based on his Second World War experiences in China.

Harry Sternberg (1904–   ): American painter and graphic artist. He studied at the Art Students League and with Harry Wickey. After some travels in Mexico and Canada, in 1933 he joined the faculty of the Art Students League and taught easel painting and printmaking there for thirty-five years. He also taught at the New School for Social Research (1942–45 and 1950–51) and other in-

276

stitutions. During the Depression, he worked for the WPA's Federal Art Project and produced murals for post offices in Sellersville and Chester, Pennsylvania. In 1960 he directed and produced the film *The Many Worlds of Art*. His work is in a number of collections in the United States and in Europe.

Laurette Taylor (1884–1946): American stage actress who first made a name for herself in 1912 as Peg in *Peg O' My Heart*. In 1938 she played Mrs. Midgit in *Outward Bound*, and in 1945 won acclaim for the performance of the mother in *The Glass Menagerie* by Tennessee Williams.

Ellen Van Volkenburgh: American actress and producer born in Michigan. With her husband, Maurice Browne, she founded the Chicago Little Theatre in 1912—the first in the United States. In 1915 she toured as Hecuba in *The Trojan Women;* in 1920 appeared as Medea in New York; and produced *Mr. Faust* in 1922 at the Provincetown Theatre in New York. In London, she starred for Browne in a number of West End productions. Together they put on *The Unknown Warrior* (1928), *Othello* (1930), and *The Venetian* (1931). Both worked for Leonard and Dorothy (Strait) Elmhirst at Dartington Hall and, before that, for Nellie Cornish in Seattle. In their later years she and Browne were divorced but remained professionally on good terms. The Elmhirsts settled a large lifetime income on "Nellie Van."

Glenway Wescott (1901–   ): author of *The Grandmothers*, a popular novel which won the Harper Prize in 1927. *Apartment in Athens* (1945) is probably his most well-known novel.

Richard Whorf (1906–1966): stage, screen, and television actor and director. "A protean man of the theatre" (Brooks Atkinson), he acted, sang, danced, wrote, designed, and directed his way through a career that spanned forty-four years. He first stepped on stage to play the Artful Dodger in *Oliver Twist* in Boston. There he played 200 different roles, before arriving in New York City in 1927 to play an eighty-five-year-old eccentric in *Monkey*. In 1935 he was Christopher Sly in the Lunt production of *The Taming of the Shrew*. Through most of the 1930's and 1940's he worked with the Lunts, appearing with them in *Amphitryon 38, The Sea Gull, Idiot's Delight,* and *There Shall Be No Night,* for which he also designed the scenery. After the Second World War he worked with the New York City Center Theatre, designing sets and costumes for a 1953 production of *Cyrano de Bergerac* and a 1953–54 production of *Ondine.* In 1951 he was secretary of Actors Equity.

Helen Wills and **Helen Jacobs:** outstanding American Lawn Tennis champions in the late 1920's and 1930's. Wills won eight singles titles at Wimbledon, seven at Forest Hills, and four in Paris. Jacobs won the U.S. singles title four times and the Wimbledon title once, in 1936, losing to Wills in the Wimbledon finals of 1935 and 1938.

Jerome Zerbe (1904–   ): society writer and photographer. A 1928 graduate of Yale, he became an art editor of *Parade* magazine in Cleveland in 1931. In 1932 he began a long association with *Town and Country,* first as a photographer and later as society editor. He wrote two books on celebrities: *People on Parade* (1934) and *El Morocco Family Album* (1937). After serving as a chief photographer's mate in the U.S. Navy, he continued to work for *Town and Country* and also as social columnist for the New York *Journal-American* and *Palm Beach Illustrated* (1967), and published several other books.